P9-EEL-788

Talking
Computers and
Telecommunications

Talking
Computers and
Telecommunications

John A. Kuecken

VNR VAN NOSTRAND REINHOLD COMPANY
NEW YORK CINCINNATI TORONTO LONDON MELBOURNE

Published by Van Nostrand Reinhold Company Inc.
135 West 50th Street, New York, N.Y. 10020

Van Nostrand Reinhold Publishing
1410 Birchmount Road
Scarborough, Ontario M1P 2E7, Canada

Van Nostrand Reinhold
480 Latrobe Street
Melbourne, Victoria 3000, Australia

Van Nostrand Reinhold Company Limited
Molly Millars Lane
Wokingham, Berkshire, England

15 14 13 12 11 10 9 8 7 6 5 4 3 2 1

Library of Congress Cataloging in Publication Data

Kuecken, John A.
    Talking computers and telecommunications.

    Includes index.
    1. Telephone. I. Title.
TK6161.K83   621.385   82-2715
ISBN 0-442-24721-4   AACR2

Introduction

A casual study of sales figures for the electronics industry will reveal that the field of telecommunications is the fastest growing portion of the industry. This trend began about 1977 and is expected to persist at least until the late 1980s. At that point the rapid growth may have fallen off to about par with other industry segments, but the overall volume is predicted to be very high and the telecommunications portion is expected to occupy something in excess of 20% of all electronics sales. As noted in the title, this text is concerned with this rapidly growing field and some of the devices contributing to its surge of growth.

The potential for very rapid growth in telecommunications was first pointed out to me circa 1975 by salesmen and marketing types who have reason to stay with or anticipate trends in industry. My initial response was a little bewilderment at what they meant by "telecommunications." Having spent many years working on radar, microwave links, shortwave, mobile radio, and finally satellite communication links, I thought that telecommunications simply meant *communicating at a distance.* Surely these arts had matured to the point where rapid growth was not particularly likely. My astonishment continued to grow when I discovered that these people and the trade journals in electronics were defining the term *telecommunications* to mean *communication over the in-situ telephone network.*

It has always seemed to me that there is a natural succession in the affairs of a particular branch of science or technology just as in the affairs of men. In infancy, a few loving parents and friends can nurture and foresee the possibilities. This is followed by a period of rapid adolescent growth during which powers and capabilities rapidly develop. This, in turn, is followed by a period of mature development when the capabilities come into full flower, after which the growth may continue but at a slower rate.

In technology, the parallel sometimes continues. The reciprocating steam engine remains mainly as an antique curiosity. The piston-engine propellor-driven airplane is a less severe case since most of the lightplanes flown by private pilots remain in this class. However, the development of these craft is very slow compared to other areas of the aircraft industry.

In the mid-1970s it seemed likely to most electronics engineers that the telephone system represented a fully mature art practiced by a small and specialized segment of the engineering community. A rapid growth, which would involve nontelephone engineers, did not seem very likely. The more mature engineer could remember the introduction of the dial telephone in the early 1930s and realized that it took nearly thirty more years before the introduction of the direct-distance dialing. More than fifteen years after the introduction of dual-tone multifrequency signaling, only a fraction of the telephones were push-button types. It was true that the communications satellite had opened up a whole new field of engineering; however, those involved in the design of the antennas, ground stations, and the satellites remained a very small and specialized group concentrated in only a few firms. Furthermore, the change in the telephone system was one of degree rather than of basic nature. It had become easier, less expensive, and more convenient to call Brussels from Rochester but the nature of the service was the same.

What then was to be the motivating force behind a rapid growth in telephone communications that would drag engineers and technicians into the art? The answer to this question is not simple and cannot be pinpointed in only one location. A number of forces working in concert have been responsible, and their sources are as diverse as social pressure, economic pressure, and technological availability.

On the social side, the single most outstanding factor has been the widespread growth in education in both the developed and the undeveloped (or developing) nations. Since the time of World War II the number of highly educated people has been rapidly increasing. Particularly in the developed nations, this has led to an increase in mobility and an increase in expectations of the people. Today's college graduate will frequently seek out employment far from his home, as testified by the migration to the sun belt in the U.S.

On the economic side, the increase in social expectations has had a number of effects. First of all, the protracted period of prosperity after World War II led most of industry into a period of expansion as production blossomed to fill the demand for material goods in the developed nations. During this period many, and perhaps most, of the major businesses became multinational in nature. The spread and diversity of business throughout the world naturally brought with it an increased need for communications. It simply takes more communications to manage a company spread over three continents than were required for a single plant in Ashtabula, Ohio.

At the same time the rising social expectations of the people made it progressively more difficult to get help to handle some of the more mundane business tasks. In the early 1950s the typical engineering group of 20 engineers would have one or two secretaries to handle typing, record keeping, etc. Today it is not unusual to find the ratio closer to one in forty or fifty. The expectations concerning job achievement have changed and the job of the steno or secretary is no longer held in such high esteem.

A similar pressure is at work in the factory. Many manufacturing operations used to operate with a large staff of low-skilled people and a smaller group of craftsmen who were capable of making the tools or keeping the machinery going. As these craftsmen retired they were replaced by technicians educated in the ways of numeric-control machinery and automation. As the automation increased, so also did the educational requirements of those who would program and repair the equipment.

These same pressures have been reflected in the developing nations. The requirements for petroleum and raw metals have been widely felt in the economy of these nations. A particular case in point is the requirement for handcraft skills in the assembly of integrated circuits. The actual creation of a large-scale integrated circuit such as a memory chip or a microprocessor is a highly technical and heavily automated procedure to the chip stage. The bonding of the multiple connections of the chip into the carrier package is, conversely, a handicraft-type operation. Thus, we find that large numbers of these products will be stamped "Made in Malaysia" or "Made in Hong Kong," etc. The presence of a large work force skilled at and willing to perform handcraft labor has drawn this industry.

These factors have reflected upon the telephone industry in several ways. On the pull side, the presence of an increasingly mobile society and the rapid growth of far-flung business ventures have led inexorably to requirements for faster and better communications to be achieved with less intervention by operators. In the Rochester area, a major plant used to have five telephone operators to handle incoming and outgoing calls. Today the same plant has an electronic Private Office Branch Exchange (PABX), which handles the task faster and better than the operators did. An outside caller simply dials MMM WXYZ (where WXYZ is the extension number of the desired phone) and the telephone rings directly on the desk of the party you wish to reach. Only in a case where the caller does not know the extension number is operator intervention necessary. This is handled by the receptionist. There are no longer *any* operators.

This system presents a number of other advantages. If party WXYZ knows that he will be spending the next few hours at a meeting at extension ABCD, this information can be keyed into the system and all calls to WXYZ will be forwarded automatically to ABCD. If the party is away from the desk and the phone rings three times without an answer, the PABX can be programmed to automatically forward the call to the department secretary. If WXYZ attempts to call ABCD and finds the line busy, he can "camp on" the number and the system will automatically try periodically and call him only when the connection has succeeded. If ABCD is busy, ABCD receives a signal indicating that someone else is attempting to reach him. For outside calls, the system will remember the last number called and can try the number again at the push of a single button. This is only a partial listing of some of the features of the system. It can be seen that such systems can greatly reduce the time and effort required to get in touch with an individual.

In this text we will discuss some of the problems of telecommunications and some of the innovative solutions that have been made available through advances in the electronic arts.

This particular art is one I have found to be fascinating, with immense possibilities for future growth. I can only hope the reader enjoys the possibilities as much.

JOHN A. KUECKEN

Contents

INTRODUCTION   v

SECTION 1. TELECOMMUNICATIONS

1. TELEPHONY – A BRIEF HISTORY. The struggles of Bell, Gray,
   and Edison are briefly recounted.   3
2. BASIC TECHNIQUES. This chapter deals with basic telephone
   problems, definitions, crossbar switching, and DTMF signaling.   20
3. TONE DETECTORS. The subject of tone detection as used in
   telephony is treated in some detail, including an organization of
   the DTMF dialing tones and the supervisory tones.   39
4. THE DTMF DETECTOR, THE DTMF GENERATOR AND
   THE HYBRID TRANSFORMER   55
5. SURGE AND TEST VOLTAGES. A discussion of surges due to
   operation signaling and external sources such as lightning is
   presented.   71
6. SECURITY TECHNIQUES. A discussion of operational security
   to prevent unauthorized operation of telephone remote-control
   systems is presented.   77

SECTION 2. SOUND, WAVEFORMS AND SPEECH

7. SOUND AND HEARING. The nature of sound waves and sound
   propagation is discussed. The nature of the human ear and its
   response to sound is treated.   85
8. SOUNDS. Some of the human responses to sounds are discussed.
   The concepts of harmony and dissonance and the makeup of the
   musical scale are briefly treated.   97
9. THE PRODUCTION OF SOUND. Pneumatic and mechanical
   mechanisms for the production of sound are treated and related
   to the production of human speech and song. The part played
   by standing waves is treated and an introduction to the phoneme
   concept is presented.   112

10. HUMAN SPEECH CHARACTERISTICS. The concepts of pitch, formats and phonemes is further developed. The spectra of human speech are analyzed. The concept of "windowing" in the Fourier analysis is studied, and an FFT/IFT program is presented.   133

11. SPEECH DIGITIZATION. The techniques of reducing sound to a digital wavetrain and reproducing the wavetrain from the sound are treated and limitations discussed. The concept of data compression is introduced. Hardware as well as software principles are presented.   163

12. MOSER ENCODING. Both the hardware and the software techniques used in this patented form of speech synthesis are treated. This is used in the "blind calculator" and the National Semiconductor "Digitalker."   181

13. LINEAR PREDICTIVE CODING. This sophisticated technique for speech synthesis is treated at some length with a presentation of the principle features of the technique.   199

14. SPEECH RECOGNITION. The nature of the fundamental problems of accurate speech recognition are treated and an assessment of current status is presented. Fundamental goals and the requirements for accuracy are discussed.   225

INDEX   235

Talking
Computers and
Telecommunications

SECTION 1
TELECOMMUNICATIONS

1
Telephony — A Brief History

If asked about the origin of the telephone system, the typical reader would respond that the telephone was invented by Alexander Graham Bell. Those a little longer in the tooth might have some gag about Don Ameche (who played Bell in the movie version of Bell's autobiography). One can also find learned observations to the effect that the telephone was not developed by the telegraph industry, which was already a large and powerful force at the time of the invention of the telephone. This is often cited as an example of the fact that big business does not innovate! (Note that the writer himself has used this argument!)

As a matter of fact these discussions miss a great deal of the point. The case is actually considerably more complex (and in the writer's opinion more interesting) than that. To begin with, a small discussion of history is in order; and we may discover why it was that Bell is the inventor of the telephone by act of the Supreme Court of the United States of America.

To set the stage for this drama, a brief listing of events is in order. The chronology is as follows:

600 B.C.   Thales of Miletos records the property of rubbed amber to attract lint, dust, and light particles.

1296 A.D.   Marco Polo brings a magnetic compass to Venice from the Court of the Kublai Khan.

1600   William Gilbert, in *De Magnete,* describes the difference between electrostatic and magnetic attraction.

1646   Sir Thomas Brown uses the word *electricity* for the first time.

1733   Charles Du Fay discovers two kinds of electricity, the "resinous" and the "vitreous." Du Fay notes that objects charged with one kind of electricity repel one another, and when charged with opposite kinds attract one another.

1746   Benjamin Franklin terms the kinds of electricity "positive" and "negative." A slightly unfortunate choice since negative electricity corresponds to an excess of electrons and positive electricity to a deficiency of electrons!

1752   Benjamin Franklin discovers the electrical nature of lightning with his kite-and-key experiment. By good fortune Franklin survived, but many who attempted to duplicate this experiment were electrocuted!

3

1800   Alessandro Volta develops the battery, or voltaic cell. For the first time, experimenters have a source of continuously flowing electric current.

1820   Hans Christian Oersted discovers electromagnetism when he finds that a current flowing through a wire will deflect a compass needle.

1822   Andre Marie Ampere forms the law describing the quantitive force between wires carrying electric current. For the first time, electrical measurements are placed on a quantitive basis.

1826   Georg Simon Ohm formulates the law describing the relationship between voltage, current, and resistance.

1831   Michael Faraday in England and Joseph Henry in the U. S. simultaneously discover electromagnetic induction. Faraday also experiments with the idea that if electricity can be used to produce magnetism, magnetism can be used to produce electricity, and he invents the dynamo-electric machine.

1832   Hypolite Pixii invents the first practical generator. This machine represents the first mechanism for coupling the power of steam into electrical energy. The high-pressure steam engine had been invented by Oliver Evans of Philadelphia in 1815.

1841   Arc lights are demonstrated in the streets of Paris.

1844   Samuel F. B. Morse and Alfred Vail exhange the first long-distance telegraph message between Washington and Baltimore.

1861   Western Union work crews from California and Nebraska meet at Salt Lake City, Utah, and the first transcontinental telegram is sent by Stephen J. Field to President Lincoln, declaring California's loyalty to the Union. Joseph Wilson Swan patents the first incandescent lamp in the U. S.

1869   Thomas Alva Edison invents the improved stock ticker, or automatic printing telegraph receiver.

The principal object of this little review is to point out that Bell was not operating in a vacuum. By the time Bell appeared on the scene, there was a large and flourishing electrical industry in the country, and a number of people were working on new ideas and products. There are a number of different names involved in the drama; some familiar and others less familiar. The drama involved figures both large and small in high and low places.

In 1866, the Western Union Company was formed by consolidating the leading telegraph companys in the U. S. By 1873 it would transmit more than 90% of the telegraph business in the U. S. over a network consisting of more than 150,000 miles of wire. At that point Western Union owned more miles of wire than all of the rest of the world combined! At the time, this was the greatest growth industry and it was rapidly becoming one of the most powerful interests in the country.

Some grasp of what is meant by the term *growth industry* can be had from the fact that the July 10 issue of the *New York Times* gives the wire mileage of Western Union at 175,000 miles! If the two figures are accurate, the wire mileage of Western Union would seem to have been growing at a rate of 11% per year. This can be translated into a doubling of the system mileage every 6.74 years.

A significant technical factor plays into the story. Wire, poles, and insulators cost money. They cost money to buy initially, they cost money to install, and they cost money to maintain. They can be blown down by the wind or can sag and break because of sleet storms. They can be struck by lightning and vaporized. They can be stolen by vandals. In short, the maintenance of an extensive system of lines is an expensive process requiring constant attention and service. Obviously, a system that would permit more telegrams to be sent over a given wire system would be worth a great deal of money to Western Union. Accordingly, it is not surprising to find that a number of enterprising individuals were working on the problem of making multiple use of telegraph lines.

THE BUSINESSMEN INVOLVED

William Orton (1826-1878) had studied to be a teacher. His college thesis was written on the subject of the magnetic telegraph and was illustrated with a model he had built. After teaching for a few years, he went into the printing and publishing business. In 1862 he was appointed New York City Collector of Internal Revenue and in 1865 as Commissioner of Internal Revenue. Obviously the man had a few political connections. In the fall of 1865 he accepted the position of president of a leading private telegraph company, only to find that rapid expansion and poor financial management had it on the brink of bankruptcy. It could only be saved by a merger with Western Union, whose position was really not all that much better due to the unbridled growth of the giant. In 1865 he accepted the presidency of Western Union and found himself in a position described by his obituary writer as "onerous." Through a series of relatively shrewd financial maneuvers Orton managed to get Western Union back on the track.

Gardiner G. Hubbard was a Boston patent lawyer turned promoter. He had made a considerable fortune by bringing the street railway and gas lighting to Cambridge, Mass. Hubbard was also a man of some vision and considerable ambition. Between 1868 and 1874 Hubbard lobbied strenuously and continuously in both Boston and Washington for a private postal telegraph company. He intended to build telegraph lines along the nation's rail and post roads and to contract with the post office to send telegrams on its wires at rates about half those charged by Western Union. In his favor it was argued that Western Union was gaining inordinate control of the dissemination of news, and thereby control of public opinion and the price of gold and other commodities. Against his position it was argued that the federal government would take most of the risks and put up most of the capital, and that Hubbard and associates would become fabulously wealthy if the effort succeeded.

In 1874 Congress defeated what was described as a "swindling scheme" and the Western Union telegraph monopoly was firmly established. Hubbard had earned only the undying antagonism of Orton for his efforts.

Jay Gould (1836–1892) is perhaps the best known of the businessmen involved in the telephone drama. It has struck me as noteworthy that the chapter in high-school American History in which Jay Gould was described was titled "The Robber Barons."

In 1860 Gould bought the Rutland and Washington Railroad. He sold this at a profit and parlayed the fortune by buying and selling other small railroads. In 1867 Gould and James Fisk joined Daniel Drew on the board of directors of the Erie railroad. Through a series of out-and-out stock swindles in which they issued themselves stock, they kept Cornelius Vanderbilt out of control of the line and made millions for themselves in the process.

In 1869, on Friday, September 24, the U. S. stock market was shaken by a crash that ruined many investors. In an attempt to corner the market on gold, Gould and Fisk made use of the fact that transactions could be reported by telegraph much faster than funds could be transferred. Gold hit 162 1/2 on the ticker and continued rising. The U. S. Treasury put $4 million in gold on the market. This action broke the "corner" and the price of gold fell sharply. Gould had been warned in advance by telegraph and had sold short. Fisk saved his fortune by refusing to honor his contracts. It is estimated that the two men made $11 million in the single day.

In 1872 Gould was forced to withdraw from the Erie and to return $3.4 million in embezzled funds. He then turned to Western railroads. He eventually came to own or control the Union Pacific, Kansas Pacific, Denver Pacific, Texas and Pacific, Missouri Pacific, Central Pacific, St. Louis, Southwestern, and Wabash railroads. In 1880 Gould was reputed to own 1 of every 10 miles of railroad in the U. S. In 1881 he gained control of Western Union.

THE INVENTORS

Elisha Gray (1835–1901) was one of the cofounders of the Western Electric Company, which today is the manufacturing arm of the American Telephone and

Telegraph Company. Gray was a professional electrician and inventor. He is known for a great many inventions in the telegraph and telephone field, including the harmonic telegraph and the telautograph. Gray was born in Barnesville, Ohio, and had studied at Oberlin College.

Emile Berliner (1851-1929) is remembered only slightly by the general public. However, he developed a number of inventions that are commonplace household items today. Among these is the flat disk record with lateral recording. The original Edison records were made by causing the point of a sharp stylus to dig deeper or shallower into a foil coating upon a cylinder. This technique had a great many drawbacks in terms of fidelity since the high pressures corresponded to a deep groove and the low pressures to a shallow one. This tended to make the cutter experience more resistance at high pressure and correspondingly to cause some slowing of the cylinder. In contrast, the Berliner record was not a cylinder but a flat disk with a spiral groove. The groove was deflected from side to side to record the sound vibrations. Since the groove was of constant depth, the resistance to cutting was also constant. Berliner also invented a technique of mass producing the records by a chemical etching process. Berliner was born in Hanover, Germany, and came to the U. S. in 1870.

Thomas Alva Edison (1847-1931) was born in Milan, Ohio, and moved with his parents to Port Huron, Michigan, at the age of 7. At the age of 12, he began working as a candy butcher on the Port Huron-Detroit train. An experiment with phosphorus set fire to the baggage car and earned him a boxing of the ears from the conductor that may have caused his later deafness. However, Edison himself attributed the affliction to a later incident in which he was running to catch a train and the conductor reached to help pull him aboard. Edison maintained that the conductor had grasped him by the ears and he heard something snap in his head, and that his hearing deteriorated steadily thereafter. In his last years he could barely hear a shout. It is noteworthy that the hearing impairment of Edison and several others plays a notable part in our story.

Edison's inventions are too numerous to list here. However, his improved stock ticker had set him up comfortably in business. Edison considered his greatest invention to be not one of his machines but the invention of the industrial research laboratory. His invention of the electric incandescent lamp in 1879, the motion picture camera in 1887, and the phonograph in 1877 were sufficient to ensure his memory. However, these constitute only a small portion of his contributions. Edison was also a cofounder of the General Electric Company.

Alexander Graham Bell (1847-1922) is, of course, the principal inventor in this saga since he was adjudicated to the eventual winner (although the outcome was by no means certain during the course of the game). In order to fully savor Bell it is necessary that we look at his forebears.

His grandfather, Alexander Bell, was a Shakesperean actor and a teacher of elocution. He was also the author of a book, *Elegant Extracts,* which was to be found on every fashionable Victorian table. At the age of 14 Alex Bell spent a year with his grandfather in London attending elocution classes and being educated from his grandfather's library.

Alex was the second of three sons born to Elysa Grace Symonds, a portrait painter and musician of some note, and Alexander Melville Bell, one of the foremost elocutionists and teachers of the time. The Bell family lived in Edinburgh, Scotland, at the time and Melville taught at the University of Edinburgh. The boys grew up in a home filled with art and music.

A most significant contribution to our story stems from the invention of "visible speech" by Melville Bell. This invention codified the positions of tongue, lips, teeth, mouth action, and vocal cords to characterize human speech. Using the Bell technique one could convey, on the printed page, the sounds of English, German, Chinese, or Choctaw in phonetic symbols so that one could learn to utter words and phrases in these (or any other language for that matter) without ever having heard the language spoken. The use of visible speech in teaching deaf-mutes was obvious, and Melville Bell was one of the foremost teachers of the time.

To place the matter in perspective, it should be remembered that Bell lived in a British Empire that was extremely class conscious. One of the paths to social and business success in mid-Victorian England was the possession of proper speaking skills and a "U" accent. The study of elocution was therefore viewed as a road to material and social success. As a matter of fact, George Bernard Shaw used Melville Bell's system to transform a guttersnipe into a lady in *Pygmalion.*

Bell must have been a remarkable student. At the age of 16 he applied for a position as a teacher-student at a school in Elgin, and by the next year he was resident-master at the Weston House Academy. During the next two years Alex and his two brothers studied and lectured extensively throughout England and Scotland on the subject of visible speech. In 1870 both of the brothers died of tuberculosis and Alex was on the verge of a nervous breakdown. In an attempt to preserve the remains of the family, Melville Bell abandoned his position as professor of elocution at the University of London. Melville moved the family to Brantford, Ontario, in search of what he felt to be a more salubrious climate. Alex soon recovered his strength and Melville held forth in the University at Brantford.

In 1871 Melville was invited by Sarah Fuller, the principal of the School for the Deaf in Boston, to show her pupils how to use visible speech. Due to teaching commitments, Melville could not accommodate, but recommended Alex in his place. In April 1872 Bell opened a school for teachers of the deaf in Boston. The following year he became a professor at Boston University. The teaching of deaf students was to give Bell two important financial connections and associates who played a significant part in his developing the telephone.

One of the associations was with Thomas Sanders, a successful merchant and patent attorney. Sanders had a son who was deaf and brought the boy to Bell as a private student. The second association was with Gardiner G. Hubbard. Hubbard was President of the Boston School for the Deaf. Hubbard had a daughter Mabel, then 15, who had been rendered deaf at the age of 5 by diphtheria (some sources say scarlet fever). At the time Graham Bell was 25.

The youthful Bell rapidly became a well-known figure in Boston society because of his work and published papers, including "Visible Speech as a Means of Communicating Articulation to Deaf-mutes," published in 1872. In it he quotes a paper by Melville Bell, "The Principles Of Speech," dated 1849.

THE HARMONIC TELEGRAPH

As noted earlier, the telegraph system in the U. S. was a very large and rapidly growing business in 1874, with lines being added to the system at the rate of about 19,500 miles per year, at a cost of about $100 to $150 per mile for materials alone. It is therefore little wonder that a number of inventors were attracted to the possibility of using the wires for more than one message at a time. Gray, Edison, and Bell were all attracted to the lucrative possibility of giving Western Union the ability to multiply its system capacity without adding more miles of wire.

In addition to his work at the school for the deaf and his lectures, Bell had been working on an idea to accomplish this end. In the fall of 1874, Bell paid a social call on the Hubbards. According to Helen E. Waite, in an authorized biography, Bell had taught Mabel Hubbard at the school for the deaf, but had turned her teaching over to Miss Abbie Locke because of a growing attachment for the attractive teenager. Bell himself was then 25 but looked much older. In any event Bell became a welcome guest in the Hubbard home on Brattle Street in Cambridge.

Bell, who was an accomplished musician, had finished playing the piano when he remarked to Hubbard that as he sang, the piano stings turned to the same note would vibrate in sympathy with the vibrations of his voice in the air. He commented that not only was this true but that if a telegraph wire were connected with the piano wire and a sounding board or musical instrument, the sound could be transferred electrically over some distance. One could use one note for a dot and a different note for a dash. (Note that this was a clear description of frequency shift keying, one of the commonest modes of digital transmission in use today.) When Hubbard asked the value of this procedure, Bell replied that it would permit a single telegraph wire to do the work of thirty or forty. Hubbard responded that he had been interested for many years in postal telegraphy and telegraphy in general and that he would be interested in funding experiments in this area.

To this point, Bell had been performing experiments in the home of Mr. Thomas Sanders. Bell had taught Sanders' son George, who was deaf, and Sanders was so impressed with the young man that he agreed to finance the experiments on the harmonic telegraph for a half-interest in the invention. Hubbard suggested to Sanders that it might be good for Bell to have more than one backer. Sanders was a prosperous leather merchant and the investment so far had been small; therefore he agreed. As matters turned out, this was a fortunate choice since the growing need for investment brought the Hubbard resources perilously low, and at one point Sanders was faced with a debt of $110,000.

On July 10, 1874, the *New York Times* had carried two articles of great significance to Bell. The top article carried a description of an invention by Edison that could simultaneously send two messages in both directions on a single telegraph wire. Of the quadruplex telegraph, the article said: "In an instant it will quadruple the usefulness of the 175,000 miles of wire owned by Western Union."

The lower article described an experiment in which Elisha Gray had transmitted musical tones that were "clearly audible at the receiving point over an unbroken circuit of 2,400 miles." A Western Union official was quoted as saying that "in time the operators will transmit their own voices over the wires and will talk with one another instead of telegraphing."

Bell too had an interest in sending human voices over the wires, but considered that the harmonic telegraph was the more potentially lucrative invention. With the backing of Hubbard and Sanders, Bell took the specifications for his transmitter and receiver to the Charles Williams Electrical Shop in Boston. This small firm had a skilled force of electricians and machinists and specialized in building experimental electrical apparatus. Just six years before, Edison had worked in the same shop on his stock telegraph.

This move was a boon to Bell. Previously Bell had been compelled by financial necessity to make his own apparatus. Unfortunately he was not much of a mechanic and perhaps less of an electrician and the experiments went slowly. With the professional aid of the Williams staff, the device leaped ahead. The first model of the telegraph was built by a 20-year-old mechanic named Tom Watson. Bell was so impressed with the young man that he asked Watson to become his assistant.

The exact details of that first instrument are somewhat controversial. However, it was probably similar to the system patented in 1876 on March 7 by Bell. Figure 1-1 shows the cover illustration for this patent. In it we see a series of three relay-type devices labeled a, b, and c, with corresponding primed and double-primed devices arrayed to the right. The entire assemblage is connected in series. The operation was as follows:

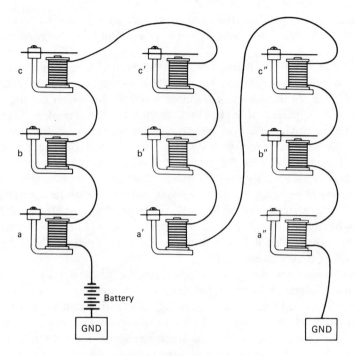

Figure 1-1. The Bell harmonic telegraph.

Instead of having a swinging armature like an ordinary relay, these units have a spring armature like the reeds in a music box. Units a, a′, and a″ are all tuned to the same frequency. The b units are all synchronized to a different frequency and the c units are similarly synchronized to yet another note. When the battery is connected the coils generate a magnetic attraction for the reeds, which bend downward somewhat but do not touch the pole piece.

The magnetic flux in the pole pieces is directly proportional to the current in the coil and the number of turns. It is inversely proportional to the airgap between the reed and the pole. If the reed is mechanically pulled up away from the pole, the flux must decrease. Therefore, during the motion a voltage is generated which bucks the battery, the battery voltage then temporarily reducing the current in the series string. If the reed on the b unit is mechanically "twanged," the current disturbance will be a relatively pure sinewave and all of the b reeds will vibrate in sympathy. The a and c reeds will respond little if at all since they cannot swing at the proper frequency. Obviously, this achieves the harmonic telegraph action Bell was after. There are certain practical limitations on the number of different frequencies that could be used due to the "Q," or response bandwidth, of the reeds and the addition of resistance due to the other coils. However, in principle, one could make use of a considerably larger number of tones.

By February of 1875, Bell and Watson had been able to get the harmonic telegraph working. On February 19, they took their apparatus to Washington, D.C., and set it up in Hubbard's Washington home. No sooner did they have the apparatus unpacked than Hubbard announced that President Orton of Western Union would be arriving shortly. Bell demonstrated a four-frequency model of the harmonic telegraph and Orton was duly impressed, but noted that he had to leave for New York that evening.

Two days later, Orton stopped Bell on the street and informed him that Western Union would be happy to place their very considerable lab facilities at Bell's disposal for the perfecting of the harmonic telegraph. The possible use of rooms full of batteries and miles of lines and the assistance of the finest electricians and mechanics fairly dazzled Bell. Furthermore, Orton told Bell that he had no interest in Elisha Gray's invention.

Orton's actions were eventually to contradict this position. However, in the same letter of March 5 in which Bell described the meeting to his parents, he noted that Orton had some reason for interest. Western Union had developed a near-monopoly on telecommunications. However, another firm, the Pacific Line, had purchased a patent for a quadruplex telegraph for $750,000, and the economies had made it possible for them to undercut the Western Union price structure. Bell felt that he could achieve a thirty- or forty-tone system that would permit Western Union to make up lost ground.

During the Washington visit, Bell had also seen Joseph Henry. Professor Henry was, of course, the inventor of the electromagnet and the codiscoveror of electromagnetic induction. Henry was then the president of the Smithsonian and was considered by many to be the leading physicist of the day. Bell described experiments in which he had shown that a coil of insulated wire produced an audible tone when excited with an alternating current. He also described to Henry his belief that it would be possible to transmit human speech over a telegraph line if a means were devised to make the current fluctuate in the same way as the air pressure of the speech. Bell asked whether he should publish his results or pursue the idea himself. Henry replied that he thought Bell had the germ of a great invention and that he should perfect it himself.

Following the meeting with Orton, Bell began spending every Saturday and Sunday in New York at the Western Union building, setting up a demonstration with a Mr. Prescott. By mid-March a series of transmission tests were set up. Orton and Prescott discussed the whole plan from a theoretical point of view. At a morning test, Bell remarked that the system went "like clockwork." The signals "though feeble, came sharply and concisely through 200 miles of line wire."

By the same afternoon, the mood had changed sharply. Orton casually announced that Elisha Gray had just visited and that Bell's apparatus was crude by comparison. Orton further pointed out what a great power Western Union was, and noted that an inventor was apt to overestimate the value of his invention. To cap the matter, Orton asked directly whether Hubbard had any financial interest in the invention. When Bell admitted that he had, Orton told Bell that "the Western Union will never take up a scheme which will benefit Mr. Hubbard." During the postal telegraph ruckus, Orton had suggested that if Hubbard should not be scalped he should at least have his head shaved! The animosity seemed to die hard. Hubbard offered to withdraw from the operation, but Bell would not hear of it.

At Hubbard's suggestion, Bell threatened to take his invention to the Pacific Line. This caused Orton to back down somewhat to the position of saying that while Western Union would not back something to benefit Hubbard, neither would personal feelings be allowed to keep the company from buying a desirable invention. Orton further stated that while he would back Gray if Bell went to the competition, no such agreement existed at the time nor was any contemplated.

In the spring of 1875, Bell told Watson of his hope to make a device in which the current could be modulated in a replica of the sound pressure of human speech. On June 2 of 1875, the day on which Bell and Mable Hubbard became engaged, a technical breakthrough materialized. The exact details of the apparatus are a bit obscure, but it would seem that the tuned interrupter shown in Figure 1-2 approximates the apparatus. When the telegraph key is closed, the current from the local battery increases the magnetization of the coil. As the reed deflects downward, the contact between the reed armature and the adjustable stationary contact is broken. The reed overshoots its equilibrium position and then springs up to remake the contact at its natural resonant frequency.

Watson and Bell were laboring over the apparatus in the attic of the Williams shop when, in Watson's words: "I was in charge of transmitters as usual, setting them squealing one after another while Bell was retuning the receiver springs one by one pressing them against his ear . . . . One of the transmitter springs I was attending to stopped vibrating and I plucked it, to start again. It didn't start and I kept plucking it, when suddenly I heard a shout from Bell in the next room, and then out he came with a rush demanding, "What did you do then? Don't change anything! Let me see?" I showed him. It was very simple. The make-and-break points of the transmitter spring I was trying to start had welded together so that when I snapped the spring the circuit had remained unbroken while that strip of magnetized steel by its vibration over the pole of its magnet, was generating that marvelous conception of Bell's — a current of electricity that varied in intensity precisely as the air was varying in density within hearing distance of that spring.

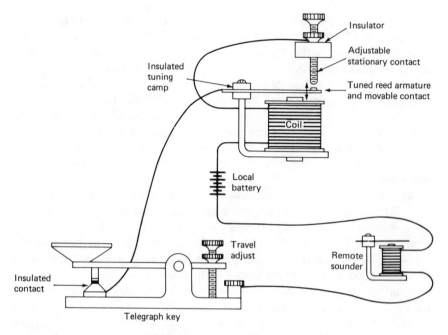

Figure 1-2. Tuned Interrupter.

"That undulatory current had passed through the connecting wire to the distant receiver which, fortunately, was a mechanism that could transform that current back into an extremely faint echo of the sound of the vibrating spring which had generated it, but what was still more fortunate, the right man had that mechanism at his ear during that fleeting instant and recognized the transcendent importance of that faint sound . . . . The shout that I heard and his excited rush into my room were the result of that recognition. The speaking telephone was born at that moment."

The welded contacts play a very important part in the drama. For interrupters such as this, the operation is very ragged. When the points close, the device draws a sharp slug of current, and when the points break the circuit there is a considerable amount of arcing as the magnetic field in the interrupter and the remote sounder collapse. Watson's use of the term "squealing" is appropriate since the remote instrument would tend to reproduce the entire ragged spectrum of the transmitter. The thing that excited Bell was that he heard a pure musical tone, which he, as a musician, probably recognized as a harmonic of the reed frequency. In normal operation the points would be open and no current would flow during this part of the cycle.

Bell became so excited over this discovery that he began to devote his efforts toward the telephone, at the expense of work on the harmonic telegraph. Hubbard was skeptical about the activity because it abandoned an invention for which there was a clear and very lucrative market for an unproven idea whose financial future was considerably more in doubt.

The original Bell telephone was a direct outgrowth of this work. The apparatus is shown in Figure 1-3. At the transmitter end, a small horn connects via a filament to the armature of what could be a conventional relay without a spring and contacts. As the pressure of the sound moves the diaphragm back and forth, the armature follows, thereby changing the airgap. The change in airgap causes the magnetic flux in the pole to vary, and this in turn induces the voltage in the coil that modulates the system current in imitation of the sound. At the receiver end the process is reversed. The fluctuating current strengthens and weakens the tension on the filament, causing the diaphragm to move in imitation of the sound at the transmitter end.

Bell filed the patent application on February 14, 1876, and the patent was issued on March 7, a remarkably short span. The rapid response of the patent office attests to the fact that there was little conflicting or prior matter. By a remarkable coincidence Elisha Gray filed a Caveat (an announcement of an intention to file) on the telephone only a few hours after Bell filed. This was to bring Bell no end of grief subsequently.

There are some fairly obvious deficiencies in the original Bell telephone when it is viewed from the standpoint of modern technology. One example is the use of the relatively heavy iron armature. In order to respond to the higher frequencies, this structure should have as little inertia as possible. A second deficiency is that the actual energy in the undulating current had to be extracted from the sound waves. This severely limited the power. Bell attacked this problem by designing a telephone in which a platinum wire was dipped into a small vial of acid. The motion of the diaphragm altered the depth of penetration, and therefore the

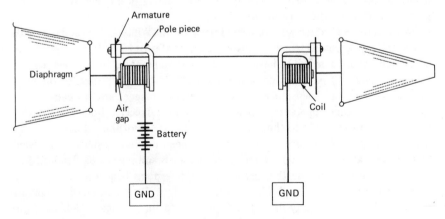

Figure 1-3.

resistance, of the transmitter circuit. This is an important concept since this transmitter was no longer required to extract all of the energy for the electric signal from the sound wave. The transmitter was in fact a parametric amplifier. The sound wave merely alters the resistance and the battery does all of the work.

As summer approached Bell and Watson made rapid progress. Watson recalled, ". . . and during the summer of 1876 the telephone was talking so well that one didn't have to ask the other man to say it over again more than three or four times before one could understand quite well, if the sentences were simple."

In June, the first Centennial Exhibition was to be held in Philadelphia. It took a great deal of persuasion and finally tears on the part of Mabel Hubbard to coax Bell into going. When he arrived he was awed by the gigantic Corliss Engine and the variety of machinery. Also, he was nearly prostrated by the heat. The passing crowds paid little attention to the exhibit, which said "A Graham Bell: Telegraphic & Telephonic Apparatus and Visible Speech." The exhibition judges came around to judge the exhibit late on Saturday, the hottest day of the entire summer, and were about to give up when a portly, well-dressed man stepped from the group and embraced Bell. It was no less than His Majesty Dom Pedro, the Emperor of Brazil. The emperor had visited Bell at the School for the Deaf and had been most impressed with the success of his teaching method. As the flabbergasted judges watched, nothing would do except that the emperor clamber into the overheated organ loft to be at the receiving end of the one-way system. Among the judges were Sir William Thompson (Lord Kelvin) and Joseph Henry. Dom Pedro exclaimed, "My God! It speaks!" The judges examined and tested the device for four hours in the sweltering heat, and finally Sir William announced: "Gentlemen, this is the most wonderful thing I have seen in America." The sensation rapidly spread and the telephone was national news.

In January 1877 Bell received the patent on the acid transmitter. The device itself was never widely used because it was messy and critical to adjust. However, it did play a part in the litigation to follow.

In April of 1877 a line was connected between the Williams shop and the Bell's home, the first practical telephone installation. In May of 1877 the first telephone advertisement appeared. Hubbard offered to lease telephones for $20 per year for residences and $40 per year for business places. In these instruments, the magnetizing current had been replaced by a permanent magnet and no battery was required. The same apparatus was used to transmit and receive, holding the device alternately to the ear or to the mouth. The elimination of the battery was critical for this application since few homes or businesses would have been interested in a device that required them to regularly mix acids and replace electrodes.

The expense of getting the instrument to this point had produced a heavy drain on the finances of both Hubbard and Sanders. By March of 1878 Sanders had sunk $110,000, nearly his entire fortune, into the business. Hubbard conceived of a solution in offering the Bell patents to Western Union for $100,000.

There is considerable question as to whether such an offer was actually made; however, there is some substantial evidence that it was. Chauncey Depew later confessed that Hubbard had offered him a one-sixth interest for $10,000, and that he had let Orton dissuade him. He later described this as the biggest mistake he had ever made.

Orton's position becomes a little more understandable in view of his great confidence in Edison. After all, Edison had invented the stock ticker and the quadruplex telegraph for Western Union. After his visit with Bell in Washington in 1875, Orton engaged Edison to look into the "acoustical telegraph" that Bell and Gray were pursuing. On January 14, 1876, Edison filed a caveat that included an apparatus for analyzing sound waves. Figure 1-4 shows this device. It consists of a solenoid with an iron plunger connected to a diaphragm mounted in a glass resonator. Edison intended to use this for a harmonic telegraph and only later did he test it for reproducing speech. It did reproduce speech, although poorly.

In March of 1876 Orton put Edison on a retainer of $500 per month to "take hold of Bell's telephone and make it commercial." According to Edison, attempts to introduce the telephone commercially "failed on account of its faintness and the extraneous sounds which came in on its wires."

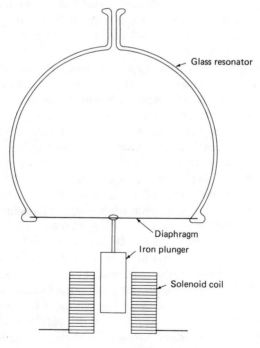

Glass resonator

Diaphragm

Iron plunger

Solenoid coil

Figure 1-4.

In April of 1877 Edison filed a patent on a transmitter he termed "more perfect than Bell's." This transmitter used a graphite impregnated electrode set and an inductance coil. In February of 1878 Edison filed a patent for a transmitter consisting of a button of carbon attached to a light metal diaphragm. As the diaphragm vibrated in sympathy with the sound, the compression altered the resistance of the carbon over a considerable range. As with the acid microphone, this device is a parametric amplifier and the energy in the undulating current can be considerably greater than the sound energy extracted from the sound wave. It was this transmitter that really advanced the telephone since it has an output many times as great as the sound-powered electromagnetic transmitter used by Bell.

The Bell Company was organized formally in July of 1877, just two days before the wedding of Alex and Mabel. By the fall of the year, they had more than 1,000 telephones in operation. In August Orton ordered Western Union's top expert (and Edison's first partner), Franklin Pope, to study the telephone situation. Pope concluded that Elisha Gray's patents would control the telephone and recommended their acquisition. Orton formed the American Speaking Telephone Company and bought up the rights to Edison's, Gray's, and others' patents. This was a giant organization for its day, capitalized at $40 million. It opened its own telephone exchanges and offered cut-price service in an attempt to crush the tiny Bell organization. Edison summarized the battle: "Western Union pirated the Bell receiver and Bell pirated the Western Union Transmitter."

Under this pressure, the Bell forces fought back in both the technological and the legal arenas. Tom Watson, who had become superintendent of all telephone and manufacturing operations, hired Emile Berliner. Berliner had filed a caveat for a pressure-sensitive carbon transmitter 14 days in advance of Edison. This enabled Bell to file an interference on the Edison patent, and this tied the transmitter patent up in litigation that was not settled until 1892.

In March of 1878 Western Union filed a block of interferences against Bell's patents on behalf of Gray and other inventors. There were more than 600 suits fought in high and low courts over the next 18 years. Bell was ultimately upheld in all of these cases, but they caused him a great deal of personal anguish.

Probably the most important of the cases was filed in 1878 against Peter Dowd, who was renting Western Union telephones in Massachusetts. When the suit was settled by consent in the fall of 1879, Western Union had in effect admitted the validity of the Bell patents. On February 8, 1878, there was a move afoot to merge Bell with Western Union. However, this merger fell apart within a few weeks. It seems likely that Orton's antagonism again triumphed.

In April of 1879 Orton died while riding in Central Park. In January of 1879 testimony had begun in the Dowd case. The tack taken by George Gifford, the chief counsel for Western Union, was that the Bell patents controlled the telephone proper, but that the Edison microphone transmitter made the telephone commercially feasible. Gifford proposed a merger, with each company having a fifty percent share. Bell Company refused.

On November 10, 1879, Western Union suddenly caved in. It admitted the validity of the Bell patents and agreed to retire from the telephone business and to turn over all of its patents to the Bell Company. In return, the Bell Company agreed to pay Western Union twenty percent of all royalties received from the rental of telephones over the next 17 years and to keep out of the public-message telegraph business.

Much of the speculation about the sudden reversal of position by Western Union centers about Jay Gould. After the Black Friday scandal, Gould was described in the *New York Times* as the "most hated man in America." In May of 1879 Gould launched another of a series of attacks against Western Union. He organized a competing telegraph company and began buying telephone exchanges and making motions in support of Bell Company in its fight against Western Union. The fears of the stockholders depressed the stock of Western Union sharply, and it was felt that the long and hazardous litigation against the Bell Company could seriously challenge the survival of Western Union and at the very least make them easy pickings for Gould.

As a matter of fact, the decision was profitable for Western Union since it received over $7 million in royalties from Bell in the course of the 17 years.

As for saving them from the predations of Gould, that effort was not so successful. In 1881, in a series of maneuvers, Gould obtained direct control of Western Union. Edison withdrew from association with Western Union after the Gould takeover in 1881 since he felt that "nothing further of value can be done there."

REFERENCES

Due to the very widespread legal controversy involved in the affairs of Bell, the Bell Company, and Western Union, and due also to the immense success the businesses enjoyed, a plethora of information about these affairs exists. Furthermore, the accounts given are often in complete and utter discord regarding some very specific events. Particular examples are the $100,000 offer and the question of the harmonic telegraph. Several sources say that after receiving the patent on the telephone, Bell abandoned the harmonic telegraph; however, U. S. Patent 174,405, issued March 7, 1876, indicates otherwise.

The writer has chosen to accept accounts of affairs, largely as given, in:

Make a Joyful Sound, by Helen E. Waite. Scholastic Book Services, 1961.

Celebrating Bell's 100th: The Marriage That Almost Was, by Michael F. Wolff. The IEEE Spectrum, February 1976, pp. 40–51.

Edison – His Life And Inventions, by F. Dyer, T. Martin, and W. Meadowcroft. Harper and Bros., 1929.

2
Basic Techniques

The original offering of the telephone to the public was based upon the idea that people who wanted to communicate between two separate buildings or points would lease a pair of telephones and erect a line. However, before the year was out Bell had pretty well formulated the form of service and the nature of organization that exists today.

The original concept held by Orton was simply an extension of the telegraph service. The company would simply have offices in different cities and the operators would communicate between offices by speaking rather than by Morse code. This is actually a pretty poor way to use the telephone system. If you want to convince yourself of this, try an experiment something like this:

My name is K-U-E-C-K-E-N, account number 123-456-7890. I want to enquire about a credit draft issued to me by the Standard Electric Lorenz Company in P-F-O-R-Z-H-E-I-M Germany.

If you can manage to get the spelling correct and the information conveyed in less than five tries, your bank clerks are a great deal more astute than those I deal with.

The simple truth of the matter is that there are many types of business communications that can be transacted much faster and more accurately by means of skilled operators using Morse code. In addition to this, one has a document with a written record of the communication. For this reason the telephone did not rapidly replace the telegraph service, and to this day most business firms that do business outside of their own city will have a teletype in the office.

Another advantage of the teletype is that it will operate unattended. This is particularly important when trying to do business over several time zones. For example, Pforzheim, Germany, operates on a time six hours earlier than Rochester, New York. There are only two hours during the working day when we are both in the office to speak to each other. A teletype message will be on the desk in the morning, and the time overlap problem is eliminated.

It is noteworthy that most European countries have delegated the operation of the telephone system to the post office, and the general mode of operation is much more akin to the telegraph operation than it is to the Bell system.

Bell had a somewhat different view of the nature of the telephone service. Telephones would be distributed among homes and businesses with the linkage to be accomplished through a central node or exchange. There are certain problems associated with this form of organization which, surprisingly, have not yet fully yielded to even modern mathematical analysis. Most of these difficulties are a matter of scale, that is, a system that works well with a small number of subscribers may become horrendously expensive and complex as the number of subscribers increases.

If one has ony two telephones to connect in a system, A and B, one obviously simply strings a line between them. But now let us suppose that a third telephone is added. We could string lines AB, AC, and BC. With the addition of a fourth, the list would grow to AB, AC, AD, BC, BD, and CD. In other words, the addition of the Nth telephone would require the addition of $N - 1$ lines. The system grows out of proportion to the number of additions.

There are two basic systems in use today that are somewhat more economical of wire. The top of Figure 2-1 shows a ring, or party-line, system. All of the subscribers, A through H, are on a single party line so that a message passing from A to D must pass through nodes B and C, or the other way around through H, etc. Years ago some telephones were organized this way, and the various parties would be assigned a different "ring" pattern so they could identify calls intended for them. For example, two longs and a short was the Baker's, etc. The big disadvantage to this scheme is, of course, that only one conversation at a time can take place. If G has a message for E, he has to wait until A and D are finished. If the ring is broken, say between A and H, this becomes a "bus" structure similar to that found in most computers. In this case A may be the CPU (Central Processing Unit), B and C may be memories, etc. Another disadvantage to this structure is that a failed node can put the whole net out of action.

One of the foremost uses for the ring architecture today is in the Xerox Ethernet. Ethernet is a mechanism for connecting computers, printers, displays and

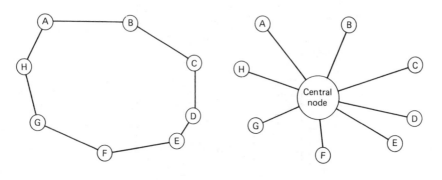

The ring or party-line network   The star or nodal network

Figure 2-1.

similar digital equipment together. This is described as a "contention driven" network. If device A wishes to communicate with device D, it listens first. If the line is busy it waits and tries again. However, suppose that G wishes to talk with F and attempts to start at the same instant as A. In this case both devices back off and wait for a random period. If another contention develops, both wait some random period longer. If the usage of the ring is relatively light, and if exchanges are brief, this, like the party-line telephone, works quite well. However, as the traffic begins to pile up or the exchanges get longer, the system can arrive at the condition where most of the time is spent in resolving contentions and most of the devices are in the wait state.

The STAR network at the bottom of Figure 2-1 resolves this problem in a somewhat different manner — by adding a central node. All communications pass through the central node. The central node can of course be equipped to connect more than two parties, but this implies some form of intelligent decision on the part of the central node. For example, A can call and say, "Hello, Central, give me D," and G can call and say, "Hello, Central, give me F." As a matter of fact, this was just what one did on the telephone in most places until the early 1930s.

However, there is somewhat of a built-in problem here as well. In Figure 2-2 we see a series of lines arranged in a crossbar pattern. If an operator could place a jumper at any of the crossings, it is apparent that the switch can be configured to connect any subscriber to any other subscriber. This works well for a small number of subscribers. However, it can be seen that the number of switch or patch facilities grows very rapidly as the number of subscribers increases. At first

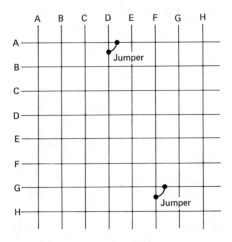

Figure 2-2. The crossbar switch arrangement.

glance it would seem that N^2 switches are required. However, it would not make much sense to connect any line to itself. Therefore, the number is actually $N^2 - N$. In order to add one subscriber it would be necessary to add $2N$, and the total becomes:

$$(N + 1)^2 - (N + 1) = N^2 + N \text{ switches}$$

This total grows very rapidly as N increases. For the example shown with $N = 8$, the array would require 56 switches. If the number were doubled so that $N = 16$, the array would become $256 - 16 = 240$ switches.

Now let us suppose that we were to add one more column to the array and label it T. In order to connect T to any of the inputs, we would have to add N switches, so our number for the array would become N^2. Now if two such arrays were connected together via T, we could serve $2N$ subscribers. For the value $N = 8$, we see that $2(8^2) = 128$ switches would suffice. Of course, this comes with the penalty that only one subscriber on the first array could speak to the second array at any instant in time.

Now let us suppose that we have M crossbar arrays, each of which has N subscribers. The system could then serve a total of $M \times N$ subscribers. Now, we can provide a central crossbar switch so that any of the M arrays can talk to any other array. Then the total number of switches in the system becomes: $M(N)^2 + M^2 - M$. Let us suppose that we want to handle 128 subscribers. We could have the following relationship.

M	N	$M(N)^2$	$M^2 - M$	Total Switches
0 (crossbar)	128			16,256
2	64	8,192	2	8,194
4	32	4,096	12	4,108
8	16	2,048	52	2,096
16	8	1,024	240	1,264
32	4	512	992	1,504
64	2	256	4,032	4,288

From the tabular data, one can see the economy possible with central-to-central switching. However, in the example given, it may be seen that any matrix may call any other matrix, but only on one line at a time. On even an eight-subscriber matrix, this would probably mean that one would frequently have to wait to place a call. It is more than likely that more than one line would be required from any matrix to central. A fairly typical small manufacturing business with which the writer is associated has an office staff of about 20 and a factory work force of perhaps 35. There are about 25 telephone instruments scattered about the place and four incoming lines. It is not unusual to have to wait a few minutes to place a call at certain times of the day.

The object of this exercise has been to show that the design of an optimum switched network is always a trade-off between the economics of the system and the level of service to be delivered. It is simply not feasible to design a system so that any telephone can be connected to any other telephone at any instant in time. Most people are willing to put up with a brief wait on Mother's Day or New Year's Eve.

Furthermore, it is interesting to note that the design of an optimum telephone system is not a trivial task mathematically. The theory of optimizing switched networks is an area of mathematics actively studied by a number of people today.

By the early 1900s the telephone had taken on the basic characteristics shown in Figure 2-3. The receiver basically followed Bell's pattern, except that the diaphragm had become a disk of spring steel that was directly attracted by the magnet, which had assumed a horseshoe form. The carbon button transmitter followed closely upon Edison's patent. It would assume a resistance that varied between about 200 Ω and 400 Ω depending upon the sound pressure. Two basic items had been added: the ringer, which was more or less tuned to follow a 20-Hz square wave, and the ringer magneto, which was designed to produce an approximately 20-Hz square wave at 70 V to 100 V.

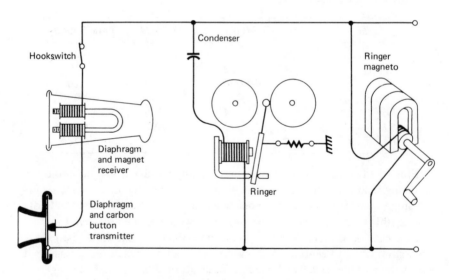

Figure 2-3. The basic telephone.

In the case of the ringer, the inductance of the coil was so large that it had little shunting effect upon the voice frequency currents. However, the dc resistance was so low that it would have essentially shorted out the current that flowed through the microphone. To prevent this, a $1\text{-}\mu\text{F}$ condenser was added in series.

The ringer magneto was a geared component equipped with a centrifugal switch to keep it from shorting the line when it was not in use. It also had a centrifugal governor to regulate the speed and an interrupter to yield the square wave. When you wanted to use the telephone you gave a brisk spin to the magneto handle and picked the receiver off the hookswitch. The magneto has disappeared, but the other elements remain in telephones to this day.

The impedance of the telephone ran to about 600 Ω, which was altered up and down by the changing resistance of the microphone. One might have expected the inductive reactance of the receiver to rise linearly with frequency; however, the shorted turn effect of the magnet and the large resistance of the fine-wire winding tended to keep the inductive-reactance effect down. The 600-Ω (nominal) characteristic remains with us to this day.

The characteristics of the telephone system as a whole are a mite tricky. For one thing the carbon button transmitter is not an electrically linear device. If measured with one of the modern digital ohmeters (which operate by passing a small fixed current through a resistance such that the full-scale reading on any range corresponds to a voltage drop of 200 mV) one will come to the conclusion that the resistance of the transmitter varies between about 700 Ω and more than 20,000 Ω.

On the other hand, when measured at a current on the order of 20 to 30 mA, the instrument's resistance seems to swing between something like 170 and 242 Ω.

The fact of the matter is that the entire system is generally dominated by the line resistance. The telephone line coming into my office in a suburb south of Rochester, New York, shows an open circuit voltage of 49.6 V. When loaded with a 100-Ω resistor (actually 99.7 Ω), the voltage drops to 3.00 V. The current through the resistor is 0.0301 A. For a line drop of 49.6 V - 3.0 = 46.6 V, this implies a line resistance of 1,549 Ω. With no speech input, the average voltage on the telephone is 4.91 V for a 44.6 V drop in the line. This implies a current through the instrument of 28.8 mA and a resistance of 170.2 Ω.

On the other hand, if I blow into the microphone, I can drive the voltage drop across the instrument to 6.70 V on the average. This, in turn, implies a current of 28 mA and a resistance of 242.5 Ω.

Viewed dynamically on the oscilloscope, and using a "true" rms digital voltmeter, the picture becomes a bit more complex, but perhaps clearer. The oscillogram of Figure 2-4 was approximately the view obtained when the writer pronounced the trailing r of the word four into a relatively modern telephone.

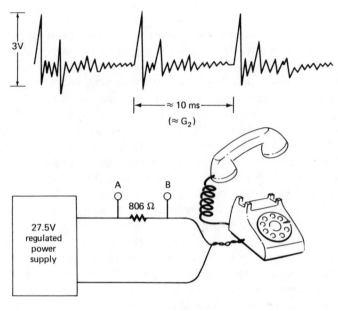

Figure 2-4.

The 3-V peak-to-peak swing was accompanied by an approximately 250-mV rms reading from the digital voltmeter. There are several points of interest here.

First among the considerations is that the trailing *r* is one of the strongest sounds made in the English language. This had long been known by folks who develop single sideband radios. The power in a single sideband radio is proportional to the speech power entering the microphone, and most old practitioners have learned that the word *four,* pronounced slowly with the *r* drawn out, will generate the most amount of power. If anything will cause the antenna coupler or the final amplifier to break down, this will. Notice that the ratio of the peak voltage to the rms voltage is 1.5/0.25 = 6, which amounts to 15.56 db.

There is a reason for this. Try saying *four* with the final *r* drawn out, and you will find yourself with your mouth open and rounded and your tongue tip pressed against the base of your lower teeth. Your vocal tract is presenting an optimum passage for the sounds generated by the vocal cords to the microphone or telephone transmitter. This is the loudest voiced sound because it is the most open.

By comparison the sound of *n,* as in *no,* is formed with the tongue tightly sealing the palate, and the sound proceeds largely through the nose. When you have a cold you can scarcely pronounce *no.* Compared to the *r* of *four,* the sound generated by the writer on *n* was only a few millivolts rms less than the *r,* but the peak-to-peak voltage was only about a volt. The waveform was nearly sinusoidal and the period was closer to 6 msec. The peak-to-rms ratio was only about 6 db. In short, the nasal *n* was a much more nearly sinusoidal waveform, and although the peak voltage was much smaller, the average power in the wave stayed nearly the same. In fact, the two sounded nearly alike in loudness. In both cases the power developed in the 806-Ω resistor was approximately 10^{-4} watts or –10 dbm. The *n* was higher pitched at approximately 166 Hz, or an E_1. It should be noted that the writer is a bass. The pitch for a tenor would have been E_1 and B_1, and a sorprano would have said the same phrase at approximately an E and an A.

We shall be going further into the electrical characteristics of speech waveforms in subsequent chapters. For the moment suffice it to say that the waveforms are very complex and they vary not only from speaker to speaker but also from expression to expression for the same speaker.

CAPTURING THE TELEPHONE LINE

When one wishes to capture the telephone line, either to answer an incoming call or to initiate an outgoing call, the only thing required is to place a current on the line by completing the circuit between the tip and ring conductors. (we shall be defining tip and ring shortly). A dc path that will conduct approximately 25 mA will trip a current-sensing relay at the exchange and inform the telephone system that your telephone is "off hook," meaning active. In the case where you wish to place an outgoing call, the system will respond by giving you a dial tone. After this you can commence to place the call by means of either a rotary-pulse sequence or by means of the Touch-Tone® code (provided you are paying the extra fee for the tone-dialing service). In the case of an incoming call, the off-hook condition will terminate the ringing and commence to connect you with the caller.

Anyone seriously interested in designing telecommunications equipment should have copies of a number of American Telephone and Telegraph Company publications. One which will be referred to in this chapter is Pub 47001- Electrical Characteristics of Bell System Network Facilities at the Interface with Voice-band Ancillary and Data Equipment. This publication, or "spec," notes that the battery voltage applied to the ring conductor is 42.75 to 52.5 V negative with respect to earth. The source resistance in the ring lead (placed in the central office to limit the current) can vary from 500 to 2,500 Ω. The tip lead is normally grounded in the central office. However, it may have a resistance of 0 to 700 Ω to ground at that point. In addition to this, the user end of the line will experience the resistance of the wires themselves. The total loop resistance is typically 0 to 1,300 Ω but can be as much as 2,500 Ω on unigauge design loops and 3,600 Ω on long route loops.

The specification states that a 200-Ω resistor is adequate for capturing the line. However, the writer has found that a 150-Ω 2-W carbon resistor is more likely to do the trick. It turns out that not all telephone companies maintain their equipment to Bell standards. The 200-Ω resistor may not be quite adequate to capture the line in some cases; therefore, the smaller resistor is advisable.

Another item worthy of note is that the resistance of the tip conductor is sufficient so that the tip terminal will not be at local ground potential when the resistor is drawing off-hook current. Neither of the lines should be grounded, and it is generally good practice to provide complete electrical isolation between your own equipment and the telephone company's equipment. In the case of the off-hook resistor, this can generally be done by using a relay to place the resistance across the line. The relay will provide the isolation between your electrical system and the telephone company's.

THE TIP AND RING

The "ring" in the tip and ring set does not refer to the ringer or ringing of the telephone at all. The terminology is very old and refers to the plugs the telephone operators used to connect callers. Before the time of automatic dial switching, the switches in the networks were not actually switches. The telephone operator used to sit in front of a large array matrix of jacks or sockets. To connect a caller to one of the lines, she would insert a plug. Often the system had jumpers to patch one jack to another. The plug itself had a construction similar to Figure 2-5. One of the conductors was connected to the end contact, or tip, and the other was attached to the second, or ring. Since the tip or outermost part was the most likely to be accidentally touched, it was made the grounded end of the circuit. The terms *tip* and *ring* have been perpetuated even though the usage of the plugs has long vanished.

POLARITY REVERSAL

In the design of equipment that operates on the telephone line, it is important to note that test voltages up to 202 V will sometimes be placed on the line and that line polarity will sometimes be reversed. It is therefore important that all

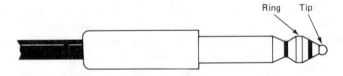

Figure 2-5. The phone plug.

equipment be designed so that polarity reversal will not cause failure of the equipment.

THE DIAL TONE

The dial tone actually consists of two separate sinusoids at 350 (F) and 440 (A) Hz. There were some older standards; however, these can be largely ignored in modern designs. In general, an off-hook interval on the order of a second will produce a dial tone. However, if the central is very busy, a longer wait may be required. Before initiating dialing it is important that the dial tone be present, otherwise the first character may be mangled or lost. It is usually useful to build a dial-tone detector into telephone interface systems since the dial tone signifies that the telephone system is ready to accept dial signals. The tone dissappears at the start of the first rotary dial pulse or on receipt of the first tone signal. Failure of the dial tone to dissappear signals that the telephone system has not accepted the first digit.

On a telephone answering system, the detection of the dial tone is equally important since a disconnect of the calling party is signaled by the insertion of a dial tone. This is not at all unusual on a telephone answering machine. A storm-window salesman or solicitor will call and hang up immediately upon hearing the machine. After about 30 seconds the telephone company will put a dial tone on the line to indicate that the party has disconnected. After about 5 seconds of this the telephone system will place a raucous series of four tones on the line consisting of 1,400 Hz (F^2) plus 2,060 Hz (C^3b) plus 2,450 Hz ($D^3\#$) plus 2,600 (E^3b) Hz. The ensemble is pulsed on and off 5 times per second. This is called the precision Receiver-off-Hook (ROH) tone. The object is to attract the customer to a telephone accidentally left off the hook and induce him to put it on the hook.

In the case of a machine using the telephone line, it is reasonably important to detect this tone since a great many people will hang up as soon as they determine that they have reached a machine. If a dial-tone detector is continuously monitored, the machine can be arranged to go on-hook whenever a dial tone is detected after a connection has been initiated. In this case the ROH tone will seldom be heard since it usually follows a dial tone. On the other hand the ROH tone is very simple to detect due to the high amplitude and the pulsing at five times per second.

The detector shown in Figure 2-6 will do the trick rather nicely. The top circuit shows a voltage doubler rectifier. The capacitors, which serve to dc-isolate the circuit from tip and ring, also limit the response to high frequencies. The time constant of the output filter is fast enough so that the output of the circuit is essentially a 5-Hz square wave biased only slightly above ground. In

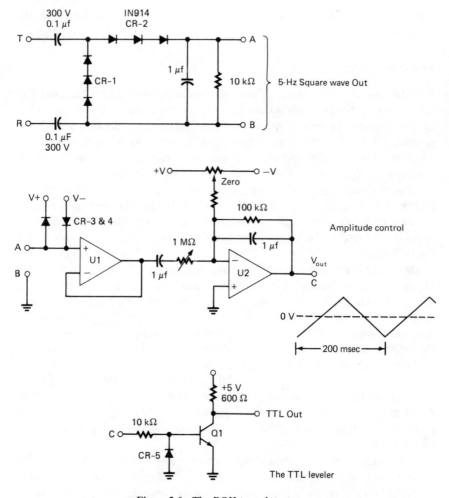

Figure 2-6. The ROH tone detector.

general, the amplitude of the square wave will pulse from near zero to about 3 V or more positive; thus it could be used directly in a TTL-level sensing circuit.

The circuit labeled "Amplitude Control," shown in the lower portion of the figure, provides a little more positive control. U1 is a voltage follower to avoid loading of the circuit, and U2 forms an active low-pass filter. The output of this circuit will be a triangular wave more or less symmetrical about zero with the amplitude adjustable through the 1-M Ω pot.

The bottom circuit labeled "TTL Leveler," serves to give a solid TTL output pulse that does not go below zero or above 5 V and produces a negative-going output pulse. This circuit need only be sampled every 50 msec or so to determine whether the ROH tone is present. The zero offset control on U2 can be used to ensure that Q1 will not fire on normal speech.

It should be noted that there are several features about this circuit that are generally good for telephone-connected devices. First of all, it provides complete dc isolation between your circuit and tip and ring. Secondly, it faces the line with relatively high voltage rating components. Thirdly, it is provided with a mechanism to distinguish the signaling from ordinary speech; it is resistant to "talk-off." Finally, the circuit is arranged to protect itself from disturbances normally encountered on the telephone line. Diodes CR-3 and CR-4 prevent the input of U1 from being driven outside of the supply rails.

It should be noted that this simple circuit will not work with certain types of modems on line. We shall be treating this subject later.

In a relatively sophisticated microprocessor-controlled machine, the output of Q1 could be monitored to ensure that is was firing every 200 msec or so and was low in between before initiating a disconnect. On the other hand, monitoring every 50 msec or so and going on-hook on the first firing of Q1 is also possible, but will yield a few more false disconnects. Using the output of Q1 to initiate an interrupt is perhaps the most likely to produce false disconnects.

ROTARY DIALING

The use of rotary dialing is always easy to accomplish, although it is relatively slow. The ease comes from the fact that the dialing can be accomplished by simply keying the off-hook connect relay to interrupt the line current.

The dial pulses are nominally insued at a rate of 10 pulses per second (pps); however, 8 to 11 will be accepted if they are uniform throughout the character. The "percent break" time, or percentage of time spent on-hook, should be slightly longer than the time off-hook and should be between 58% and 64%. A character is identified by counting the number of breaks; thus, a 1 is a single break and a nine is nine breaks. It does not make much sense to have a zero equal to no breaks at all; therefore a zero represents ten breaks.

The characters are separated by 600 msec to 3 sec. However, some older step-by-step systems require as much as 700-msec separation. A machine designed for general distribution should generally operate with a 750-msec interval between characters. Dialing should not commence sooner than 70 msec after the dial tone appears, and it is safer to allow 100 msec.

On this basis we can compute the time required to dial a call. The longest 7-digit number would be 900-0000. The time taken would be:

$$(8.5 + (6 \times 9.5))100 \text{ msec} + 6 \times 750 \text{ msec} + 70 \text{ msec} = 11.12 \text{ sec}$$

For a direct-distance-dialed call to 1-900-900-0000 the time is 16.92 sec. We shall see shortly that Touch-Tone® dialing is a great deal faster.

In order to effectively signal, the system should draw at least 26 mA, and 30 mA is actually preferable. In the on-hook condition the impedances between tip and ring, or either one and ground, should be at least 150 k Ω. However, in order to avoid sparking at the relay contacts, a resistor-condenser circuit should shunt the line. A 50-k Ω resistor with a 0.01-uF capacitor represents the smallest acceptable load. Larger resistors and smaller capacitors are acceptable. The contacts should not bounce for more than 3 msec at the initiation of a "make," or off-hook condition, and should not arc for more than 0.2 msec on a break. Spurious breaks, other than a contact bounce, should not exceed 1 msec, and spurious makes during a break are completely unacceptable. In general, most reed relays are quite suitable for the off-hook and dialing duty. Conventional open-frame iron-armature relays will generally have longer bounce times unless they are rather small.

The Bell spec notes that no. 1 and no. 5 crossbar and ESS offices can accept dialing at rates up to 17 to 21 pulses per second, which would halve dialing time. However, equipment designed for general usage would not be able to take advantage of this.

The equipment should not generate breaks in excess of 300 msec during the course of a call. When a call is terminated by going on-hook, a new off-hook condition can be generated in less than 2 seconds.

It is noteworthy that the dial pulses do not propagate through the system farther than the local exchange office. They can thus not be used to propagate information through the system. On the other hand, Touch-Tones propagate freely through the system and thus may be used for signaling. However, only a conditioned (and extra charge) exchange will accept Touch-Tone dialing. For the widest application, equipment should be designed to permit either type dialing. All tone-dialed systems will also accept rotary signaling; therefore if speed is not required, the safest course would be to always pulse dial, although the option of tone dialing is an attractive one where possible. Pulse dialing seems awfully slow when a machine is doing it, and one sits and waits for it to finish.

TOUCH-TONE DIALING

The generic term for Touch-Tone dialing is dual-tone Multifrequency (DTMF) dialing. The term Touch-Tone is a registered trademark of the Bell System and cannot be used in descriptions of your product without reference to the trademark condition or without license. The system was evolved to permit voiceband propagation of dialing signals through the system. The system uses two simultaneous tones at a time, one each from a "high group" and a "low group," to uniquely define each digit.

The reason for the use of dual tones is that the tones were selected on the basis of two criteria:

1. Equal energy in both groups is seldom present in ordinary speech. The system is therefore highly resistant to "talk-off."
2. The presence of two simultaneous, relatively pure tones provides an effective "signature" to identify the fact that signaling is taking place rather than music.

The tones are selected so that they are not harmonically related in a simple way. This is particularly important when they enter the telephone system from some nontelephone source; for example, a mobile radio telephone repeater. In such devices the complete elimination of intermodulation can be quite difficult; therefore, sum and difference terms can appear when two tones are simultaneously present. The tones are selected so that chances of misreading are minimized.

The listing of the tones is generally presented in matrix form. Your signals to Ma Bell for dialing will be done using ten tone-pairs although twelve are actually present on most tone-dialed telephones. In actuality, the system is hexadecimal in nature and there are sixteen tone-pairs possible in the Bell standards. The matrix is as shown below:

		High Group Tones Hz (Notes are Approximations)			
		1,209 (C^2b)	1,336 (F^2b)	1,447 ($F^2\#$)	1,633 ($G^2\#$)
Low	697 (F^1)	1	2	3	A
Group	770 (G^1b)	4	5	6	B
Tones	852 ($G^1\#$)	7	8	9	C
(Hz)	941 ($A^1\#$)	*	0	#	D

Note: $\#$ = sharp.

The first three columns will be recognized as the markings on the telephone keyboard. These are available at any public telephone with tone signaling. They are of particular interest to us here because they are not to be found in any telephone number. Therefore, if your system is intended to provide for direct data entry into a computer, the * and # symbols (usually referred to as "star" and "pounds") can be used to identify data as distinguished from telephone numbers.

In keeping with telephone practice, from the rotary system the zero is decoded as a 10 (hex $0A). On commercial decoders there is no overriding standard, but * is generally decoded as an 11 (hex $0B) and # is decoded as a 12 (hex $0C). The remainder of the characters are often decoded as $0D, $0E, $0F, and $00, reading from top to bottom on the right-hand column. It may be seen that the characters are a bit scrambled from a hexadecimal point of view. In a number of data entry systems the writer has used * = CLEAR and # = ENTER. They can also be used in combinations. For example, in a file register system:

MMMM NN NNNNNNN

might represent an entry under heading MMMM. The three leading #'s tell the computer that this is an entry, and the trailing # tells the computer that the entry is complete. The use of a terminator allows the use of variable-length entries.

On the other hand, the use of:

MMMM

tells the computer that I would like to have it read the contents of file MMMM to me. A * entered at any point would clear the system for a restart.

Those familiar with such matters will recognize the fact that the use of ### and # contains some redundant information. However, there is an advantage to this inclusion. The machine can be instructed to go on-hook, that is, hang up, if the leading character is not a #. This does a great deal to eliminate, or at least minimize, the amount of time that the machine is occupied with people who have reached a wrong number and decide to play with the machine.

The nominal level for the sine-wave tones is –6 to –4 dbm (db with respect to one-milliwatt.) The minimum acceptable level for a low-group tone is –10 dbm, and for a high group tone it is –8 dbm. The maximum level for the two tones is +2 dbm. The difference in level, or "skew," between the tones should not exceed 4 db, and the level of the high-group tone should equal or exceed the level of the low-group tone. The frequencies should be within ±1.5%, and preferably within ±1.2%.

The minimum duration of the two-frequency signal should be 50 msec, and the minimum interdigital time should be greater than 45 msec. The minimum cycle time is 100 msec. Since all digits take the same time, we see that any seven-digit number may be dialed in 0.7 sec minimum. The ten digits of a long distance number can be dialed in one second. The Bell spec does not say so but the writer has found that it is advisable to stretch the 45 msec pause after the initial "1" for direct-distance-dialing to 150 msec.

The Bell spec requires voice tones to be suppressed at least 45 db relative to the signaling tone-pair and all energy above 500 Hz to be at least 20-db suppressed. Both frequencies should attain 90% of full amplitude within 5 msec (preferably 3 msec). Any transient overshoot should be confined to the first 5 msec of the burst and should be no greater than 12 db above the zero-to-peak maximum of the tone-pair. More will be said of this later.

If one has the service available, the time savings accruing to the use of tone dialing are obvious. The speedup from 11.12 sec to perhaps 750 msec in local calling is significant.

For data transfer the DTMF signaling also works quite well since the tones will propagate freely through the Bell (and for that matter non-Bell) systems. For a simple system using only the keys available on the telephone keyboard, namely 0 through 9, * and #, one could send messages in alphanumeric code in a variety of ways. Referring to Figure 2-7, you will note that keys 2 through 9 each carry three letters. The comptete alphabet, except for Q and Z, is present. One could send all four meanings of a key by two keystrokes rather than one. For example, 15 would represent the numberal 5, while 25 would represent the letter J, 35 the letter K, and 45 the letter L.

The letter Q could be represented by 57, and the letter Z by 59. A given word could be started with a # and ended with a *. A period could be represented by two stars: **.

With a little practice, people can "type" messages on this keyboard at the rate of about two keys per second, and three is not that difficult to achieve. Assuming that the average word represents 5 characters (and that a starting # and a closing * are added), we see that there are 13 keys to be pressed. At two keys per second this comes out to 9 words per minute, and at three keys per second it works out to about 14 words per minute. In the case of machine talking to machine via the DTMF code, it is possible to reduce the detection time and achieve very low error rates at about 100 msec/character, or 10 char/sec for a transfer rate of more than 100 words per minute, which is faster than a conventional teletype.

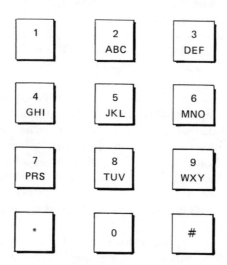

Figure 2-7. Standard DTMF keyboard.

At first glance one might be inclined to ask why anyone would want to use a telephone in such a clumsy fashion. The answers are manifold. For example, a man with a wife who is hearing-impaired would suddenly find it possible to communicate with her over the telephone if he simply has a home computer equipped with a DTMF decoder. He need carry nothing with him except the change for the telephone call, and the message would appear on the screen. Whereas a speech-recognition system for a single speaker with a vocabulary of only a few tens of words is hardly likely to achieve an error rate better than 2 of 10 words, the DTMF system could print pages without a telephone-electronic error. Most of the errors would be typing errors on the part of the sender.

For a second example, consider a firm with a large number of salesmen scattered throughout the country. These salesmen call in daily to enter orders. The orders must carry a customer name and address, both of which must be properly spelled, and a product name or number and quantity. With a machine-decoding DTMF code, the salesmen can achieve high-accuracy order entry into an unattended machine at any time of the day or night (when long distance rates are lower).

One of the first questions asked in this situation is usually, "Why use an expensive computer machine when you could simply use a cheap electronics store tape-answering machine?" The answer is very simple: accuracy! Imagine getting the following message correctly off of a tape made from a long distance phone: The customer name is Irmgard Fotzengargle, buyer for Zanzibar Widgets, Inc., at 23956 Malamute Street, Piqua, Ohio. She needs 1,300 Chanion pins, model 2A43791, shipped air express tomorrow morning. This looks like a real live account so get those pins to her tomorrow at all costs! I will be traveling and unavailable till 7:30 P.M.

Note that you cannot ask him to repeat or spell, and anything rendered indistinguishable by noise in the message is unverifiable until it's too late to do anything about it. This is a horrible example but it is not too unlikely to happen from time to time.

Regional accents can also enter in. For example, Piqua, Ohio, is pronounced PICK-WAY by the people who live (and sell) there. Chili, N.Y., is pronounced CHY-LIE, and the Texas salesman who gives an address on ORAL street expects the order clerk in Boston to transcribe the address on *Oil* street.

Error rates on the order of one in 10^4 and better are achievable using Touch-Tone telephones and a decoder on otherwise unconditioned lines. With a speech synthesizer the machine can be made to read back the data for verification and/or correction, spelling letters one at a time in proper names and words not on the vocabulary list.

The remote user can operate without any equipment at all or he can use a repertory memory dialer which acoustically couples into the telephone transmitter. The latter units are inexpensive and can be pocket-size.

THE BUSY SIGNAL

Any device that is used to originate telephone calls should be equipped with a mechanism to recognize the busy signal. The busy signal consists of two tones, 480 Hz (A#) and 620 Hz (D#). The tones are interrupted with an on period of 0.5 ± 0.05 sec and an off period of 0.5 ± 0.05 sec, for a 1-Hz nominal total. The busy signal is considerably softer than the dial tone, running –28.5 to –25.5 dbm per tone. By comparison, the dial tone runs –17.5 to –14.5 dbm per tone. You will note that the dial tone at 440 Hz is not very far removed from the busy tone at 480 Hz, a difference of only 9.1%. All of the signaling tones have a tolerance of ±0.5% in frequency. Therefore, the 440-Hz tone could actually be 442.2 Hz, and the 480-Hz tone could actually be 477.6 Hz, thereby reducing the spread to 8% in the worst case. We shall shortly be discussing the techniques for tone detection.

Upon receipt of a busy signal, the equipment should go on-hook and not attempt another off-hook operation for 2 seconds. Depending upon the purpose of the machine, the following action varies. For example, if this is a repertory dialer, it may simply try the same number again. However, if the machine is an automatic alarm monitor, it may have a list of numbers to call to report the alarm condition (such as oven temperature too high, intruder, etc.).

THE AUDIBLE RING

When you hear the telephone ringing at the other end of the line, what you hear is not the actual ringing voltage sent to the remote telephone set but rather a pair of tones inserted to let you know that the central is attempting to reach the called number. The tones are 440 Hz and 480 Hz at a level of –23.5 to –20.5 dbm per tone. You will note that the audible ring shares the 440 Hz with the dial tone and the 480 Hz with the busy tone. The tones are interrupted, with a 2-second on-time and a 4-second off-time, which aids in distinguishing ringing. In general, the ringing is detected by sampling the two detectors.

After the number has been dialed, if ringing does not commence within 5 seconds it is usually a sign that the central has not been able to place the call for some reason. The usual strategy is to go on-hook and redial after a 2-second wait. If ringing is established, the strategy becomes somewhat different and is more dependent upon the actual machine usage. If a human being is to be called it is usually a good idea to allow 6 to 8 rings, which amounts to 36 to 48 seconds to give the person time to get to the phone. If a machine is intended to answer, the time allowance is dependent upon the arrangement of the answering machine. The ring detector can be made to respond on the first cycle of the ringing voltage. However, this may not be advisable, as will be shown shortly. Also, some machines deliberately delay answering for 12 to 15 seconds to allow a human operator to answer if present.

The cessation of ringing is a fairly good indication that the telephone has been answered at the far end. However, this has several drawbacks in that it is slow and does not give positive indication of an answer. The slowness is due to the fact that the ringing will have a 4-second off-period. At the end of a ringing interval the machine has to wait 4 for seconds before it can determine whether the phone has been answered. This is actually a fairly long time compared to the normal response. Typically, a person will say "Hello" in 500 to 700 msec after picking up the telephone. The detection of a human response by the machine is also somewhat more difficult than would be expected. If possible, a far more reliable technique is to have the responding party answer by sending something distinctive, such as # or *.

THE MISDIAL TONE

It is virtually impossible to detect a wrong number by machine when the phone is supposed to be answered by a human being. However, on occasion, the dialed number may be mangled and there will be an attempt to reach a nonexistant exchange, etc. In this case the central may place a loud, sustained swept tone which sounds something like a siren. Any loud (greater than –17.5 dbm) tone sustained for more than 1.5 sec is cause to go on-hook. Central will, on occation, mangle your dialing and misdirect a call, and provision for disconnect chould be included. When a person answers a misdialed call, they will probably hang up shortly and the machine will then go on-hook when it detects a dial tone or an ROH signal.

In the next chapter we will treat the subject of the various tone and ring detectors.

3
Tone Detectors

In the previous chapter, we discussed the various tones and voltages present upon the line. In this chapter we will discuss some of the mechanism whereby these tones and signals may be unambiguously detected and utilized. We shall be discussing incoming ringing first since this is the easiest to do.

THE INCOMING RING DETECTOR

The incoming ring is the easiest to detect since this is the highest voltage signal encountered on the telephone line. Your machine will be on-hook and in a high-impedance condition and the tip-ring voltage will be around 50 V. The ringing voltage is 86 ± 2 V rms at 20 ± 3 Hz with a dc component added. In some cases the ac voltage can vary from 65 to 130 V, and the dc component can go from 35 to 75 V negative. During the ring period, which is generally 2 seconds out of 6, the dc bias makes the ac term essentially unipolar, that is, not actually reversing in polarity.

Because of the high voltage, one of the simplest ring detectors consists of a neon lamp and a phototransistor. This arrangement has some great advantages for ring detection:

1. It offers complete isolation between the telephone line and your equipment. Commercially available neon opto-isolators are typically guaranteed for 1,500 V isolation between input and output sides. All of the coupling takes place via the light emitted by the neon lamp.
2. The neon lamp has a well-defined threshold at about 67 V. A signal less than this will simply not light the lamp. The unit is therefore immune to all of the normal signaling on the line.
3. The circuit has minimal parts count and cost.
4. The output transistor can be arranged to give solid, well-defined TTL output levels.
5. The loading on the line is negligible and the detector does not need to be removed when the system is off-hook since the impedance of the neon lamp is very high, near infinity, when the voltage is below 67 V.

When the ringing voltage is detected, the lamp lights and drives transistor Q1 into saturation (Figure 3-1). The $\overline{\text{RINGING}}$ (say ringing-NOT) signal goes from

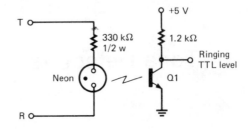

The neon detector

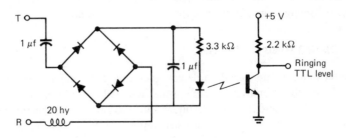

The LED detector

Figure 3-1. The ringing detector.

5 V to nearly 0, probably on the order of 0.3 V, so the device is active-low. This low signal can be taken as indication that the phone line is ringing.

There are a few tips about using this device. First of all, the detector is fast enough so that it actually follows the 20-Hz ringing pulses. A capacitor can be added across Q1 to prevent this, however, it can also be handled by software. The signal will actually spend 25 msec low and 25 msec high. If RINGING is sampled on perhaps a 5-msec time base, the presence of multiple lows will suffice to indicate ringing. Typically, the machine will catch the first cycle of the ring signal.

If the machine is intended to talk to human beings, it is well to put some delay in the answer since it is rather disconcerting to have the telephone answered before the caller hears the ring. Without the delay, a ring is not perceived by the caller.

A second point to note is that the machine should not begin its salutation until at least 600 msec to 1 sec after going off-hook since a fast central connection will not give the caller time to get the receiver to his ear. This problem is accentuated when the caller has a DTMF telephone with the buttons on the handpiece.

Upon completion of the call, the machine should ignore the ringer for at least 1 sec after going on-hook since a voltage transient will frequently follow the disconnect and briefly fire the detector. On a manual telephone, this is often heard as a single "ding" following hang-up. Failure to observe this delay will result in having the machine go on-hook and almost immediately go off-hook again with the final on-hook occurring due to a timeout or a dial tone.

The opto-isolated detector is a relatively high impedance device; therefore, it has a low *ringer equivalence number* (REN). The REN is one of the items which is stipulated in Section 68.312 of part 68 of the FCC rules governing type approval of devices to be attached to the telephone lines. All very small REN numbers are arbitrarily rated at 0.1 REN. In essence a REN of 1 implies the equivalent of a 25-hy inductor in series with a 23,333-Ω resistor. A 12.5-hy inductor in series with an 11,667-Ω resistor would be a ringer equivalent of 2, etc. In general, it is advisable to keep the REN as small as practical. It should be noted that all components attached between tip and ring in the on-hook condition are included in calculating the REN. The REN of all type approved devices must appear on the nameplate.

There are a number of other types of isolated devices that can be used for ring detection, which still supply high levels of isolation. For example, a bridge rectifier that is ac-coupled to the line through a condenser can be used to operate a high-impedance relay. Your machine can then sense a contact closure. Unfortunately, this scheme is a great deal more expensive than the neon isolator that sells for less than a dollar in quantity. Furthermore, the relay contacts are subject to bounce and therefore require either hardware or software debounce measures. In addition to this, the relay is much more subject to burnout due to transients on the line.

Ring detection and isolation can also be accomplished with a LED photoisolator as shown in the lower half of Figure 3-1. Equivalent isolation and action can be obtained, however, only at a cost of higher parts count and a higher REN. The reason for this is that the LED is a low-voltage high-current device compared to the neon lamp. The phototransistor requires about the same amount of input power to the lamp in order to saturate. However, for the neon lamp this amounts to only a few microamps. In the case of the LED isolator, the transistor current will be about 5 times the diode current for a sensitive isolator with a photodarlington, so the LED must draw several mA. The inductor is added to bring the REN to 1. By comparison, the neon detector will drive about 10 TTL loads, whereas the LED detector is probably confined to LSTTL or MOS devices.

THE DECIBEL

Fairly early in his studies of the telephone as a working instrument, Alexander Graham Bell discovered that the normal human ear is a highly nonlinear device. Among the human senses the ear has the greatest dynamic range. A person with normal hearing can easily hear the rustle of leaves in a gentle breeze that corresponds to a radiated sound intensity of about 4×10^{-15} W/cm² and acute hearing extends down to 10^{-16} W/cm². A normal conversation proceeds at about 10^{-10} W/cm², and the painful noise 100 meters behind a jet airliner represents about 10^{-3} W/cm². In all, this represents a range of 10^{13}, a ratio larger than the ratio between a penny and the national debt by several orders of magnitude. The fact that the normal conversation is a million times stronger than the smallest detectable sound and a rock concert is a million times stronger than the conversation gives some feel for the range of the human ear.

In the course of his studies, Bell found that the perceived loudness about doubles when the actual power incident upon the ear increases by a factor of ten; that is, the response of the ear is logarithmic. For this reason, it made a little sense to talk of the "speech power" in a telephone since even doubling the power gave a perceived change in loudness that was just perceptible. Instead, he found it much more meaningful to talk about power on a logarithmic scale. Accordingly, the *bel* was described as the logarithm to the base 10 of the ratio of the powers.

Now, whereas the ear may tell one that a sound is 4 times as loud when the power is increased 100 times, this is a pretty coarse measurement for electrical work because a 100 times increase in power is a big change in the voltages and currents going into a device. There is a lot of difference between applying 40 volts and 400 volts to the telephone. Accordingly, the unit adopted was the *decibel*, which strikes somewhat more of a medium between the very nonlinear properties of the ear and the linear dependence of electrical machinery upon power.

The decibel is defined as ten times the log to the base ten of the ratio of two powers measured across the same or identical resistors. Mathematically this is written:

$$\text{Ratio in db} = 10 \log \frac{P_2}{P_1}$$

For example, if we double the power so that $P_2 = 2P_1$, we find that the logarithm of $2 = 0.30103$, and multiplied by 10 this gives us 3 db. For $P_2 = 4P_1$, the result is 6.02 db, and for a ratio of 10 it is 10 db. A ratio of 100 is 20 db, and a ratio of 1,000 is 30 db.

One sometimes hears engineers who should know better ask something like "Is that a voltage db or a power db?" A DB IS A DB IS A DB. And the decibel is a measure of power ratio. There is no such thing as a "voltage db"! Engineers will frequently determine the power in a resistor by measuring the voltage drop across the resistor and using the formula:

$$\text{Power (watts)} = \frac{(\text{Voltage drop})^2 \ (\text{volts})}{\text{Resistance (ohms)}}$$

Note that the power is proportional to the square of the voltage. Now we can substitute for the power in the decibel equation to obtain:

$$db = 10 \log \frac{\dfrac{(E_1)^2}{R_1}}{\dfrac{(E_2)^2}{R_2}} \qquad (3\text{-}1)$$

but:
$$\text{Log } (N)^M = M \log (N)$$
Now, only if $R_1 = R_2$ may we simplify equation 3-1 to:

$$db = 20 \log \frac{E_1}{E_2} \qquad (3\text{-}2)$$

To illustrate the necessity for considering power in db calculation, let us assume that we have a record amplifier (a phonograph, stereo/2, hi-fi, etc.) Let us assume that the pickup arm is delivering 1 V into the 1-MΩ input of the amplifier is delivering 1 V into the 1-Ω output speaker. What is the gain of the amplifier in db? If one applies equation 3-2 without regard to the difference of impedance, one would come to the conclusion that the amplifier has a gain of zero db, or unity. This is obvious nonsense and can be shown to be such by trying to have the pickup drive the speaker directly; the result would be silence. The input power to the amplifier is one volt squared divided by 10^6 ohms, or 10^{-6} W. The output power to the speaker is one volt squared divided by one ohm, or one watt. The power gain of the amplifier is therefore 10^6. One might, at this point, describe the gain of the amplifier as 60 db. However, this would tell a misleading story about what the amplifier is actually doing. The use of gain or loss descriptions in db should be confined to systems in which the impedance is constant.

The telephone system is nominally designated as a 600-Ω system, and power measurements are usually made using a 600-Ω resistor. The powers are often described in terms of dbm, or db with respect to one milliwatt. One milliwatt is about 10 times as strong as loud speech over the telephone. On a 600-Ω resistor one milliwatt corresponds to 0.775 V rms (or 1.1 V peak) for a sine wave. One milliwatt is –30 dbW.

In terms of acoustic power, the zero-db reference is commonly taken as 10^{-16} W/cm², or –130 dbm/cm². This refers to noise power in the air.

Another commonly used reference is *reference noise*. The telephone system can pick up noise and interference in a variety of ways and in a variety of degrees. The noise is frequently measured with a noise-measurement test set. For calibration purposes the reference noise is not noise at all but rather a 1,000-Hz tone at a level of –90 dbm. The noise measured on an actual system is then given in db with respect to reference noise, or dbrn. The most commonly used test sets are the Western Electric 3-type Noise Measuring Set or the Hewlett-Packard Transmission and Noise Measuring Set Model 3555B. When used with the C-type message filter, which drops steeply below 800 Hz and above 2,600 Hz, the noise level is designated as dbrnC or dBrnC. In general, the noise increases with the path length. The noise at the interface is given by:

Circuit length, mi	Noise dBrnC
0–50	31
51–100	34
100–400	37
400–1,000	41
1,000–1,500	43
1,500–2,500	45
2,500–4,000	47

At the interface, the maximum power your equipment should deliver, averaged over a 3-second interval, is given as –13 dbm for speech. Considering the 2,500–4,000 mile circuit, the noise in the speech band is 47 db above the –90 dbm reference noise, –43 dbm. Compared to the –13-dbm speech, this would give an average S/N ratio of 30 db. The desired actual speaking power is –16 dbm for the long-term average so the S/N would be about 3 db less.

THE DETECTION OF TONES

The dial tones operate at a level of –17 dbm minimum, which is approximately 60 μW. The tone voltage is therefore on the order of 0.109 V rms. The busy tone is smaller, at –28.5 dbm or 1.41 μW, giving a voltage of 29 mV rms. Obviously, these tones require some amplification to bring them up to logic levels for detection. The amplification can either be separate or it can be a part of the tone-detection scheme. The dial tone is roughly equivalent to normal voice power. However, most of the others are lower except for ROH and the misdial siren.

In the previous discussion, we treated the tones and tone-pairs separately. It is instructive to consider the various tones in spectral order to permit a better assessment of the detection problem. Figure 3-2 lists all of the tones in use in modern telephone systems. In this case the illustration is constructed in the form of a truth table with a X designating usage.

One of the first things that catches the eye is the fact that the 1,400-Hz tone splits the DTMF high group precisely in two. Most of the other tones for signaling are below or above the DTMF groups. Another point of interest is the fact that * represents something of a detection problem since it contains the closest

	350	440	480	620	697	770	852	941	1209	1336	1400	1477	1633	2060	2450	2600
Dial tone	X	X														
Busy			X	X												
Ringing		X	X													
Call waiting		X														
Rcvr off hook (ROH)											X			X	X	X
Recorder conn.											X					
High tone			X													
DTMF tones 1					X				X							
2					X					X						
3					X							X				
A					X								X			
4						X			X							
5						X				X						
6						X						X				
B						X							X			
7							X		X							
8							X			X						
9							X					X				
C							X						X			
*								X	X							
0								X		X						
#								X				X				
D								X					X			

Figure 3-2. Tone usage.

of the DTMF tones to occur simultaneously. Of course, it may not be necessary for any given machine to detect all of these tones. For example, a machine that does not originate calls need not detect RINGING or BUSY. On the other hand, it probably should detect DIAL TONE and perhpas ROH if it is to hang up promptly on a disconnect from the other end. The actual decision of which of these tones is to be monitored is very machine-specific and very dependent upon the application.

Probably the oldest form of frequency-selective circuit is the LC-resonant circuit, which operates like the frequency preselector at the front (antenna) end of your radio. Unfortunately, it would take a rather high Q multipole filter to give a reasonable suppression or immunity from 480 Hz energy when the object was to detect 440 Hz energy. Furthermore, the inductors would be rather large and expensive. In modern practice, the use of LC fliters has been almost entirely replaced by the use of solid-state active filters for reasons of convenience, size and cost. We will therefore not pursue the subject of LC filters here.

THE ACTIVE FILTER

Active filters are generally constructed using one or more opamps to provide isolation between stages of filtering and to develop the near-zero or near-infinite impedances required for some forms of filtering. These filters generally employ only resistors and capacitors, thereby eliminating the size and expense of large inductors.

The circuit shown in Figure 3-3 shows an active low-pass filter, in one of the simpler formats. The op amp acts to isolate the two filter sections and provides a very low impedance output. At frequencies below the cutoff frequency, the attenuation of the circuit is essentially zero. The attenuation is about 12 db at twice the cutoff frequency, and eventually settles to about 40 db per decade.

Two different designs are shown. Using the Butterworth design results in a somewhat faster falloff, whereas the linear phase design optimizes response to impulses. Since the output impedance is near zero, two or more sections may be cascaded for faster cutoff.

It is fairly common to design these filters with $C_1 = 2C_2$ and $R_1 = R_2$. For a 3-kHz cutoff frequency in the Butterworth design:

$$C_1 = 0.002 \ \mu F$$
$$C_2 = 0.001 \ \mu F$$
$$R_1 = R_2 = 37.5 \ k\Omega$$

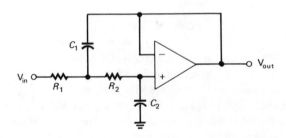

Butterworth design
$$C_1 = \frac{R_1 + R_2}{\sqrt{2} \ R_1 R_2 \omega_c}$$
and
$$C_2 = \frac{\sqrt{2}}{(R_1 + R_2)\omega_c}$$

Linear phase design
$$C_1 = \frac{R_1 + R_2}{\sqrt{3} \ R_1 R_2 \omega_c}$$
and
$$C_2 = \frac{\sqrt{3}}{(R_1 + R_2)\omega_c}$$

ω_c = Cutoff frequency $\times 2\pi$

Figure 3-3. A low-pass active filter.

Two such sections cascaded will give –6 db at 3 kHz and –24 db at 6 kHz, which is just about ideal for the voiceband top-end cutoff for your machine. As a practical matter it is usually more convenient to pick the values so that the capacitors come out to be standard sizes, and then determine the resistor values accordingly.

It is worth noting that the cutoff frequency of the filter is linearly related to capacitor size and resistor size. As a result, if the filter is to be stable with temperature, it is necessary that attention be given to the temperature coefficients of the parts. For stability, silvered mica capacitors are generally used for sizes below a few thousand picofarads and metallized polycarbonate capacitors for larger sizes.

The high-pass active filter is constructed simply by swapping C_1 for R_1 and C_2 for R_2. Figure 3-4 shows an active high-pass filter with the components selected for cutoff at 250 Hz. Two such stages will give –6 db at 250 Hz and –24 db at 125 Hz in the linear phase design. It may be seen that while the capacitor values are standard, the resistor values are not and it may be necessary to obtain the required resistance by using more than one standard resistor. Two such filter units cascaded will yield a nearly optimum low-end voiceband filter. It may be seen that the full required voiceband filtering can be obtained with eight resistors, eight capacitors, and a quad op-amp package.

From the discussion of the falloff rates, it can be seen that it would take an impractical number of sections to separate 440 Hz from 480 Hz by simply filtering, although the task could probably be accomplished using active filters. To separate two closely spaced tones, it is usually more practical to employ a notch filter, which sharply rejects one or the other.

Figure 3-5 shows a notch filter. The RC circuit will be recongized as the "bridged-T" circuit. This operates by having a phase shift through the capacitive branch 180 degrees out of phase with the resistive branch. The filter can be seen to represent a high-pass and a low-pass section. U1 actually serves only to provide a high impedance to the filter and a low-impedance output. The action of U2 is a bit more sophisticated.

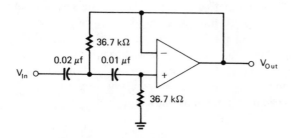

Figure 3-4. A high-pass active filter.

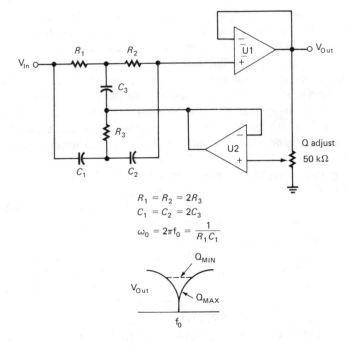

Figure 3-5. The notch filter.

In the usual bridged-T circuit, the junction of C_3 and R_3 is grounded. In this circuit, the action of U2 is to hold the juction of C_3 and R_3 at the potential of the tap on the potentiometer labeled "Q adjust." At the ground end of the potentiometer, the action is identical to the normal bridged T. However, at the top end of the potentiometer, the Q of the filter is minimized.

The notch filter can be used to sharply notch out or discriminate against any single given frequency. The 480-Hz detector leg could contain a 440-Hz notch filter, and the 440-Hz detector could contain a 480-Hz notch.

It should be noted that nearly all of the RC filters work from an input impedance of zero and work into an output impedance of infinity. Otherwise the source impedance and the load impedance become part of the filter and can cause detuning. It is therefore usually wise to drive any filter or group of filters with a voltage follower. The natural action of most of the active filters provides a near-zero output impedance, so this generally takes care of itself and the filters can be cascaded without detuning due to the load.

THE PHASE-LOCKED-LOOP TONE DETECTOR

In recent years, a number of phase-locked loop (PLL) chips have been developed. Most of these chips contain a voltage-controlled oscillator (VCO) and a digital phase detector along with some op amps, etc. The output of the phase detector is used to drive the VCO into phase synchronism with the incoming signal. Let us first examine the operation of one of the simpler types of phase detectors.

The exclusive-OR phase detector is shown in Figure 3-6. This can be an actual Boolean exclusive-OR digital logic chip. The output, C, is high when either A or B, but not both, are high. The timing diagrams at the bottom of the figure

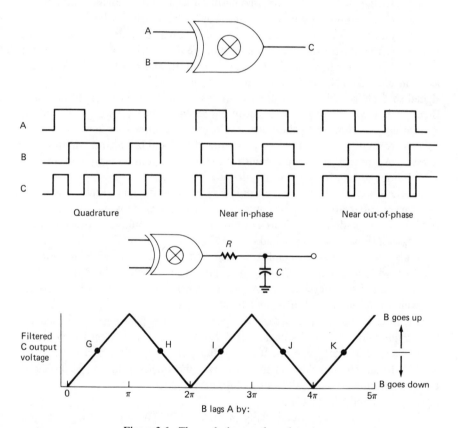

Figure 3-6. The exclusive- or phase detector.

show the action. When A and B are in quadrature, we see that output C is high just half of the time. When A and B are nearly in phase, we see that the output is low nearly all of the time. And if A and B were perfectly in phase, the output would be low all of the time.

Conversely, when A and B are nearly out of phase, we see that the output is high most of the time. And if A and B are exactly out of phase, the output would be high all of the time.

If a low-pass filter or integrating filter were attached to C so that the average voltage was presented at the filter output, we can see that the quadrature condition would be represented by an average value of one-half of the full output swing. Moving closer to an in-phase condition would give a smaller voltage, and moving toward an out-of-phase condition would give a higher voltage.

If we plot the filtered C output, we would obtain a curve similar to that at the bottom of the illustration. As B lags A by more than a half wave, it starts to get more and more in phase, so the voltage drops until at 2π radians the waves are again in phase and the output is zero. It may be seen that if the circuit were designed so that for voltages less than G the oscillator frequency would decrease, then the B wave would slowly begin to lag behind A and thus drive the output voltage up. Conversely, if the output voltage at the filter rose above G, the oscillator frequency would begin to pick up and B would begin to catch up to the phase in A, thereby restoring the output to G. Thus, point G represents a stable equilibrium, and so, for that matter, do points I and K.

On the other hand, we see that points H and J present an unstable equilibrium since a departure below H would cause B to slow, thereby increasing the departure from quadrature and driving the output lower still. The process could not cease until point I was reached.

It may be seen that the stabilizing action of the circuit keeps B in a precise lockstep with A, trailing it by exactly a quarter of a cycle. The differences in instantaneous frequency between A and B will generally not persist long enough for even a quarter-wave of difference to accumulate.

One note of caution is in order. The phase detector operating in the exclusive-OR mode really only works linearly if A and B are almost perfect square waves with precise 50% duty cycles. If one or both of the waves depart much from this condition, glitches develop that can make the output nonlinear or displaced from quadrature. Some of the PLL chips have a detector that will tolerate non-square waves, but others will not.

The system is shown conceptually in Figure 3-7. The input voltage (A) and the VCO voltage are compared in the phase detector. If the VCO is not operating in the correct phase relationship, a filtered output signal is derived to change the oscillator frequency in the correct direction to eliminate the phase error.

The VCO can by any of a number of types. However, in this case it is shown as an RC oscillator whose frequency is controlled by the values of R_1 and C_1.

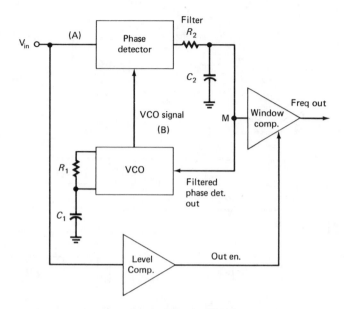

Figure 3-7. The PLL tone detector.

If the RC values are adjusted so that the oscillator will freely run at the frequency we desire to detect with the output of phase detector at voltage G, then insertion of higher frequency will drive the voltage at M up and a lower frequency will drive the voltage at M down. Only when the frequency is equal to the desired frequency will the control voltage be G.

The window detector can be used to determine when the filter output is close enough to G to accept the tone. The level detector is used because in the absence of any signal the level of M will gravitate toward G. Suppose, for example, that A, the input signal, were stuck low, that is, zero voltage. During half of each cycle B would be different from A; thus, the phase detector output would be a square wave with a 50% duty cycle, and the average voltage at M would be identical with the condition obtained when the unit is in perfect phase lock. An ac-level detector could be used to disable the output as shown in the circuit.

A more elegant system would derive from a somewhat different property. In Figure 3-6 we observed that in the phase locked condition, the output of the phase detector is a square wave of twice the frequency of either A or B. Conversely, with A stuck at either zero or one, the output of the phase detector is a square wave of the same frequency as B, and either in phase or out of phase.

One mechanism for detecting the absence or presence of A is shown in Figure 3-8. A D-type flip-flop is supplied with a sample of A, then squared and standardized with a Schmitt trigger. The clock is supplied with a signal from the

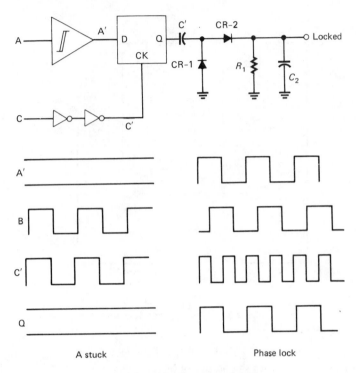

Figure 3-8. A-signal presence detector.

phase detector output C, which is delayed with respect to A' by a few spare in-
verters. Now if A is not large enough to trigger the Schmitt, A' will stick either
high or low. However, if A' is toggling, then the Q output will toggle as well.

The voltage-doubler rectifier attached to Q will not respond to a steady voltage
at Q. However, if the output is toggling, the rectifier will develop a voltage approximately twice as large as the high voltage at Q.

If the time constant at R_1, C_2 is equal to about three halves of the period of
A, the voltage will be relatively steady at the high level when the detector is
locked. However, when the detector is unlocked, an ac component equal to
the difference in frequency between A and B will be present. This difference is
due to the modulation presented at C, which is due to the difference frequency.
A second voltage-doubler detector can be used to detect this unlocked condition.
An isolation amplifier should be placed between the detectors.

THE 567 TONE DECODER PHASE-LOCKED LOOP

Both Signetics and National Semiconductor produce a chip intended to be used in tone-detection applications. The 567 is available in either an 8-pin TO-5 or an 8-pin DIP package. The chip is equipped with both a quardrature and an in-phase detector, a current-controlled oscillator, and several op amps.

The frequency of free oscillation is controlled by R_1 and C_1, as shown on Figure 3-9. The capture bandwidth is controlled by C_2 and C_3. With small values of C_2 and C_3 the capture bandwidth can rise up to about 14% of the operating frequency for voltages at the input on the order of 200 mV and decreasing with smaller input voltages. The values given at the bottom of the figure are recommended by Signetics for DTMF detection. The detector for each tone is identical except for the value of R_1.

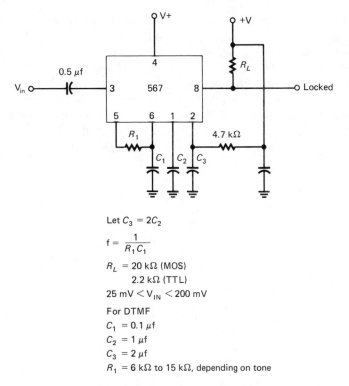

Let $C_3 = 2C_2$

$$f = \frac{1}{R_1 C_1}$$

$R_L = 20$ kΩ (MOS)
$\quad\quad$ 2.2 kΩ (TTL)

25 mV $< V_{IN} <$ 200 mV

For DTMF
$C_1 = 0.1$ μf
$C_2 = 1$ μf
$C_3 = 2$ μf
$R_1 = 6$ kΩ to 15 kΩ, depending on tone

Figure 3-9. The 567 tone detector.

The output of the device is an open-collector transistor (NPN), which can sink up to 100 mA. Therefore, a pull-up resistor is required. An array of seven or eight of these can be used to construct a DTMF decoder. The Signetics manual shows a hardwired logic circuit using OR gates to decode to one of ten or one of sixteen.

Unfortunately, the unit is running in the region where the bandwidth for lock-in is level-sensitive. The device begins to operate successfully with an input in excess of about 15 mV. However, at these low signals the pull-in range is only about ±2%. This is actually good since the DTMF tones are separated by about 10% in frequency. Unfortunately, as the signal level exceeds about 150 mV, the pull-in range gets up to about 10%. If one of the tones is low, it is possible for a stronger signal to simultaneously fire two of the detectors tuned adjacent to one another. As a matter of fact it is possible to fire three of the detectors with a stronger signal.

It has been the writer's experience that this detector is suitable for detecting the dial tones and the busy signal using 440-Hz notch filters, but the detector is a little unsophisticated for high-accuracy DTMF decoding. In the next chapter we will deal specifically with a low-error-rate DTFM decoder.

For voiceband filtering it has been the practice of the writer to use a Butterworth-type low-pass filter to establish the high-end rolloff and a linear-phase-type filter to establish low-end roll-off. The low-end filter is prone to have a settling time about fifteen times as long as the high-end filter; therefore, it is advantageous to employ the faster settling design in the low-end high-pass filter.

4

The DTMF Detector,
the DTMF Generator and
the Hybrid Transformer

As noted in chapter 2, the DTMF tones are generated at a rather substantial level compared to speech level on the telephone. The specifications call for the nominal level to be -6 to -4 dbm, or 388 mV for the lower level. The minimum level in the low group is -10 dbm (about 245 mV), and -8 dbm in the high group. The maximum level is specified at + 2 dbm (975 mV) for the pair.

One can expect an incoming telephone-line signal to be on the order of 50 to 200 mV. If the signal is coming from a radio link, however, the values can be lower or higher, and some AGC (automatic gain control) may be required.

The minimum duration of the two-frequency signal is specified at 50 msec, and the minimum interdigital time at 45 msec. The maximum interdigital time is specified at 3 seconds, and the minimum cycle time at 100 msec.

In practice the writer has found that for direct distance dialing it is advisable to stretch the interdigit time for a cycle interval of not less than 110 msec, and 150 msec is actually better. In a series of tests, I have also found that some people can "peck" a single key for a closure time on the order of 40 msec. If one is expecting manual inputs, a detection time on the order of 35 msec is advisable.

Another point is worthy of note. A number of the older DTMF telephones make use of LC tuned oscillators. If one pecks the keys too fast, it is sometimes possible to cause the system to "false" since the oscillators do not "ring up" to full amplitude at the same rate. In particular, the low-group oscillators are slow in starting. The interdigit interval is not a problem with manual inputs, except in the case where a digit is to be repeated, and then one can seldom approach 45 msec if the key is truly opened.

The combination of possible contact bounce and start-up time make the first 3 to 5 msec of the tones suspect; for this reason it is usually advisable to reject this portion of the tones if a counting-type detection scheme is employed. This permits the tones to rise up to a steady-state value and settle in frequency.

The idea of using a frequency counter to detect the tones and identify which of the tones is present seems relatively straightforward. However, it should also be relatively obvious that it is necessary to separate the high-group from the low-group tone in order that the counters provide an unambiguous count. Figure 4-1 shows a sine wave to which has been added an antiphased third harmonic and a fifth harmonic component. The simulation was run on an Apple II+. The magnitude of the components is in the order in which they occur in a sin x/x distribution, the magnitudes that would be obtained if the fundamental sine-wave train were chopped in a square-wave fashion (except for the phase reversal of the third harmonic). It may be seen that if the fifth harmonic were twice the amplitude, there would actually have been extraneous zero crossings. Since the tones are actually keyed on and off in the DTMF signaling, this tells us that the filters should be able to suppress the harmonics of the tones to avoid the possibility of ambiguous readings.

```
]LIST 100,250

100   REM  THIS PROGRAM PLOTS THE WAVEFORM RESULTING FROM THE FIRST THREE
      TERMS OF A SIN(X)/X EXPANSION.
110   REM  THE THIRD HARMONIC COMPONENT IS REVERSED IN PHASE IN THIS WAVEFORM
120   HGR
130   HCOLOR= 3
140   POKE  - 12524,0
145   REM  THIS PLOTS BLACK ON WHITE
150   FOR Q = 0 TO 12.56638 STEP .01
160   LET B = 3 * Q
170   LET F = 5 * Q
180   LET A = (.6366 *  SIN (Q)) - (.2122 *  SIN (B)) + (.1273 *  SIN (F))
190   LET X = (140 / 6.2831) * Q
200   LET Y = (A * 75) + 85
205   REM  SCALING OF ILLUSTRATION
210   LET X% = X
220   LET Y% = Y
225   REM  APPLE WILL ONLY PLOT INTEGERS
240   HPLOT X%,Y%
250   NEXT Q

]PR#0
```

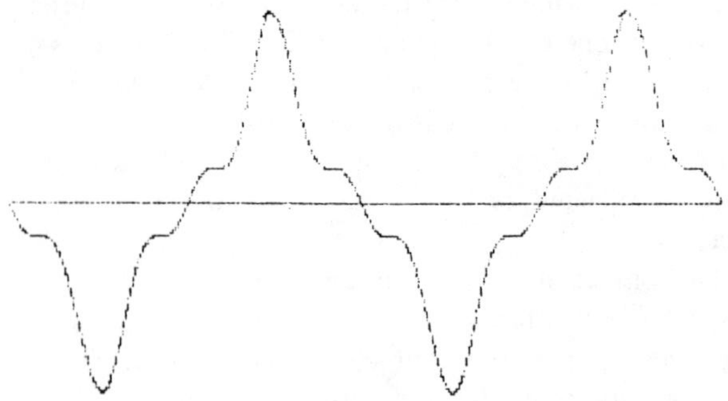

Figure 4-1.

The Bell spec also requires that speech should be suppressed at least 45 db relative to the normal level during DTMF signal transmission, and that the total power of all extraneous frequencies in the voiceband above 500 Hz should be at least 20 db below the level of the frequency pair.

Because the potential market for these telephone items is very high, the development of DTMF items has been subject to a substantial effort on the part of a number of the silicon houses. There is a very substantial inventory of devices that have been developed to meet this market. The products are such that it scarcely makes economic sense to develop a system on your own for a given application since the available devices are so good and low cost. Accordingly, we shall concentrate on the commercially available devices.

Figure 4-2 shows a complete DTMF detector system. At the front end the signal is split into the high-group and the low-group tones by a pair of bandpass filters. These filters may be either ceramic, passive crystal, or active types.

The filters are followed by an automatic level control (ALC) system. This is followed in turn by a zero-crossing counter, which employs a crystal oscillator time base. The output of the two counters is decoded to provide data and control logic signals. We shall treat the functions separately.

The response of the bandpass filters is shown in Figure 4-3 in a schematic presentation. It can be seen that the filters provide a minimum of 33-db attenuation for signals of the opposite group. Also, the dial tone is suppressed a minimum of 18 db for the 440 Hz and 33 db for the 350 Hz tones of the dial tone. This response is adequate to ensure reliable detection.

It is also noteworthy that the third harmonic of the 697-Hz tone falls at about –29 db, and none of the other odd harmonics of the low group are more than –33 db. The keying transients of the tones are thus strongly suppressed.

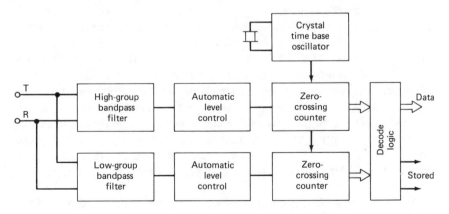

Figure 4-2. The DTMF detector system.

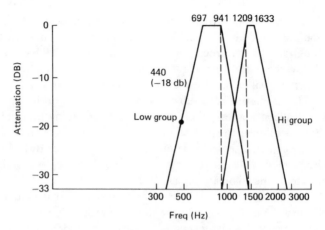

Figure 4-3. DTMF band-split filters.

Filters with such performance are available from a number of vendors, including General Instrument, ITT, North Electric, CTS, Beckman, Cermtek, BEI, and Amperex. One could probably design a filter for this duty. However, attaining the performance achieved with these units is not a trivial task, and maintaining the performance in production is harder still. At least in the opinion of this writer, the commercially available units are a bargain.

The three blocks to the right-hand side of the unit, along with the oscillator and the decoder, are available in a 16-pin DIP from a number of vendors and in a hybrid package from a number of others. The monolithic units are slightly inferior in performance to the hybrids, and are also considerably cheaper.

Most of the units operate as follows: The unit waits for a signal of sufficient amplitude to qualify as a tone. Upon this detection a delay of about 5 msec is inserted. The low- and high-group counters are then enabled, and the zero crossings are counted for a period of 30 msec or so. During this time a 697-Hz tone would have between 41 and 43 zero crossings, and a 770-Hz tone would have between 45 and 47 zero crossings, assuming that the tones are within the ±1.5% tolerance. The high-group tones are somewhat easier to resolve because of the larger count. A 1,633-Hz tone would have between 96 and 99 crossings. In general, the nominal count ±1 gives a tolerance equal to the Bell spec. It may be seen that the resolution of this arrangement is somewhat limited at the low end since a low-end error on the 700-Hz tone could give a count of 45, and a high-end error on the 697-Hz tone could give a count of 43. Thus, only 44 crossings is rejected as an invalid tone.

An alternative scheme is one in which the tone counter is preset for a fixed number of cycles and the much faster clock is counted. Suppose that a 4-MHz crystal clock is used and the counter for the low group is set to count 42 cross-ings. In this case the bind comes at the high end of the band where a low-error 941-Hz tone would have 90,626 clock cycles, and an 852-Hz tone would have between 97,134 and 100,092 clock cycles. In this case the circuitry could be set to reject a wider range as invalid.

From the user standpoint the internal mechanism of the decoder is not avail-able. One has only the choice of chip, with the internal workings being deter-mined entirely by the chip manufacturer. Probably the best tool for evaluation of the relative merits of the various decoders is the number of "hits" experienced with a Mitel test tape. This tape is available from the:

Mitel Corporation
PO Box 13089, Kanata, Ottowa
Canada K2K1X3

This tape consists of a series of tests featuring conversation, noise, crosstalk, switching transients, and other extraneous sounds encountered on a telephone line played at representative amplitudes. The instructions for using the test and establishing the reference level are given in voice on the tape. The tape is simply set up and played and the instances of a "hit" or "talk-off" are recorded on the tape for a test length of approximately 20 minutes.

A DTMF detector built with 8 PLLs and no preselection will typically score more than 100 hits, whereas a very good counting-type detector can often score less than ten, and some will actually score zero hits.

In order to reduce hits, some of the chips, such as the Mitel MT8820 and the Mostek 5102, require that the counts in two successive periods agree before the logic is enabled to signal a decoded character.

It should be noted that a single isolated hit need not provide a "hard" error. If the logic following the detector is arranged to reject any inputs in which de-tected tones are separated by more than three seconds, many of the hits on the PLL detector system would have been rejected as invalid and ignored by the ma-chine. This is usually easily accomplished in the computer software by means of a timing loop. The three seconds does not represent an inordinate strain for manual input since an entire seven-digit telephone number known by the keyer is frequently input in less than three seconds. A three-second pause between keys is really quite long.

The Mostek 5102(N)-5 integrated tone receiver is roughly characteristic of the single-chip DTMF detectors of high quality. The unit uses a 3.579545-MHz colorburst crystal. Because of their widespread use on television receivers, these crystals are very inexpensive. You will note that this is a good speed to run a

6502 or 6800 family processor. Therefore, a single crystal can be used for both the DTMF detector and the processor itself.

In this chip the zero crossings are counted in clock cycles for several periods and averaged over a longer period. The unit waits until it has accumulated 33 msec of valid DTMF tones before latching data to the output. When a valid digit is no longer detected, the strobe will return low and the data will remain latched in the outputs until a new valid digit it latched through.

It may be seen that it is necessary to catch the strobe output when it is high in order to detect the digit properly. It is also necessary to debounce the data by reading a low strobe in between digits. This prevents the multiple recording of the same digit. The flow chart of Figure 4-4 shows a routine I have used for this operation.

This routine is based upon a machine language program run in a 6800 family microprocessor. It easily adapts to a 6502. However, the 6502 does not have the two independent accumulators; therefore, a temporary memory location must be used instead.

Starting at node 1 the unit loops until the strobe goes high. When the strobe goes high, indicating the successful decoding of a DTMF signal, the strobe flag is set and the data acquired. If the strobe flag does not go low before three-second time-out, the data is destroyed and all registers are cleared. If, on the other hand, the strobe goes low, indicating that the key has been released, then the data is stored in memory at the address given by the index register. The index register is then incremented and tested to see whether the full length of the message has been received. It is presumed that the messages are of fixed length in this routine.

You will note that this routine yields a definite "toggle" action. One must first press the key to enter the two-tone character and then release the key to have the machine accept it. Furthermore, it has an "N-Key Rollover" feature. Suppose that I were to depress, say, the 5 key on the telephone. Then, before releasing the 5, I were to depress the 7, subsequently letting 5 up. Since the data is acquired about 30 microseconds after the strobe flags a valid digit, the 5 would be entered correctly. What would happen next depends upon the details of the particular DTMF decoder.

Another point worthy of note is that the machine has a way of escaping a stuck key. Suppose a prankster calls and wedges a toothpick in one of the keys. In three seconds the system will abort the detection process and presumably hang up, thereby avoiding a system tieup. He can call again but the joke would be on him, and he would have to be pretty persistent if he could tie the machine up for no more than three seconds at a time.

As written, the program assumes that the DTMF detector would be read through a peripheral interface adapter, like a 6821. If the DTMF detectors follow the course set by the A/D converter and D/A converter, the second-generation

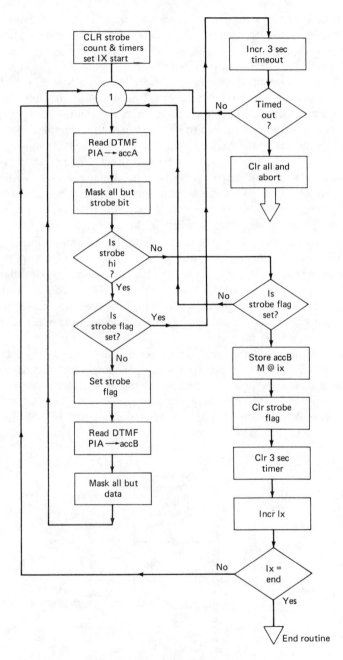

Figure 4-4. DTMF read and store.

chips will probably be able to interface directly with the microprocessor address and data lines. However, such is not the case for the present generation and a PIA is required.

The 5102 has a format control input that has three states. Set at V+ potential, the four-digit output lines read in hexadecimal notation with zero decoded as a hex $A and * = $B and # = $C. With the control pin floating, the data is output in a dual two-bit row-column code. With the control pin at ground potential, the chip output is tri-stated to high impedance. Using the V+ and ground terms as a chip select, the device could probably be used for direct data-bus application provided that the strobe were also fitted with a tri-state gate since the strobe is not itself tri-stated. It has been the preference of the writer to operate the chip through a PIA. It has also usually proved simpler to accept the data in the hexadecimal format since it then fits with other data in the processor.

The 5102 likes to receive its data best in the form of square waves of 0.9 V peak-to-peak amplitude. The little circuit of Figure 4-5 will perform this trick. At the bottom end, the amplifier will show a voltage gain of 100 so that only 9 mV peak-to-peak is required. At the top end, voltages up to about the supply rails will produce the desired 0.9 V since the 1N914s will conduct and reduce the effective gain of the amplifier to near zero. One could not treat speech data this way, but signals going to a frequency counter do not need much of anything but zero crossings preserved.

One should note that the input impedance of the circuit is only a thousand ohms. If the output of the group filter needs something higher, a voltage follower can be used to raise the input impedance to near infinity. The circuit is not fussy about the op amp used. Something like a 558 or a pair of 741s will work fine. The 558 is handy since the op amps for the low-group and the high-group ALC amps can be had in a single 8-pin dip.

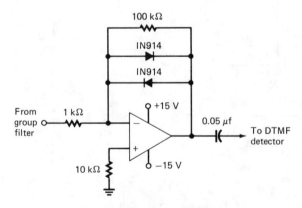

Figure 4-5. The ALC amp.

The 5102 will generally operate with an interdigit spacing of 35 msec with the prescribed filtering, and an 18-db signal-to-noise ratio. At this ratio the detection bandwidth is nominally ±2.5%, but can be as low as 2% and as high as 2.9%. This allows a bit more error than the Bell specs for the worst frequency error on a single tone. The unit will also accept as much as 6 db of "twist," or difference in amplitude between the tones. The twist can arise from out-of-spec transmission facilities.

With regard to the twist, it should be noted that an FM radio will frequently add preemphasis and subsequent deemphasis on reception, which will add a considerable amount of twist to the tones. This effect is one of the principal causes of malfunction for radio-operated DTMF systems.

THE ERROR RATE

For teletype and similar digital detecting systems, one of the most critical factors is the *bit error rate*. In general, the BER is a function of the extent of noise corruption of the channel and the rate at which the bits are sent. For an ordinary teletype or radio teletype (RTTY) using *frequency shift keying* (FSK) of 850 Hz, a BER of 10^{-5} is often specified at a *Baud* (bits per second) rate of about 100 and a signal-to-noise ratio of 3 db.

One has to be a bit careful about trying to transfer these figures into DTMF signaling. First of all, the BER for the RTTY is specified on the bit rate for a machine transmitting Baudot (5-bit code). To begin with, the Baudot code uses 5 bits to specify one of 32 characters. Actually, only 30 characters are available since two are assigned unique meanings as "letters" and "numbers." The beginning of a message is interpreted as letters until a "numbers" character is received, whereupon all subsequent characters are interpreted as numbers (or punctuation, control, etc.) until a subsequent "letters" character is received.

In usual RTTY practice, no message is signified by a continuous "marking" condition. The start of a character is designated by a "space." After this, follow the 5 bits designating the marks and spaces that define the character and the two stop bits (marks) designating the end of the character. This means that a character actually consists of eight bits.

From the above we see that 100 Baud actually correspond to only about 12.5 characters per second. A single bit error in the Baudot code will certainly destroy the character in which it occurs. However, if the code is being sent by machine so that only two stop bits are sent (that, is there is no protracted marking period between characters), then an error that causes a start bit (a space) to be interpreted as a mark will occur. If by chance the first bit or the first several bits of the character are marks, it is possible for the system to get a half character or more out of synchronism. This means that the single bit error can destroy a whole string of characters. Thus, the message error rate or number of incorrect characters in a string is, on the average, much larger than the BER. This discrepancy is a factor of at least ten.

As noted earlier, the DTMF code only uniquely defines four bits, or sixteen distinct items. Therefore, it is necessary to receive two characters in a row correctly to define a character of complexity similar to the Baudot code. If a 20-minute talk-off test scores only two isolated hits, this would most probably destroy two separate characters. If we assume a machine sent DTMF two-symbol code, this can probably be operated at something in excess of 5 characters per second, or a total of 6,000 characters, covering the 20-minute period for an error rate of 1 in 3,000 or 3.33×10^{-4}, which is about comparable to the character rate for the RTTY.

A typical printed page of this book will have about 470 words consisting, on the average, of 5 letters and one space, or 2,820 characters. A two-hit DTMF detector would be expected to have an average of nearly one character per page in error. Actual tests over the telephone system have shown that the error rate is generally significantly better than this. However, the accumulation of statistically significant data is difficult because of the slowness of the transmission.

DTMF TONE GENERATION

There are a number of function generator or oscillator chips that could be used for generating the DTMF tones. As a matter of fact, many of the older DTMF telephones make use of discrete transistors and an LC circuit to generate the tones. As noted from the earlier recital of the specifications, the tones should be pretty accurate and reasonably pure sine waves. By the time that one provides the necessary temperature compensation and component stability, this tends to make the straightforward approach fairly expensive.

In recent years the silicon houses have come to the rescue of this situation with large-scale integration. A number of chips are offered for this purpose. Figure 4-6 shows the organization of one of the more common chips, the National Semiconductor 53130 DTMF Generator. With very few external components, this chip will do the whole job of generating both tones.

This chip, like the detector discussed earlier, is designed to employ a 3.579545-MHz TV colorburst crystal. If you have the detector in the circuit, or if the computer is operating at this frequency, a second crystal is not required and the clock can be fed in on the OSC-IN terminal.

Basically, the unit operates by dividing the crystal clock frequency down to obtain the desired frequency. It would be possible to divide right down to the desired frequency and then filter the square-wave output of the digital counter. However, this would take a great deal of filtering and a large number of external components. Instead, the crystal frequency is counted down only part way and then fed to a waveform generator.

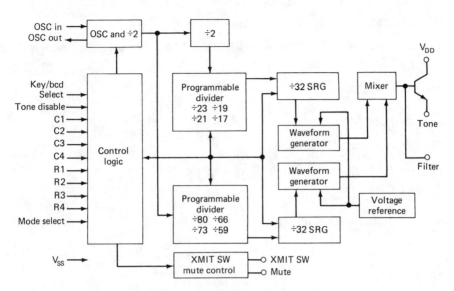

Figure 4-6. The DTMF generator.

In Figure 4-6, we see that the oscillator is first divided by two. Now suppose that one of the input keys is depressed, calling for 697 Hz. The logic would set the lower programmable divider to divide by 80. The final divider divides by 32 to make sure that the output is a true square wave. The result is:

$$\frac{3,579,545}{2 * 80 * 32} = 699.12988 \text{ Hz}$$

which is actually 0.3% high, well within specs. The block labeled $\div 32$ SRG is actually not a divider in the normal flip-flop sense of the word. Instead, it is generally some form of shift register and ROM (read only memory). The waveform generator is a digital-to-analog converter, which converts the digital output of the SRG into a stepwise approximation of a sine wave.

The waveform of Figure 4-7 shows this stepwise approximation. It may be seen that the approximation is fairly good. One can consider that the output of the device consists of two components, an ideal sine wave and a little ragged wave made up of the errors. You will note that the error waveform is made up of the series of little triangular pieces where the stairstep approximation failed to match the pure sine wave. The energy of this error waveform is clustered about the 16th harmonic of the tone. Because it is so high in frequency, it is relatively easy to filter out. For the 53130, the total harmonic distortion (THD) is specified at 4% typical.

```
]LIST 100,300

100   REM   THIS PROGRAM PLOTS A DIGITALLY SYNTHESIZED WAVEFORM AND THE ERRO
      R TERM
110   HGR
120   HCOLOR= 3
130   POKE  - 12524,0
131 P = 0
135   LET N% = 0
136   LET M% = 66
140   FOR Q = 0 TO 6.2382 STEP .0243679588
150   LET X = (256 / 6.2382) * Q
160   LET Y = (64 *  SIN ( - Q)) + 66
170   LET X% = X
180   LET Y% = Y
181   LET P = P + 1
182   IF P <  = 9 THEN  GOTO 240
183   LET P = 0
190   HPLOT N%,M% TO X%,M% TO X%,Y%
200   LET M% = Y%
210   LET N% = X%
220   NEXT Q
240   LET Z% = Y% - M% + 66
250   HPLOT X%,Z%
260   NEXT Q

]24

]TEXT

]240

]PR#0
```

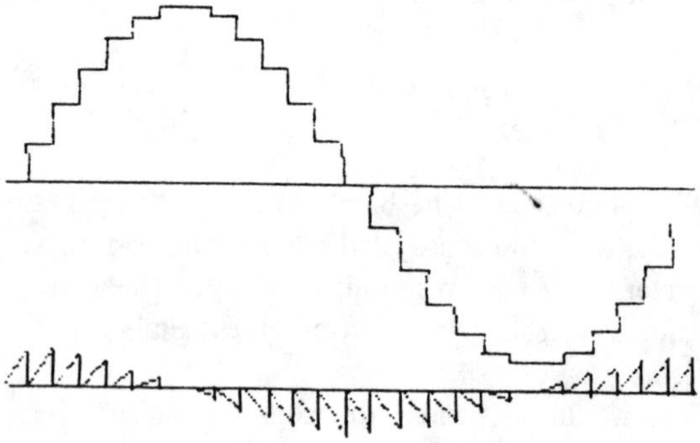

Figure 4-7.

The chip (Figure 4-8) is designed to operate from 3 V to 8 V, and it can be powered directly from the phone line. It draws 2 mA when outputting into an infinite impedance, working from a 3-V supply. Working into a 150-Ω resistor, the device will develop 1,000 mV p-p on the high-band tone, and 820 mV on the low-band tone, with both tones measured alone.

Obviously the counting sequence takes a while to get cranked up. The device delays 3 to 4 msec after the switch closure before the tone starts to emerge. The chip is equipped with a XMT SW lead and a MUTE lead. The XMT SW lead is high during the period when the tones are actually present, and the MUTE lead is high shortly after key depression and remains high about 0.5 msec after the keying is removed. The muting is useful in disabling the receiver, and the XMT SW is useful in disabling the transmitter.

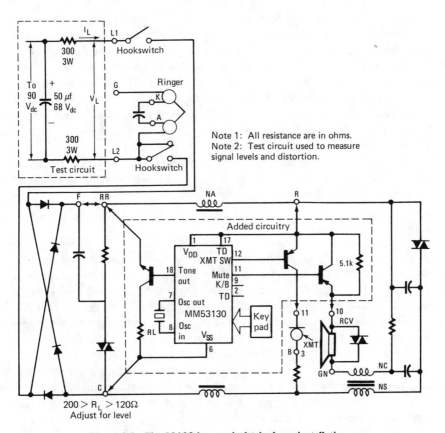

Figure 4-8. The 53130 in a typical telephone installation.

In the circuit shown a bridge rectifier is supplied to prevent the application of reverse polarity. Two transistor switches are also added to accomplish the XMT SW and MUTE functions. Another transistor is used as a tone-driver amplifier. In this application the chip draws all of its power from the telephone line and no other power source is required. Since one is required to draw some current to capture and hold the line, it might as well be used for something useful.

One of the features that make this particular device of interest in computer-based applications is that it is equipped with several options on the input keying. When the KEY/BINARY SEL lead is tied low, the device will select tone-pairs based on the binary word present at the ROW inputs. One may simply write the binary word to the four row inputs and then pull the KEY/BIN lead low to transmit the tone. After the suitable transmission period of 40 msec or more, the KEY/BIN lead is set high again to stop the tone. This type of operation avoids start-up glitches when changing characters.

Another nice feature for testing and adjustment is that a single tone may be generated in the binary operation mode. Normally in the binary mode the column switches are simply left open. If $C1$ is grounded, the device will only transmit the low-group tone. If $C2$ is grounded the device will only transmit the high-group tone. It is much easier to make and interpret voltage measurements if only a single tone is present. In addition, the use of this added degree of freedom could be used in signaling if the DTMF detector will decode it. However, in the latter case the high rejection of voice signals inherent in the use of the dual tones is defeated.

The 53130 is more or less typical of the current generation of DTMF generators available from a variety of sources. It is particularly suitable for computer drive because of the inclusion of the binary mode.

THE HYBRID ISOLATOR

It was noted earlier that neither the tip nor the ring conductor from the telephone line should be connected to local earth ground. When the generator is powered by the telephone line, this is fairly easy to do. One could drive the chip through a series of opto-isolators from the computer logic. However, this is also a reasonably clumsy thing to do since it requires a fair number of isolators. There are certain advantages to isolating the generator with a hybrid transformer.

Figure 4-9 shows the hybrid transformer. Although it is generally referred to as a transformer, we see from the illustration that it is actually made up of two separate transformers, T1 and T2. The operation proceeds as follows:

Suppose that we were to apply a current through winding A. This will induce a voltage in windings B and C, and since the winding are identical, the voltages will be identical in amplitude and phase.

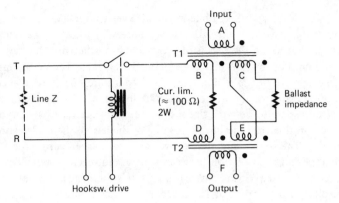

Figure 4-9. The hybrid isolator.

Now, if the total impedance viewed by winding B is identical to the total impedance viewed by winding C, then equal currents will flow in the two windings. Since the connections between C and E are reversed with respect to the connections between B and D, the currents will flow in opposite directions in D and E will exactly cancel at the output winding F. Inputs A and F are completely isolated.

The isolation between A and F is nice to have in a number of situations. For one thing, transistor amplifiers do not like to have large signals applied to their inputs, and it is handy to be able to isolate the more sensitive input circuitry from the output circuitry. For another thing, we see that both A and F are dc-isolated from both tip and ring so that now the tone generator and the detector and a possible speech amplifier for either speech input or output can be operated at a local earth ground potential, and from a local power supply associated with the computer or other devices.

Miniature telephone hybrid transformers are available from a number of sources. Typically these will occupy a cube about 2 cm on a side. The combined winding resistance adds up to about 50 Ω, therefore the line-holding current-limit resistor should be reduced to about 100 Ω to ensure line capture.

In the real world, the isolation between A and F is never complete. For one thing, the impedance of the line is a function of frequency. One can actually measure the impedance of the line by placing a signal source on A and a voltmeter or detector on F, or vice versa. The ballast impedance is then adjusted to minimize the detected voltage. This is liable to require both resistive and reactive components in the ballast. Properly done, it is usually possible to drive the detected output 40 db or more below the input at any one frequency. The ballast impedance then equals the line impedance. This can be repeated at a number of frequencies to develop a plot of line impedance versus frequency. In order to actually work this measurement, it is usually necessary to call some number that will hold the line while the test is in progress since otherwise the measurement will be complicated by the dial tone or an ROH, etc. The actual impedance determined by this test is seldom very close to a pure 600-Ω resistance. A resistor of 600 Ω will usually provide about 20-db isolation between A and F.

It is also possible to isolate a signal source from a receiver by means of a resistive bridge. In this case the line forms one of the legs of the bridge and the ballast another. The source and the receiver are then placed across the diagonals. This accomplishes the isolation between source and receiver, but does not provide the isolation between the devices and the telephone dc potentials.

Motorola has developed an IC to accomplish the hybrid and isolation function. However, this is relatively new and is not yet in widespread use. It seems likely that an IC implementation will eventually replace the hybrid transformer because of size and cost considerations. However, this is not presently the case.

5
Surge and Test Voltages

Even prior to the Morse experiments, a number of people had been playing with telegraph signaling. Karl Friedrich Gauss had constructed a working telegraph to relay time signals from the university to the astronomical observatory, and vice versa, at Heidelberg. In the Gauss telegraph, only a single wire was used and the return current flowed through the earth.

The earth is not a particularly good conductor of electricity in most locations. However, the effective cross section of the conductor is very large. The resistance of a conductor is given by:

$$R = \rho \, l/A$$

where ρ = resistivity in ohms per meter, l = length in meters, A = cross-sectional area in meters squared.

With care and perhaps some buried conductors in a *counterpoise,* or ground, system it is generally possible to acheive a ground or earth connection with a resistance of an ohm or less. Because of the very large cross section of the earth conductor, the remaining resistance of the earth leg of the path is pretty negligible in many cases. The original Morse telegraph was constructed with a single conductor and an earth return. This not only saves one wire but it also actually has less loss than a two wire circuit. A 16-gage (B&S) wire will have a resistance of 40 Ω per mile (at 55°F); thus, a 100-mile circuit will have 4,000 Ω of wire resistance. With a ground return the total circuit resistance will generally be no higher than 4,100 Ω in good soil. Thus we see that the overwhelming majority of the resistance is in the wire and not in the earth conductor.

GROUND RESISTANCE MEASUREMENTS

The establishment of a good ground is important in a great many electrical installations, so we might take some time discussing how one goes about measuring the quality of a ground. It is not immediately obvious how one determines the resistance to the "true" earth.

Figure 5-1 shows the trick. Since we cannot attach one of our ohmmeter terminals directly to the "true" earth, we simply drive two temporary ground rods. At the left we have the permanent ground rod with a buried counterpoise and at

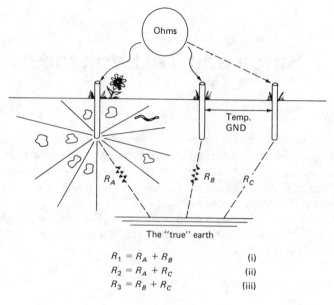

$$R_1 = R_A + R_B \qquad \text{(i)}$$
$$R_2 = R_A + R_C \qquad \text{(ii)}$$
$$R_3 = R_B + R_C \qquad \text{(iii)}$$

Figure 5-1.

the right are the two temporary ground rods. We can take our ohmmeter and measure between A and B, between A and C, and between C and B. This yields the three simultaneous equations shown. By subtracting (ii) from (i), we eliminate R_A. The result added to (iii) gives the value of R_C, which can then be used to find R_A and R_B.

In damp loamy soil an eight-foot ground rod will often show a resistance of less than an ohm with no other buried coounductors. Drier sandy soil may require a fair amount of buried noninsulated wire to obtain a low resistance. In the Sahara desert you can just about forget about trying to get a good ground.

Another point is worthy of note. For this type of measurement it is usually a good idea to use an ac ohmmeter. Commercial ground test sets often use a 20-Hz square wave. There are two reasons for this. First of all, just touching a sensitive voltmeter between the ground rods will generally show a voltage that is often on the order of 100 mV or more. This voltage will tend to bias a dc measurement and give substantial errors. The second point is that a dc current flowing in the rod will generally produce a small polarization in the soil. For a substantial ground current this effect is usually negligible, but it can give large errors in the measurement.

BACK TO THE SINGLE WIRE

In the initial work on the telephone, Bell used single wire and ground-type tele-graph circuits for his telephone, and the initial telephone circuits were all installed this way. After all, why pay for the extra conductor when it only doubled the loss in the circuit?

If you recall, at one point it was the opinion of Edison that the telephone would never be a success because of the extraneous clicks, squeaks and squawks one heard on a circuit of any appreciable length. The initial telephone circuits were very noisy.

The reasons for this noise were primarily related to the way in which the tele-phone line was constructed. Figure 5-2 shows a line with a ground return and a load at the far end. A changing magnetomotive force is facing crosswise to the loop. We see that the amount of voltage induced is directly proportional to the area of the loop.

For many practical reasons, the line was generally placed high enough above the ground to get it out of the way so that animals, people, wagons, and locomo-

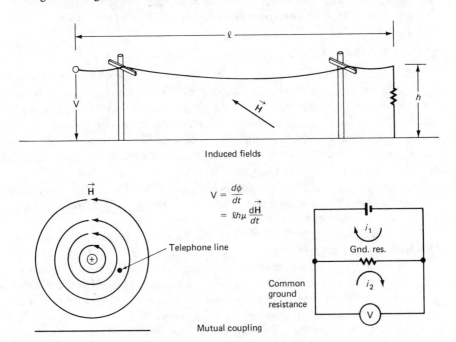

Induced fields

$$V = \frac{d\phi}{dt}$$
$$= \ell h \mu \frac{d\vec{H}}{dt}$$

Telephone line

Gnd. res.

Common ground resistance

Mutual coupling

Figure 5-2. Magnetically induced voltages.

tives could pass beneath it. By the time the length of the line exceeded a few miles, one could always measure substantial voltages at the open end. The earth's magnetic field fluctuates slightly, lightning generates large currents with attendant large magnetic fields, etc.

Another factor that significantly affected the situation was that the early telephone lines were run on the same poles as and adjacent to telegraph lines. The telegraph lines carry substantial currents that are constantly fluctuating and, in the case of multiplex circuits, changing polarity. The center illustration shows that the magnetic field that surrounded the telegraph line also linked the telephone line, thereby inducing voltage.

A final significant factor is that the telephone and the telegraph shared a common ground resistance. As shown in the lower illustration, a portion of the telegraph voltage appears directly in the telephone circuit.

Since the length of the telephone line is determined by the places it must go, the only way to reduce the area of the loop is to reduce the spacing between the line and the return. Well before the turn of the century, the practice was accepted that high-quality telephone circuits were run in adjacent pairs of wires strung on the same pole. The wires were generally run with 8-inch or 12-inch spacing.

LIGHTNING PROTECTION

The Bell system practice is to refer to the voltage between the wires as *transverse* or *metallic* voltage. Presumably, if the wires were very close together, perhaps even twisted, no outside source could induce any voltage transverse to the wires. However, the original argument about induced voltage is not changed when one considers the common-mode (*longitudinal voltage,* in Bell parlance) voltage between the wire-pair and ground. The wires are still at some height h above the ground, and the loop encloses a very large area.

It is noteworthy that the wires do not have to be directly struck in order to have a very large voltage induced on them. Just the mangetic field from a nearby strike is quite adequate to do the job.

In this day and age, disturbances from the telegraph lines are not common. However, induced voltages from the power system are. Modern telephone circuits are no longer run on open wires, they are run on shielded cable in which a conductive sheath completely surrounds the telephone circuits, effectively sealing out induced noise. However, in the final analysis, the shield itself represents a conductor in which voltages can be induced by magnetic fields.

Cross-country power lines are generally run on four air-spaced wires, with each of three wires carrying a different phase. At a distance from the set, the fields can largely cancel. However, if one phase shorts to ground, in the interval before the system shuts down, very large exterior fields are developed. The shield on the telephone line is grounded at regular intervals. However, this grounding does not have zero resistance and a substantial voltage can appear on the shield due to the induced current surge.

STATION-PROTECTOR LIMITING VOLTAGES

The Bell system entrance to most installations is equipped with either 3 mil carbon blocks, gas tubes, or a combination of both. The carbon-block arrangement consists of a set of carbon blocks for tip, ring, and ground. The short 0.003-inch spacing is intended to break down on a surge of voltage and channel the current directly to ground. The breakdown of these devices shows a bell-shaped distribution with the 50% point at 700 V and the 3-sigma points at 400 and 1,000 V respectively.

The gas tubes generally do somewhat better and will reliably fire at lower voltages. However, it is good design practice to count on the higher voltages because a great many installations still use the carbon blocks.

For protection from accidental power crossings, a standard 7-amp fuse is usually installed. However, in some cases fuses down to 0.35 A rms rating are employed.

Although they are not, in theory, supposed to occur, metallic (or transverse) voltage surges do arise. In the worst case, these may go to the limit of the carbon-block protector. These surges generally show an exponential rise and fall. About 95% have rise times longer than 1 μsec and most are on the order of 10 μsec.

The longest decays are produced by distant strokes that have undergone propagation dispersion. Upper 3-sigma limits of 2,500 μsec have been measured; however, about 70% have decay times less than 560 μsec. In a worst case, one could have a 1,000-V pulse (limited by the carbon-block arrestor) with a 10-μsec rise and a 2,500-μsec decay. However, this is quite unlikely. A much more likely waveshape would be 800 V with a 10 μsec rise time and a 560 μsec decay time.

In most cases, the current in a lightning surge is limited by the impedance of the cable. In a Bell study conducted over a 5-month period, an isolated, sheathed cable with grounding was found to have experienced 1,000 current surges. The maximum short-circuit current was found to be 60 A, and the typical current was 2 A from conductor to ground. Good design practice should probably allow for occasional 100-A surges.

Longitudinal voltages and currents tend, in general, to be larger then metallic currents and voltages. Among other things, because both conductors are contributing, the impedance of the circuit is halved. One would therefore expect that 200-A surges might be occasionally encountered.

A very significant point concerns the impedance of the ground wire. The resistance is really not the problem; it is mainly a matter of the inductance. For example, a 30-foot length of #14 wire has a negligible resistance of 0.08 Ω. However, it has an inductance of 0.4 μhy per foot. A 200-A surge with a 1.6 μsec rise time has a di/dt of 125 A/sec. Over the 30-foot wire this would yield a voltage drop of 1,500 V! Long ground wires are to be avoided when possible. In cases where this is not possible, the grounding should be done with the largest feasible conductors. The inductance of a straight length of wire is inversely proportional to the diameter.

YOUR EQUIPMENT

Electronic equipment designed for direct connection to the telephone line must be equipped with some form of surge protection. This can be obtained in the form of a miniature gas tube or a varistor. The gas tube fires to connect either line to ground when the ionization voltage is exceeded. The varistor acts like a bidirectional zener and will conduct only when the voltage exceeds a certain level.

The currents and voltages at your equipment interface are generally limited by the fact that they are "behind" the entrance protection and the equipment is connected to the inlet block through length of 24-AWG wire. Your equipment case should be grounded to the green power-line safety return or to a local ground.

It is permissible to mount the surge arrestor on a printed circuit card. However, the ground must be of sufficient size to withstand a substantial surge. Fuses to disconnect from tip and ring can be used but are not mandatory. The ground path should be at least the equivalent of a #18 wire. This is one of the items tested in FCC-type acceptance tests.

The lower voltage of the surge arrestor is controlled by the voltages that are liable to be encountered on the line. The maximum voltage that may be applied between tip and ring or either wire and ground is 202 Vdc. This will be found only in the on-hook state. A surge arrestor that fires at 250 V is probably about the most sensitive practical limit.

As can be seen from the discussion, the use of a substantial isolation method is probably warranted in any case where there is a significant investment in the electronics. For a small repertory dialer, the economics of the situation might not warrant significant costs for isolation. However, a mini- or microcomputer that was wiped out in a thunderstorm would represent a substantial loss.

One of the advantages of using hybrid isolation is that the transformers are designed to protect the equipment by keeping many of the transients out of the subsequent electronics.

6
Security Techniques

The convenience of a remotely controlled device that gathers data or controls items unattended which can be accessed over the telephone network has been discussed at length. However, the very convenience of access through any telephone can pose problems by itself since it means that *anyone* can access the equipment as easily. This means that some level of security must be included in many cases.

The level or requirement for security will generally depend upon the nature of the operation. For example, if the operation is one in which the equipment serves to accumulate atmospheric data such as wind velocity, temperature, pressure, etc., it probably would do no harm to have outsiders occasionally access the data. On the other hand, if the organization is a utility company that monitors the data for environmental control reasons, the management would not be too happy to have some environmental vigilance organization have free access to their instrumentation network.

On a more commercial basis, if the purpose of the network was to disseminate commodity futures price information and to collect transaction data from field buyers, it would be unattractive to have the information freely accessible to the sellers.

In addition to this, any information-only system is liable to a variety of unauthorized access attempts if information is interesting enough. Even when it is not all that terribly interesting, one has to contend with pranksters and kids. If nothing else it can sometimes become a nuisance because the authorized access can be blocked by a busy signal.

On the other hand, if something is being controlled at the far end of the line, there is the very real possibility that some damage could result from unauthorized access. The seriousness of this depends upon what is being controlled. If it is only the lighting or air conditioning, the results would not be as serious as if it were a dam gate, etc. Long experience has taught that an unattended installation should be padlocked to prevent unauthorized entry by the curious, the malicious, and thieves.

LEVELS OF SECURITY

Security is a matter of degree. There is probably no level of security that would not eventually yield to some level of intelligent attack. The power substation surrounded by a nine-foot chain link fence topped with barbed wire can be penetrated with a pair of chain cutters or a ladder. Even bank vaults sealed with time locks have been penetrated with high explosives, pneumatic drills, oxyacetylene torches and, in one case, an antitank rifle! As one attempts to raise the level of security, the process of authorized entry generally becomes progressively more difficult.

There are some valid analogies that can be drawn between the security of an electrical communication network and the security of an unattended structure. For example, the use of an unlisted telephone number is analogous to the security of having an installation in a remote location with an unobtrusive appearance. It is not unusual to have four to eight "wrong number" calls appear on an unlisted telephone number each month. The probability can increase dramatically if the unlisted number represents a transposition of some listed and busy number such as a department store. If the listed number is 444-3821 and the unlisted one is 444-3281, you can expect to have several "wrong number" calls per day.

In terms of locks, these come in several varieties using either a key or a combination. The key-type has the advantage that one does not have to remember anything. The combination lock has the advantage that one does not have to carry any special hardware.

If only a few people are to have access at any given time, the key lock has a distinct advantage since the distribution of the keys can be made by a central authority. The analog for the telephone system is a generator that produces some combination of nonstandard tones. Unfortunately, if a large number of people are to have access, this equipment must be produced for each at some expense. These little boxes can easily become lost, strayed, or stolen. They are somewhat more difficult to duplicate than a brass key, but it can be done if someone is sufficiently interested.

The combination lock is relatively easy to implement over the telephone, and it has the advantage that no extra hardware is required if the access is attempted from a DTMF telephone. Even a rotory-dial phone can be used if the user carries one of the pocket-DTMF acoustically coupled generators. These units are mass produced and therefore are relatively inexpensive compared to the custom electronic "key" generator.

In general, a combination lock becomes more secure as the length of the combination increases. For example, a three-decimal digit combination has 1,000 possibilities, from 000 to 999. If someone were to start systematically trying numbers at random, possibly using a home computer, he could crack the combination in an average of 500 tries. Assuming that it required 1.5 sec (on a DTMF system) to dial the number, 5 sec to access your machine, and 1 sec to enter the combination, the code would be cracked, on the average, in 1 hr and 2.5 min. At worst it would only take 2 hrs and 5 min.

With six digits the task becomes a little more time-consuming. With a million possible combinations, it would require 1,041.67 hours or 43.4 days on the average. This would certainly make it possible to detect the attempt at unauthorized entry and have the telephone number changed. In regard to this point, it is relatively simple to condition your answering equipment to keep a tally of unauthorized entry attempts, and it is probably advisable if there is enough at stake to warrant a six-digit combination.

An interesting point exists with regard to the response to unauthorized entry. At first glance it might seem that one would program the machine to hang up when it detects an error in the combination. This obviously saves time. Unfortunately, it seriously compromises the function of the lock. Suppose that the machine hangs up when it detects the first erroneous digit. The caller then simply tries every digit from 0 to 9 and writes down the first one which is not rejected. That digit and a second 0-to-9 try will give him the second digit, etc. A six-digit combination could thus be broken in just 300 tries on the average. In order to preserve the system integrity, the machine should patiently wait until the entire combination has been entered before hanging up, even when the first digit is not valid.

Another point is worth noting. It is usually worthwhile to place a time-out feature on the digit entry so that the machine will hang up on an incomplete entry whether it was valid or not. Three seconds is quite adequate for manual entry from a DTMF standard keyboard. If the machine does not hang up immediately after the invalid combination is completed, but rather accepts some small semirandom number of additional digits, it makes it difficult for the intruder to determine the exact length of the complete code.

The latter point is mainly of value against the prankster since the true length of the code would be given in the instruction manual and anything written down and published should be considered to be compromised. Anyone with a business or profit motive for cracking the system would know enough to get a copy of the manual if the system is marketed commercially and not a one-of-a-kind device.

THE DOUBLE LOCK

It is a fairly common practice in the military, where a strict accountability for access is required, to place more than one padlock on a device in such a way that two or more parties each have to remove their own lock to gain access. An electronic variation of this would provide one basic combination that is given to all authorized parties, along with a separate combination known only to each individual. Authorized access would then be obtained by entering both the general combination and any one of the individual combinations stored on a lookup table.

There is an important point to note regarding the entry of combinations. The combination padlocks authorized for use of files for storage of military classified documents are arranged to accept a key on the rear. When this lock is first received from the manufacturer, it comes in locked with a combination published in the instruction sheet. The lock must first be unlocked using the published combination. The working combination is then dialed in using the dial and the key to set each digit. The combination can be changed only when the lock is unlocked using the previously set combination. If the lock is never left unattended in the unlocked condition, a new combination cannot be set in by an intruder.

Translated into electronic terms, new combinations must always be entered by some means other than that used for normal entry. Otherwise, the intruder, in possession of the manual, could simply follow the procedure and enter a combination known to himself, and then unlock the system at will.

The use of a general and private combination system has several advantages in terms of accountability. The answering system can easily be arranged to account for each access. Furthermore, matters can be arranged at the time of entry so that some individuals can access data but not control and some can control only A but not B. It is not difficult to arrange the machine program so that the machine will not read back any of the private combinations.

THE WIRETAP

Combination locks can be easily compromised in any of a number of ways by disgruntled employees, carelessness (someone writes the combination on his phone pad), or poor practices (someone uses his birthdate or social security or pay number).

The telephone-based system merely adds a new electronic mechanism for compromise of security because it is subject to complete copy via a wiretap. If the communication is to be done entirely from machine to machine, it is possible to include one of the sophisticated polynomial encoding algorithms (sometimes called pseudorandom) such that a given message would never be repeated twice in the same way. For a human being such manipulations are too complex to be practical. No one is going to use the system if it requires lengthy calculations to encode the message.

A wiretap done at a high level of technical skill is virtually undetectable from measurements on the telephone line. Probably the only real defense against the wiretap is the insertion of redundant and meaningless communications with the arrangement that the machine response to the dummy messages be indistinguishable from the response to valid messages and commands. Even here the dummy messages will only delay the decoding process unless the valid messages form a statistically small faction of the total and the format of the valid message is subject to continuous change. Otherwise, a correlation can be established by careful analysis of a sufficiently long record. The coding of valid commands must be changed often enough to preclude the intruder from obtaining a record of sufficient length to establish correlation.

SUMMARY

We have attempted to outline a few of the considerations regarding security on a system operated over the public switched telephone network. The emphasis has been on human being-to-computer access rather than machine-to-machine data transactions. Because of the difficulties involved in having human beings perform an extensive data encryption on some pseudorandom basis, it has been shown that the system is inherently a rather low-security system that is rendered more vulnerable by the possibility of wiretapping.

It seems fair to conclude that only matters that do not have severe penalties due to security compromise should be controlled or accessed over the public switched telephone network.

SECTION 2
SOUND, WAVEFORMS
AND SPEECH

7
Sound and Hearing

In this section we shall be dealing with some of the more fundamental aspects of sound and to a limited extent with the properties of hearing. Although this text is not primarily concerned with the physiology of either speech or hearing, the subject matter of the text cannot be properly grasped without some understanding of these processes. This is the more so particularly because a great many of the phenomena to be dealt with in telephony hinge upon some of the details of the speech and hearing processes.

There is an old puzzle which asks, "If a tree falls in the forest and nothing is present to hear it, is there a sound?" There is a school which argues that sound is the manifestation of vibration upon an ear; thus, with no ear to hear, there is no sound. The *American Heritage Dictionary,* on the other hand, gives:

> *sound* 1. A vibratory disturbance with frequency in the approximate range between 20 and 20,000 cycles per second capable of being heard.
> 2. The sensation stimulated in the organs of hearing by such a disturbance.

For our purposes, in most cases, we will associate sound with the sensation of hearing. However, in other cases (for example, when discussing phenomena like the speed of sound), the association with hearing will not be observed, and only the vibratory process will be of interest. However, the distinction will be observed that something is sound if it could be heard either with an ear present or with an appropriate instrument to convert the disturbance into an auditory sensation.

HOW DO WE HEAR?

Superficially, the answer to this question is: "With our ears." Although this is generally correct, there are a number of other ways in which we may sense vibratory disturbances. The slow throb of the propellor on a large ship and the sonorous rumbling of a 64-foot organ pipe are sensed more through the nerves on the feet, buttocks, and perhpas the hands, if touching something. Similarly, the sonic boom of a passing aircraft is sensed as much through the lungs and pleural cavity as through the ears. However, most of the transactions between vibratory media and the brain proceed through the ears, and most of these are the result of pressure waves in the medium in which the ears are immersed.

Gaseous and liquid media can transmit only pressure waves. In the special case of the interface between a liquid and a gas (the surface of the lake or ocean), gravity waves can propagate. However, truly transverse or polarized waves like light and radio signals can propagate only in a solid that has properties such as tensile strength and bending moment. (The fact that the "aether" would have to be a solid, if it exists, is a Pandora's box that we will not open here.) On the other hand, transverse sound waves do propagate through solids like diesel engine blocks, airplane propellors, and violin strings. And they can be heard, either through the pressure waves they create or by direct physical contact. A mechanic trying to locate a bad bearing in a machine will frequently probe the machine with a screwdriver against which he rests his forehead. There are certain phenomena that can be heard quite clearly this way.

One of the unusual properties of human hearing is that of *mixing*. A human being who is shown light made up of a mixture of red and green light will perceive the color as white. A similar thing applied when yellow and blue light are mixed. As a matter of fact, the eye cannot perceive differences between different complementary-color mixtures of "white" light.

On the other hand, the human ear does not respond to mixing. It is a standard part of a musical education to be trained in "dictation." In this course the student will listen to a chord consisting of three to five notes and be expected to write each distinct note upon the staff. Obviously, with human hearing mixing does not occur. It should be noted that anyone who does not have a "tin ear" can hear a difference between an augmented and a diminished chord, even without the benefit of any musical training at all.

THE PRESSURE WAVE

Figure 7-1 was prepared in order to illustrate some of the pressure-wave phenomena that occur in a compressible medium such as a gas. Picture the parallel vertical lines as being smoke trails. Smoke trails are frequently introduced into wind tunnels to make the motion of the air particles visible. Next assume that the picture was taken with a slit-type camera in which the film travels upward. At any instant in time, a single horizontal line represents the spacing of the smoke trails. This type of camera action is similar to the "photo-finish" camera used at horse tracks. Horizontal strips at the bottom of the picture were taken at a later time than those at the top.

Starting at the upper left hand corner of the page, a piston or loudspeaker cone begins to move toward the right with a time curve of displacement equal to the Gauss error curve:

```
]LIST 100,300

100  REM  THIS PROGRAM IS INTENDED TO ILLUSTRATE A PRESSURE WAVE. THE PRES
     SURE AT ANY LOCATION IS PROPPORTIONAL TO THE RECIPROCAL OF THE TRACE
     LINE SPACING.
110  HGR
120  HCOLOR= 3
130  POKE   - 12524,0
140  LET Y% = 0
150  LET D% = 0
160  LET Q =  ABS ((D% - Y%) / 10 + 3)
165  LET Q = Q ^ 2
170  LET X = D% + 10 *  EXP ( - Q)
180  LET X% = X
190  HPLOT X%,Y%
200  LET D% = D% + 10
210  IF D% < = 255 THEN  GOTO 160
220  LET D% = 0
230  LET Y% = Y% + 1
240  IF Y% < = 160 THEN  GOTO 160
250  END
```

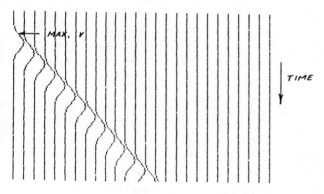

Figure 7-1.

$$\chi = k\, e^{(-t^2)}$$

The Gauss error curve does not depart significantly from a single cycle of a sine wave running from 270° through 0° to 270°. The single cycle is easier to follow than a complete sine-wave train.

As the piston moves to the right in the beginning of the cycle, the air must flee before it; however, the individual air molecules have inertia and therefore require some mechanical force to move them. The result of this is that the air immediately ahead of the piston is compressed and the smoke tracer lines are forced closer together. The pressure disturbance races ahead of the piston at the speed of sound in the medium.

At about one-half of the rightward travel of the piston, the piston velocity is maximum and the compression is also maximum. This point is noted on the figure. After this the velocity of the piston to the right begins to decrease in a nearly sinusoidal manner, reaching zero at the maximum rightward extension. Since this decrease takes the piston farther and farther from the speed of sound in the medium, the most highly compressed portion of the wavefront flees away from the piston and becomes detached.

Upon reaching maximum rightward extension the piston begins to accelerate back toward the left. This reduces the pressure at the piston and the lines begin to be stretched apart. The maximum leftward velocity is again reached at the half-travel point, and this is the point of minimum pressure on the piston and maximum stretching of the line spacing. At this time the air molecules to the left of the pressure peak are accelerated to the left because they have a higher-than-ambient pressure to their right and a lower-than-ambient pressure to their left. This pressure gradient exerts a pressure or force upon each molecule.

From the halfway point to the original rest position, the piston decelerates its leftward motion in an approximation of a sine wave. Since it is going slower and slower, the pressure depression decreases and the piston finally comes to rest in the initial position with the pressure at the piston face back at ambient level. At this point the pressure disturbance is completely detached from the piston.

For the detached pressure peak, the air molecules to both right and left are pushed and accelerated. Those to the left go to fill the depression and those to the right serve to compress the air ahead of them, thus causing the disturbance to propagate to the right without change of shape at the speed of sound in the medium. Note that after the disturbance has passed, the air molecules have returned to their original positions as designated by the smoke streaks. The pressure depression is maintained because the leftward accelerated molecules reach very high velocity and do not coast to a stop until the increasing pressure (to ambient) halts them.

If the pressure wave was confined to a tube so that it did not spread, and if there were no friction losses among the molecules, it would propagate indefinitely without change, at the speed of sound in the medium.

There are a few oversimplifications in the picture that will be briefly touched upon before the argument is dropped

Let us suppose that the detached wave collides with a completely immovable surface at the right-hand boundary of the picture. The rightward-moving molecules would rebound from the surface toward the left and, momentarily, the compression at the rigid surface would be doubled compared to the peak of the wave. The echo, or reflection, would result in a wave identical to the incident wave, but traveling in the right-to-left direction. The pressure would exert a force on the immovable surface but no work would take place since no motion resulted and work is the product of force times distance.

On the other hand, if the surface is such that it yields slightly in response to the pressure peak and depression, the wave could in fact transfer energy into the surface. As a matter of fact, if the compliance of the surface were just right, it could absorb *all* of the energy of the incident wave and no echo or reflection would result; the backward wave would completely disappear. This is the mechanism by which ears and microphones extract energy from passing sound waves. A common source of the hearing loss experienced by older people is the fact that the reflecting surface (the eardrum) ceases to have this optimum compliance and the surface becomes too rigid.

THE VELOCITY OF SOUND

It may be seen that the arguments describing the propagation of a longitudinal pressure wave apply equally to any material that can undergo compression and rarefaction. One normally tends to think of water as being imcompressible, however, this is not rigorously true. The compressibility of a material is usually described by the term *bulk modulus*. Mathematically, the bulk modulus is described by:

$$\text{bulk modulus} = \frac{\text{hydrostatic pressure}}{\text{change of volume per unit vol.}}$$

$$= \frac{P}{dV/V}$$

It may be seen that dV and V both have the same units, that is, both are measured in cubic inches or cubic centimeters, etc. The units, therefore, cancel, and only the units in the numerator remain. Bulk modulus is therefore measured in pounds per square inch or newtons per square meter, etc.

For water the bulk modulus is 310,000 lb/in² . Therefore, a pressure of 1 lb/in² would compress water by a factor of 3.23×10^{-6}, and a pressure of 3,100 lb/in² would be required to compress water 1%. By comparison the bulk modulus of mild steel is 30,000,000 lb/in², or nearly 100 times as great.

For these relatively incompressible media, it is possible to show, on theoretical grounds, that the velocity of sound is given by:

$$v = \sqrt{\frac{\text{bulk modulus}}{\text{density}}}$$

For solids, Young's modulus is used instead of the bulk modulus. From this it can be seen that a material with low density is as liable to have a high velocity as a denser but stronger material. The velocity of sound in water is approximately 4,760 ft/sec at 59°F, and the velocity of sound in steel is approximately 16,700 ft per sec, which is approximately identical to the velocity of sound in aluminum since the ratio of Young's modulus to density is nearly the same for both materials.

In gases the matter is slightly different. Whenever a gas is compressed, the temperature changes, raising for increased pressure and falling for decreased pressure. The compression and expansion follow each other so rapidly and the thermal conductivity of most gases is so small that the passage of a sound wave corresponds to an adiabatic process, and the change in pressure is larger than it would be if the compression were slow enough to take place at a constant temperature. The ratio of increase is usually specified as γ.

The value of γ depends upon the molecular structure of the gas. It can be shown that for diatomic gases $\gamma = 1.40$. This actually accounts for the majority of gases. However, for a few of the nonreactive monatomic gases, such as helium and argon, $\gamma = 1.60$. Air, which is made up largely of diatomic gases, has $\gamma = 1.4$.

The velocity of sound in a gas is given by:

$$v = \sqrt{\frac{\gamma P}{d}}$$

The velocity of sound in air works out to about 1,048 ft/sec at 32°F. According to Boyle's law, the ratio of pressure to density for gases at constant temperature is a constant. Therefore, the velocity of sound is largely unaffected by pressure changes.

On the other hand, the ratio of pressure to density does change with temperature, as given by Charles' law. Therefore, the velocity of sound in the gas changes as:

$$\frac{v_1}{v_2} = \sqrt{\frac{T_1}{T_2}}$$

A particularly striking application of this fact occurs in a dense fog over water. This is usually caused by a temperature inversion, that is, the temperature is lower at the surface than it is at some moderate altitude. Sounds passing from a slower into a faster medium tend to be refracted or bent back into the slower medium, so the sound is trapped or ducted along the surface, rather than being able to spread freely in elevation. One can thus hear voices and sounds much farther in a dense fog than in clear air.

An interesting phenomenon in speech processing involves the lighter gases. The speed of sound in hydrogen is 4,220 ft/sec due to the very low mass of the hydrogen. Helium is also low-mass and in addition, monatomic. This becomes significant in deep-sea diving. To prevent nitrogen narcosis and reduce decompression times, deep-sea divers breathe a mixture of helium and oxygen rather than normal air, which is 80% nitrogen. In this mixture the velocity of sound is on the order of 4,000 ft/sec. This high velocity completely alters the sound-producing capability of the human speech apparatus and results in an incomprehensible "Donald Duck" sound. Only after electronic processing does it become possible for divers to understand one another or be understood by those on the surface tender.

THE EAR

The ear is a remarkable organ that is considerably more complicated than a casual inspection by the layman would reveal. Figure 7-2 shows the feature usually brought out in an encyclopedia illustration for laymen (like the writer). The outer ear consists mainly of the pinna, or the part visible to others, and the auditory canal, which is the small channel through which the sound is conducted to the inner ear.

The auditory canal terminates the tympanic membrane or eardrum. This is the portion of the organ that yields to pressure and extracts energy from the sound wave. The construction of the pinna and the auditory canal is such as to concentrate the pressure, thereby increasing the sensitivity to the ear.

The eardrum is loaded by and transfers energy through three tiny ossicles, or bones, called the malleus (the hammer), the incus (the anvil), and the stapes (the stirrup). These items may be seen in Figure 7-3 in somewhat better detail. The fact that these items are used to load and transfer the sound seems fairly obvious

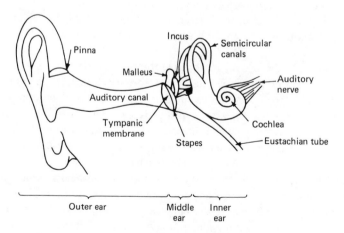

Figure 7-2. The ear.

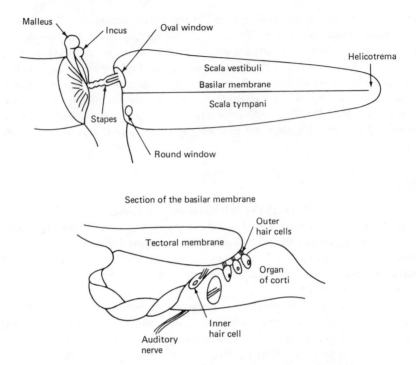

Figure 7-3. The middle and inner ear with the choclea uncoiled.

from the connection. However, a satisfactory engineering explanation of the details of this odd linkage does not seem to be present in the literature.

The semicircular canals consist of a series of looped tubes partially filled with a fluid. These seem to act in the fashion of a carpenter's bubble level, and would seem to have more to do with the properties of balance and equilibrium than with hearing.

The eustachian tube is used to equalize the pressure on the inner-ear side of the eardrum with the outside world. The eardrum is a delicate membrane and cannot withstand much continuous pressure differential. When changing altitude in an airplane or underwater depth, it is sometimes necessary to forcibly equalize this pressure by yawning or pinching the nose and blowing (note that the latter diver's trick is a bit dangerous and should not be attempted without instruction, and then only gently). When one has a cold the eustachian tube can become partly or completely blocked and a diminution of hearing will result.

The real job of hearing and transfering sound energy from the air to the nervous system is accomplished in the cochlea. This organ is tubular and coiled more or less like a snail. In the illustration of Figure 7-3 it has been "uncoiled" for clarity. Note that this is only an artistic license. It is probably not possible to uncoil a real cochlea even surgically.

The cochlea is divided into two channels, or chambers, called the scala vestibuli and the scala tympani, separated by the basilar membrane. Sound vibrations are coupled into the scala vestibuli from the stapes via the oval window. The basilar membrane does not extend quite to the apex of the cochlea, and the chambers are connected there by the helicotrema. Both chambers are filled with a fluid called the perilymph, which is related to the cerebrospinal fluid. The unrolled length of the cochlea is on the order of 32 mm (approx. 1.26 in). A pressure wave induced by pressure from the stapes travels this distance to the helicotrema and then an equal distance back to the round window, which relieves the pressure.

By the seventeenth century the phenomenon of sound resonance in strings, tuning forks, organ pipes, and a variety of other instruments was well known and it seemed to present a logical explanation for the ability to detect sound and differentiate pitches. However, this presented a difficulty. It is demonstrable that a person with acute hearing and perhaps a trained musical ear can detect differences as small as 0.3% over a range between about 20 Hz to 16,000 Hz, a dynamic range of 800 to 1. If done with separate resonators, this would require 2,231 separate resonators, or about 1,785 per inch of cochlea. It was at first suggested that the spiral lamina, which is the bony part of the basilar membrane, might be the resonator, much like the tines or reeds in a music box. Since this organ is wider at the base of the cochlea, this theory would lead to the detection of low-pitched sounds at the stapes end of the cochlea and high-pitched sounds at the apex.

An excellent summary of the history of discoveries on the subject of the hearing process is given by:

> Joseph J. Zwislocki. Sound analysis of the ear: A history of discoveries. *American Scientist Magazine*: Mar–April 1981, pp. 184–193.

Professor Zwislocki points out that the first modern theory of the functioning of the cochlea is due to Heinrich von Helmholtz. Helmholtz announced a theory in 1863 in which he proposed that the arches of Corti might be the resonators. Because these arches increase in size from the oval window to the apex, he proposed that high pitches would be detected at the stapes end and low pitches at the apex, the direct opposite of the prevailing theories.

In later work Helmholtz was made aware of the hair cells, which string the basilar membrane, being shorter at the base and longer at the apex, like the strings on a musical instrument. He then abandoned the arches as resonators and reasoned that the "strings" were better candidates.

In a series of experiments, G. Bekesy constructed enlarged models of the human cochlea, similar to that in Figure 7-3, with a small piston to excite the waves. A rubber membrane modeled the cochlear duct and the model was filled with water-glycerine solution to obtain the correct viscosity. Carbon dust was added to make the motion visible. The volume displacements were equalized with an opening that was the equivalent of the round window.

Bekesy found that, just as Helmholtz had predicted, the waves reached an amplitude maximum for high frequencies near the base and for low frequencies near the apex of the artificial cochlea. A puzzling facet of the work was that the waves traveled right through the maximum without either a significant refraction or an absorption, either or both of which would be noted when a wave encounters a high-Q resonator. Bekesy extended his work, improving dissection techniques to the point where he was able to observe the waves in post mortem preparations of human cochleas; a work which won him the Nobel Prize in 1961.

In a 1942 work on the inner ear, O. W. Ranke showed that the cochlear waves are not pressure waves, but rather surface waves like the ripples on a pond. This is a significant factor since the cochlea is entirely too tiny to support resonances in waves traveling at 3,000 to 4,000 feet per second. On the other hand, a "gravity" type of wave arising from the interaction between the stiffness of the cochlear membrane and the inertia of the cochlear fluid can propagate at rates three orders of magnitude or more lower, thus reducing the wavelengths to the dimensions of the cochlea.

In work published in 1946 and 1948, Professor Zwislocki derived the cochlear waves mathematically, and showed that the waves, due to the increasing compliance of the cochlear membrane, should increase in amplitude and decrease in wavelength with distance from the cochlear base; in other words, the propagational velocity decreases with distance. A reflection at the apex would then give rise to a standing-wave pattern. A loss of hearing at a particular frequency or band of frequencies is not too uncommon, and by post-mortem examination of the cochlea it was found that the damaged areas closely corresponded to the theoretical prediction of the resonance point. Empirically, the distance between the helicotrema and the standing wave maximum is given approximately by:

$$\text{distance (mm)} = \frac{(\log_{10} F)^3}{2}$$

This is a very nonlinear relationship.

A significant problem remained: Bekesy had found a high order of damping to exist. The damping was in fact high enough so that the standing wave did not show any sharp resonance, in agreement with his experimental model. Experiments with electrodes in the cochlea indicated that electrical potentials were found in agreement with the other localization determinations. These potentials were believed to arise from the hair cells, which carried the fibers. However, here again the resonance was not sufficient to account for the sharp distinctions in pitch.

By the late 1960s and early 1070s a number of investigators shed some new light upon the matter. Using the Mössbauer technique, which is based upon the absorption of gamma rays, Johnstone and Boyle succeeded for the first time in measuring basilar vibrations in a living animal (a guinea pig). They found two particular points of interest. First of all, in the living ear a very sharp peak, more that 10 db higher than found in post-mortem measurements, was located. Secondly, a flat-phase plateau extending from the resonance to higher frequencies was detected, indicating that the resonance frequency had been exceeded.

In the present theory, it is speculated that the tectorial membrane and the basilar membrane undergo a vibration, producing a shearing action on the outer hair cells. These, in turn, generate the electrical neural signals we perceive as sound. The exact nature of the vibration is still under investigation. It may be of a shearing nature with the basilar membrane moving in the direction opposite to the tectorial membrane, or the vibrations may be at right angles to one another.

A mechanical model is proposed by Zwislocki. In Figure 7-4 we see a loudspeaker or other damped vibrator to which has been affixed a resonant reed mounted at an angle so that there is some coupling. Without the reed the speaker is well damped and gives a constant amplitude output motion for a constant input current. When the reed is attached, at frequencies below the resonance of the reed the reed moves in phase and with an amplitude equal to the speaker. However, as the reed resonance is approached, a sharp peak in the reed amplitude occurs and it begings to swing through a large arc. This is expressed in the

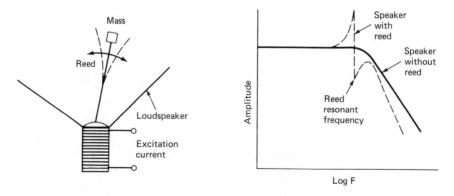

Figure 7-4. A basilar membrane resonance model.

speaker cone motion by a sharp peak below the reed frequency and a sharp dip at the frequency itself. This peak and notch characteristic is a common feature of very high Q resonant circuits, such as a quartz crystal of the type used for determining frequency in a radio. The sharply peaked response and the plateau seem very similar to the responses measured in living animals. However, certain problems remain in matching the phase response.

It would seem that the investigators are homing in on the problem of how we hear, but perhaps the final story is not yet with us. One item that does not seem to fit too well was shown by H. Spoedlin in 1969 that, at least in the cochlea of a cat, 90 to 95% of the nerve fibers terminate in the inside hair cells, which seem to be connected to nothing, and only 5 to 10% terminate in the outer hair cells, which are the connected ones. As a matter of fact, these outer hair cells seem to share nerve fibers since there are fewer fibers than hair cells. The question of why the inner hair cells get the lion's share of the nerve fibers when they do not seem to play a part in the operation of the ear (by current theory) is a discordant note, and suggests that a few things remain to be resolved.

8
Sounds

In this chapter we shall be spending a bit of time discussing sounds in general. This text is not specifically related to the generation of music by computer. However, taken as a class, the sounds of music have been studied for a much longer time than the sounds of speech, and there is more information generally available on music than there is on the sounds of speech. It is therefore worthwhile to carry a few of the concepts of music into the discussion. A recognition of some of the complex waveshapes encountered in music is helpful in understanding some of the waveshapes and sounds encountered in speech.

From the very earliest times, the basic concept of the *octave,* or a tone of twice the frequency, seems to have played a basic part in music. Stringed instruments are very old and seem to have independently evolved in different parts of the world. We probably do not really know where music first evolved. However, the record of music is at least preserved in some of the older parts of the Bible. In about 1200 B.C. we find the troops of Joshua blowing their trumpets about the walls of Jericho (Josh. 6:13-21). In about 1000 B.C., David is soothing to King Saul because he was "a cunning player upon the harp" (1 Samuel 16:16.).

The concept of the octave seems to be an inherent gift of most men. The octave can nearly always be substituted in a piece of music without spoiling the harmony. As a matter of fact, music as diverse in nature as the five-tone scale of the Pythagoreans, the seven-tone scale of India, and the twelve-tone scale of China are all based upon the octave. The people in all corners of the world seem to base their music upon the concept of the octave. As far as this writer has been able to discover, there is no music that is not, in one way or another, based upon the octave.

It seems likely that, with at least a thousand years of development, the makers and players of stringed instruments must have had to know that the pitch of a string is:

- Directly related to the tension in a string, with higher tensions yielding a higher pitch.
- Inversely related to the mass per unit length. Low mass yields a higher pitch.
- Inversely related to length. A shorter string yields a higher pitch, tension and mass being equal.

In the face of this we find that Pythagoras is credited with the first observation (ca. 530 B.C.) that halving the length of a string will double the pitch and produce the octave. Standardization of things such as weights and measures was common long before the time of Pythagoras, and probably some standardization of music was common also. It seems more likely that Pythagoras, who was a teacher and philosopher, simply taught something that was well known to musicians of the time. Each of the separate scales mentioned earlier can be derived by appropriately stopping the strings on a stringed instrument in equal intervals. It would seem that the human ear simply responds to pitch in a fashion proportional to the log to the base two of the frequency.

There is further evidence that knowledge of the relationship between tension and pitch was common in ancient times. Even the most primitive accounts of sailing record the fact that sailors (or anyone who depends upon ropes in his work) knew that when a plucked rope gave a high pitch, it was being stressed close to breaking. The expression "tight as a fiddle string" has its equivalent even among the natives of Micronesia.

WHAT IS MUSIC?

It seems fair to ask just what it is that sets music apart from all of the sounds in which we are immersed. For most of us, our waking hours are spent immersed in a barrage of sound ranging from the rumble of thunder and the blasting exhaust of diesel engine on trucks, to the quieter sounds of conversation, the Muzak in a department store, the song of birds, and the gentle rustle of leaves. It is usually only in the confines of a "quiet room" specially insulated from the sounds of the world that we can escape the deluge of sound and find the limit established, eventually, by the sound of the beating of our own heart and the rush of our own breathing. Which of the sounds constitute music and which are simply noise?

The answer to this question is rather complex since it includes elements of personal taste, the area of one's upbringing, world chronology, and perhaps education. A western citizen of bifocal age (like the writer) will generally find the strident shrieking and mind-numbing volume of a rock group unattractive, while younger people seem to appreciate such efforts, judging from the sale of tickets and records. On the other hand, my own parents did not appreciate Tommy Dorsey and Harry James. *Sic transit gloria mundi!* Probably none of the generations in this country would consider seven-tone music from India particularly attractive.

On the other hand, there is a single thread that seems to run through all of what is usually considered to be music (by at least some group of more than two). The common thread is in the closeness of tones.

Any given musical sound is usually described in terms of *quality* (or *timbre*), *intensity* (related to loudness), and *pitch* (related to frequency). We will discuss these in the following section.

To begin with, the quality of timbre of a tone refers to the fact that few if any instruments commonly used in performing music will output only a pure single tone. In most instruments the output is a wide spectrum consisting of three, five, or more tones. Among common devices the tuning fork and the pitch pipe are particularly designed to output only a single tone, and the output of these is pure but noticeably "colorless" or lacking in "character." In a series of experiments performed in the 1850s, Helmholtz showed experimentally that the quality or timbre of an instrument is related to the number and amplitude of the *overtones* present in the sound. Interestingly, Helmholtz employed a series of tuning forks and glass resonators in his analysis of sounds. Each resonator was arranged to have a slightly different resonant frequency on a logarithmic scale. Each of the resonators would respond only to a component of the sound in a narrow range near its resonant frequency. Helmholtz considered this to be a crude model of the workings of the ear.

When two sounds are well separated in frequency, they would seem to be easily distinguished by the ear. This would seem to follow from the representation of the ear as a series of independent resonators. Figure 8-1 shows the sum of two sine waves (generated by computer synthesis) separated in frequency by a ratio of 11:1. It may be seen that, even on the picture, it is simple to distinguish the separate components.

On the other hand, when two tones are very close together, the phenomenon of *beating*, or a beat note separate from either of the two and equal to their difference, is heard. A computer-generated illustration of this is shown in Figure 8-2. It is important to note that this is *not* a nonlinear phenomenon mathematically. The plot present in the picture still represents simply:

$$Y = A\sin(\omega_1 t) + A\sin(\omega_2 t)$$
$$= 2A \sin \left(\frac{\omega_1 t + \omega_2 t}{2}\right) \cos \left(\frac{\omega_1 t - \omega_2 t}{2}\right)$$

The depressed portion in the center of the plot is due to the fact that the two waves with a frequency ratio of 11:10 stay out of phase for a considerable period of time.

The trigonometric identity in the above equation tells us that we should be able to hear two tones in this waveform, one equal to half of the difference and one equal to half of the sum, or the average.

By comparison, the modulation process where the tones are multiplied gives a different result. It might seem fair to ask why one would expect the result of

```
JLIST100,210

100  REM   THE SUM OF TWO SINEWAVES
101  HGR2
110  HCOLOR= 3: REM   WHITE
120  POKE   - 12524,0: REM   BLACK ON WHITE
125  POKE   - 12529,255: REM   UNI-DIRECTIONAL
130  POKE   - 12525,64: REM   PLOT PAGE 2
131  LET M = 0
132  LET N = 85
140  FOR X = 0 TO 279 STEP 1
150  LET Q = .0224399 * X
160  LET R = .246839 * X
170  LET A = - 40 * ( SIN (Q) +   SIN (R)) + 85
180  REM   ADD THE TWO SINEWAVES
190  LET A% = A
200  HPLOT M,N TO X,A%
201  LET M = X
202  LET N = A%
205  NEXT X
210  END
```

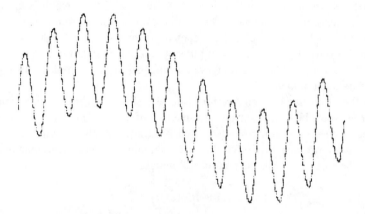

Figure 8-1.

two separate processes to be multiplicative rather than simply additive. Two trumpeters blowing slightly different notes should produce independent pressure waves in the atmosphere. The answer is that the pressure waves are in fact independent, but their effect on the ear may not be.

We have seen that Alexander Graham Bell established pretty firmly the fact that the response of the human ear is logarithmic. It is another mathematical fact that:

$$\log A + \log B = \log (AB)$$

```
]LIST 100,210

100  REM   THE SUM OF TWO SINEWAVES
101  HGR2
110  HCOLOR= 3: REM   WHITE
120  POKE  - 12524,0: REM   BLACK ON WHITE
125  POKE  - 12529,255: REM   UNI-DIRECTIONAL
130  POKE  - 12525,64: REM   PLOT PAGE 2
131  LET M = 0
132  LET N = 85
140  FOR X = 0 TO 279 STEP 1
150  LET Q = .224399 * X
160  LET R = .246839 * X
170  LET A =  - 40 * ( SIN (Q) +  SIN (R)) + 85
180  REM   ADD THE TWO SINEWAVES
190  LET A% = A
200  HPLOT M,N TO X,A%
201  LET M = X
202  LET N = A%
205  NEXT X
210  END
```

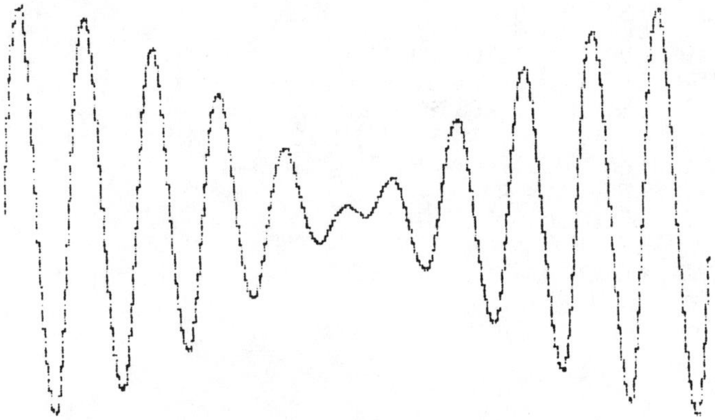

Figure 8-2.

This tells us that adding two logarithms is the same as taking the logarithm after the numbers have been multiplied. Therefore the multiplication can take place in the hearing process.

Now when we multiply two sines we obtain:

$$C\left[\sin(A)\sin(B)\right] = \frac{C}{2}\left[\sin(A + B) + \sin(A - B)\right]$$

This is a different arrangement than we had for the simple addition since it tells us that the two tones should be completely replaced by another pair of tones equal to the difference and the sum of the two original frequencies. Figure 8-3 shows the result of multiplying the same two tones that were added in Figure 8-2. You will note that statement 170 in both cases differs only in the amplitude scaling factor and the + and * (multiply in BASIC).

This difference is an interesting one since it presents the possibility that one could arrange an experiment that would definitively establish the response of the hearing mechanism. For the experiment, one would simply strike the two tones or generate them with a pair of sine-wave generators, and then have people simply write down the notes that they heard. If what they wrote down equated

```
JLIST 100,210

100  REM  THE PRODUCT OF TWO SINEWAVES
101  HGR2
110  HCOLOR= 3: REM  WHITE
120  POKE  - 12524,0: REM  BLACK ON WHITE
125  POKE  - 12529,255: REM  UNI-DIRECTIONAL
130  POKE  - 12525,64: REM  PLOT PAGE 2
131  LET M = 0
132  LET N = 85
140  FOR X = 0 TO 279 STEP 1
150  LET Q = .0224399 * X
160  LET R = .246839 * X
170  LET A =  - 80 * ( SIN (Q) *  SIN (R)) + 85
180  REM  MULTIPLY THE TWO SINEWAVES
190  LET A% = A
200  HPLOT M,N TO X,A%
201  LET M = X
202  LET N = A%
205  NEXT X
210  END
```

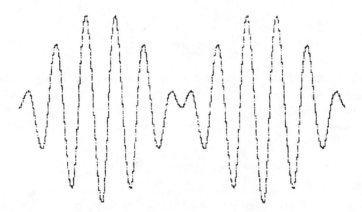

Figure 8-3.

to the sum and difference, the process would be multiplicative, and if what they wrote down corresponded to half of the difference and the average, then the process would be simply additive.

Unfortunately, there is a certain amount of difficulty involved in performing this experiment. To begin with, most people cannot take musical dictation. Therefore, your experimental group becomes limited principally to trained musicians. Secondly, even among trained musicians the gift of *absolute pitch* is fairly rare, thereby further limiting your choice of subjects. Absolute pitch is the ability, in the absence of any cues, to sing or hum a frequency and get it right on, or to identify precisely the note represented by a sine-wave oscillator. Most good musicians have a good *relative pitch,* that is, once given a cue in the form of a standardized note, they can then sing or identify the other notes in the scale. To add to the difficulty, those with the gift of absolute pitch are sensitive about it and generally do not like to be tested since any error is taken personally as a deficiency in their musicianship.

As a result of these factors, this writer has been able to perform this experiment with only a very limited number of poeple and has found no reference to the experiment being performed with pure sine-wave oscillators.

The middle G and A above middle C in the piano nominally have the frequencies 396 and 440 Hz. However, the actual sound produced by the piano string is very complex, with a number of overtones. Struck together, they produce a distinctive *dissonance,* and a pronounced undertone or beat is noted by all listeners. However, it seems difficult to determine whether the undertone is due to a 44-Hz beat, which would be the difference characteristic of a multiplicative action, or a 22-Hz tone, or half the difference characteristic of the additive process.

Most listeners will still hear the G and A. Therefore, the process is, at least in some measure, additive. The additive process yields the average of the pitches, whereas the multiplicative process does not.

At least in this writer's limited experience, few musicians will record the 836-Hz (A) tone that would be characteristic of the multiplicative process. It should be noted that this tone represents the average of the second harmonic, or octave, of the G and A that is present in the string outputs and would be present in the additive process from the complex piano tones.

Based upon a slight preference for the 22-Hz undertone and the fact that most of the subjects identified the G and A correctly, this writer is at least swayed in the direction of believing that the process is in large measure additive.

HARMONY

Whereas tones placed close together on the scale produce the effect of dissonance, there are certain spacings that provide the effect of *consonance* or *harmony;*

that is, they seem to go together and make a pleasing sound. We have dwelt upon the ratio of 2:1 or the octave; however, other consonant ratios exist as well.
These ratios are 3:2, 4:3, 5:3, 5:4, and 6:5. Our western musical scale has been
arranged to accommodate these ratios. The scales formed using these ratios in
three consonant tones are termed *triads*, or chords formed of three tones. In
such chords the octave of a tone may either accompany or replace the tone
without altering the nature of the chord.

The major scale of eight notes beginning with middle C is arranged as shown
in Figure 8-4. The frequencies of these notes are determined by the major triads
CEG, FAC, and GBD. The intervals are given by whole-number fractions as 9/8,
10/9 and 16/15. The intervals 9/8 and 10/9 are termed whole tones. The ratio
16/15 is termed a halftone.

The present Stuttgart or concert pitch is based upon a frequency of 440 Hz
for **A**, although instruments are sometimes tuned to 440.4 Hz for a more "bril-
liant" tone. This standard is fairly recent, dating since the turn of the century.
Handel is said to have used a pitch as low as 422.5 Hz for **A**.

One of the reasons the triads produce consonance is that their harmonics are
also consonant. For example, the third harmonic of C corresponds to the second
of G, and the fifth of C corresponds to the fourth of E. The sixth harmonic of
E corresponds to the fifth harmonic of G, and so forth. For this reason, the dissonance and disturbing undertones and beat notes do not develop. The fact that
difference tones are not noted lends a little further weight to the argument that
the additive process prevails for larger differences in pitch.

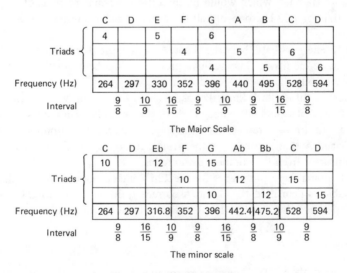

	C	D	E	F	G	A	B	C	D
Triads	4		5		6				
			4		5		6		
					4		5		6
Frequency (Hz)	264	297	330	352	396	440	495	528	594
Interval		$\frac{9}{8}$	$\frac{10}{9}$	$\frac{16}{15}$	$\frac{9}{8}$	$\frac{10}{9}$	$\frac{9}{8}$	$\frac{16}{15}$	$\frac{9}{8}$

The Major Scale

	C	D	Eb	F	G	Ab	Bb	C	D
Triads	10		12		15				
			10		12		15		
					10		12		15
Frequency (Hz)	264	297	316.8	352	396	442.4	475.2	528	594
Interval		$\frac{9}{8}$	$\frac{16}{15}$	$\frac{10}{9}$	$\frac{9}{8}$	$\frac{16}{15}$	$\frac{9}{8}$	$\frac{10}{9}$	$\frac{9}{8}$

The minor scale

Figure 8-4. The major scale.

Figure 8-5 shows the printout of three sine waves in the 4:5:6 ratio. It may be seen that this is a moderately complex waveform. Obviously it will repeat its shape in a period of time sufficient to pass four cycles of the lowest pitch, which is the time required for five cycles of the middle pitch and six of the highest.

The minor scale presents a somewhat different situation. Here the triads are set in the ratio 10:12:15. The intervals have the same values as in the major triad. The symbols in Figure 8-4, beside E, A, and B, are read "flat" since the pitch is depressed for these notes compared to the major scale. Minor-scale music is generally considered to sound sad, although the inclusion of a few minor-

```
]LIST 100,210

100  REM   THE WAVEFORM OF A MAJOR CHORD WITH FREQUENCIES IN THE RATIO 4:5:
     6
101  HGR2
110  HCOLOR= 3: REM   WHITE
120  POKE  - 12524,0: REM   BLACK ON WHITE
125  POKE  - 12529,255: REM   UNI-DIRECTIONAL
130  POKE  - 12525,64: REM   PLOT PAGE 2
131  LET M = 0
132  LET N = 85
140  FOR X = 0 TO 279 STEP 1
150  LET Q = .224399 * X
160  LET R = .280499 * X
161  LET S = .336599 * X
170  LET A =  - 26.7 * ( SIN (Q) +  SIN (R) +  SIN (S)) + 85
180  REM   ADD THE THREE SINEWAVES
190  LET A% = A
200  HPLOT M,N TO X,A%
201  LET M = X
202  LET N = A%
205  NEXT X
210  END
```

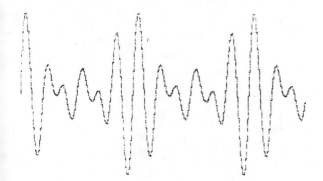

Figure 8-5.

to-major chord progressions is a very common feature of "barbershop" harmony, which is usually very lighthearted music.

Figure 8-6 shows a minor triad to the same scale as that of Figure 8-5. It may be seen that the waveform is much more complex than that of the major chord and, as a matter of fact, the pattern does not repeat in the same interval. To show the repetition, the curve of Figure 8-7 was generated with the time scale changed by a factor of two. The relative complexity compared to the major chord is striking.

```
]LIST 1900,210


]LIST 100,210
100   REM   THE WAVEFORM OF A MINOR CHORD WITH FREQUENCIES IN THE RATIO 10:1
      2:15
101   HGR2
110   HCOLOR= 3: REM   WHITE
120   POKE   - 12524,0: REM   BLACK ON WHITE
125   POKE   - 12529,255: REM   UNI-DIRECTIONAL
130   POKE   - 12525,64: REM   PLOT PAGE 2
131   LET M = 0
132   LET N = 85
140   FOR X = 0 TO 279 STEP 1
150   LET Q = .224399 * X
160   LET R = .269279 * X
161   LET S = .336599 * X
170   LET A =   - 26.7 * ( SIN (Q) +   SIN (R) +   SIN (S)) + 85
180   REM   ADD THE THREE SINEWAVES
190   LET A% = A
200   HPLOT M,N TO X,A%
201   LET M = X
202   LET N = A%
205   NEXT X
210   END
```

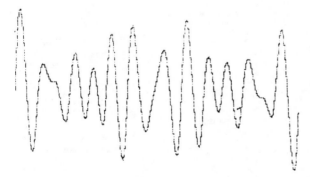

Figure 8-6.

Of course, not all musical pieces begin in the key of C nor are all voices adapted to sing in that key. Using the same sequence determined for the triads but starting with D at 297 Hz would yield a set of frequencies running:

D	E	F♯	G	A	B	C♯	D
297	334	371	396	445	495	557	594

```
]LIST 100,210

100  REM  THE WAVEFORM OF A MINOR CHORD WITH FREQUENCIES IN THE RATIO
     10:12:15
101  HGR2
110  HCOLOR= 3: REM  WHITE
120  POKE  - 12524,0: REM  BLACK ON WHITE
125  POKE  - 12529,255: REM  UNI-DIRECTIONAL
130  POKE  - 12525,64: REM  PLOT PAGE 2
131  LET M = 0
132  LET N = 85
140  FOR X = 0 TO 279 STEP 1
150  LET Q = .224399 * 2 * X
160· LET R = .269279 * 2 * X
161  LET S = .336599 * 2 * X
170  LET A = - 26.7 * ( SIN (Q) +  SIN (R) +  SIN (S)) + 85
180  REM  ADD THE THREE SINEWAVES
190  LET A% = A
200  HPLOT M,N TO X,A%
201  LET M = X
202  LET N = A%
205  NEXT X
210  END
```

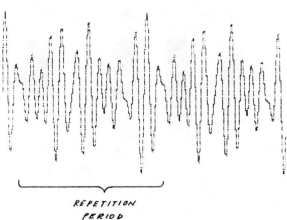

REPETITION
PERIOD

Figure 8-7.

You will note that the agreement is exact for G and B and close for E and A for the major scale in C. However, we have had to introduce two new notes. It turns out that if one were to develop similar scales for each key, there would be quite a few extra keys required on instruments like the piano and the organ; as a matter of fact, the situation would become quite impossible. Either the fixed-pitch instruments would require an impossibly large number of keys, like a Japanese pictographic typewriter, or else they would be restricted in the scales that could be played. Accordingly, the *tempered scale,* in which all half notes are spaced by the twelfth root of two, was adopted to replace the previously discussed *natural scales.* The twelfth root of 2 is 1.0594631. In the key of C major, this makes E 2.6 cycles high, G 1.6 cycles low, and B 3.36 cycles high, with all other tones falling within a fraction of a cycle of the natural scale. In the natural scale there is actually a difference between C# and Db, but there are very few people who can hear it.

Figure 8-8 shows a piano keyboard with the frequencies labeled. This keyboard is justified to the tempered scale, which is standard for modern music. The

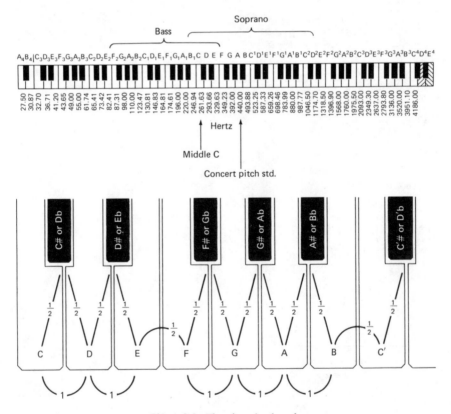

Figure 8-8. The piano keyboard.

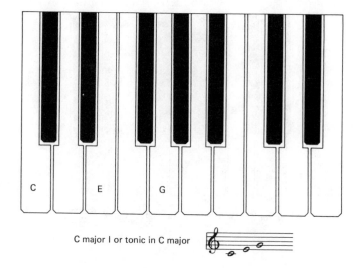

C major I or tonic in C major

Figure 8-9.

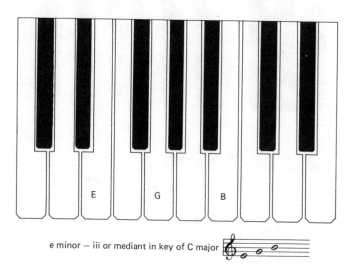

e minor — iii or mediant in key of C major

Figure 8-10.

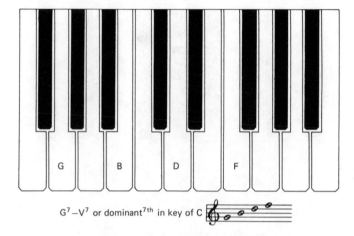

$G^7 - V^7$ or dominant^{7th} in key of C

Figure 8-11.

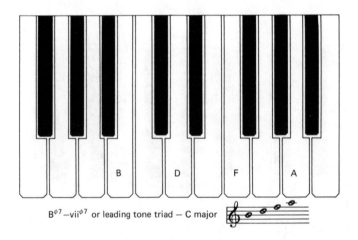

$B^{\phi 7} - vii^{\phi 7}$ or leading tone triad — C major

Figure 8-12.

enlarged section shows the center of the keyboard with the full steps and half steps labeled. This will perhaps help to explain what seems at first to be the odd arrangements of the black and white keys. The illustrations which follow in fig- gures 8-9 through 8-12 illustrate in the musical notation and the keyboard sym- bols in succession a major, minor, seventh, and a diminished chord. Each of these is to be found in the ordinary tones of human speech (from a single voice), al- though they can ordinarily be sung by a trio or quartet.

As we study the spectrograms of speech, we shall see that human voice is re- plete with overtones, which generally follow the rules of harmony in a voice that is termed "pleasant" or "musical." Speaking voices in which the overtones do not harmonize are usually considered "harsh," "abrasive," or "unpleasant." You can probably summon up examples of each type from your own acquaintances.

9
The Production of Sound

In this chapter we shall begin our discussion of the mechanisms for production of sound, including those of the human vocal tract. Because of the complexity of human speech production, it is worthwhile to concentrate on some of the simpler musical apparatus for the production of sounds, which will eventually lead us to some of the more complex mechanisms.

In general, all oscillating phenomena proceed by means of a transfer of energy from a kinetic to a potential state and vice versa. The same phenomena apply to wave propagation. For example, in the pressure wave illustration of Figure 7-1 we saw that the compressed wave front, representing a state of elevated pressure (and therefore potential energy) served to accelerate the molecules on each side of itself. Those moving to the right, the direction in which the wave was propagating, served to elevate the pressure ahead of the wave, thereby advancing the wave front. Those moving to the left accelerated a good deal more into the rarified region behind the wave front. Their energy was converted to kinetic form because of the high velocity and was finally surrendered in coasting back to the ambient pressure.

If we were to follow the history of a small packet of air molecules, they would first gain both kinetic and potential energy. At their rightmost travel they would be compacted by pressure and be stationary; all of the energy would be potential, concentrated in the elevation of pressure and temperature. The packet would then begin to expand and cool and accelerate toward the left. As the velocity increased, the pressure and temperature would both fall below the ambient and the energy would be in the kinetic form, except for the cooling. As it slowed down, the packet would begin to warm and increase in pressure until it finally came to rest at the initial position with both temperature and pressure back at ambient.

Next, let us consider the case of a single string. A simple and rather edifying experiment can be performed with a piece of nylon twine about 1 mm in diameter. This cord is quite strong, very flexible, and also very elastic. Take a length of this cord and stretch it across a room between two fixed objects, say a pair of doorknobs. Over a span of 10 feet the string will easily stand a stretch of 2 inches and will be quite taut. The string is large enough and heavy enough so that the traveling waves can be seen easily.

If one now steps to the center and pulls at right angles to the string, it will stretch and deform sideways. In this condition potential energy is stored in the string due to the tension. As the string is released, the tension accelerates the center of the string back toward the straignt-line condition. However, it reaches the straight line with a very high velocity. In this condition all of the potential energy has been converted into kinetic energy. The string will overshoot and finally come to a momentary halt on the far side with nearly all of the energy originally imparted stored in potential form again. The string will continue to oscillate visibly for perhaps 3 to 5 seconds. When the oscillation has died down to the point where the string is moving about its own diameter, you will note that all portions of the string are not oscillating equally. There will be places where the amplitude is much larger than others. Furthermore, little "shudders" will race back and forth along the string in the last decaying phases. The string will seem to have decayed to nearly a quiet state and then a small burst of activity races from one end to the other.

If the string is initially plucked about an inch from one end and the fingers lightly placed in the same location, one can feel a series of sharp impulses as the initial disturbance races down the string and rebounds from the far end, rattling back and forth along the length of the string. The disturbances can actually be seen racing along the string back and forth. If the string is felt near the end after being plucked in the middle, the disturbances come at the same rate but they are much smoother and less sharp-fronted. In short, the oscillation can be described in terms of a series of traveling waves racing in opposite directions along the length of the string. When plucked in the center, the principle excitation is in the fundamental, or lowest frequency, oscillation of the string. When plucked near the end, the string oscillates in a number of modes constrained only by the immovable attachment at the ends.

The little sharp shocks are the thing that make a violin work. Suppose that the string were excited with a rosined horsehair bow. When the bow first begins to move, the string would be deflected sideways by static friction. Eventually the tension would rise to a level sufficient to break the string loose. As the disturbance races toward the far end, the string would again stick and be deflected. The shock of the reflected disturbance would again break the string loose at the right time to reinforce the excitation of the string, and the oscillation will grow to some stable level where the string is loose from the bow most of the time and sticks just long enough to maintain the tone. The tone is not a single pure sine wave since it consists of a number of components that make up the complex traveling waves.

An air-powered oscillator can be obtained by blowing over the top of a test tube or one of the tubes that better-grade cigars come in. The illustration of Figure 9-1 shows such a whistle. As one initially blows across the top of the tube, a pressure wave is initiated that races down the tube at the speed of sound. When the wave finally reaches the bottom, the immovable end of the tube will

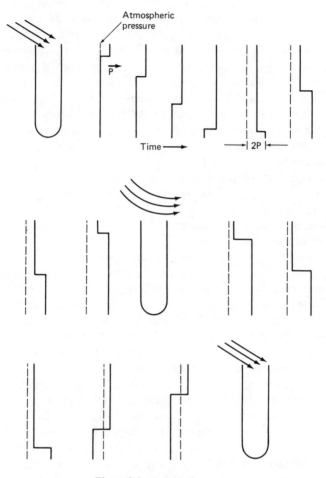

Figure 9-1. A pipe of pan.

not permit further downward movement of the compressed wave front, so the compressed front rebounds, thereby doubling the pressure. When this overpressure wave reaches the top of the tube, it deflects the airstream since the pressure is higher in the tube than in the airstream. With the drop in pressure at the top, the pressure falls to a level just sufficient to hold the airstream deflected and a negative pressure wave begins propagating down the tube. When this wave reaches the bottom, it too must reflect; therefore the upward-going wave can actually be pulled below atmospheric pressure. When this wave hits the top, the decreased pressure pulls the airstream into the tube again and the cycle begins anew.

In the process it was necessary for a wave front to traverse the length of the tube four times in order to complete a cycle; therefore, the wavelength of the sound is equal to four times the length of the tube. If the length of the tube is six inches, the wavelength would be two feet. Taking the velocity of sound in air as 1,100 ft/sec, the fundamental frequency would be 550 Hz, or approximately $C^1\#$.

Let us suppose that the far end of the tube were open to the atmosphere. In this case, when the initial pressure wave reached the far end, the pressure could not be sustained above atmospheric at the boundary, so a negative pressure wave would be reflected up the tube immediately. In this case the wave front has to traverse the length of the tube only twice, and the wavelength of the sound would be only twice the length of the tube, an octave above the tone from the closed-end tube.

The proportions are interesting from the standpoint of the physiology of the voice. We see that if the fundamental frequency of the bass voice, say 110 Hz, were to be achieved with a closed-end organ pipe, the wavelength is 10 feet and the pipe would have to be 2.5 feet long. This is considerably larger than the space allotted by nature for this function.

Before we depart from this point, let's look a little closer at the physical aspects of the situation. In Figure 9-2, we see two pressure waves, or deflection waves, in a string on a collision course. For clarity, again we have used Gauss error function waves rather than sine waves. If we consider that the deflection of the horizontal trace from a straight line is an actual deflection, the illustration becomes a series of successive pictures of the string experiment. On the other hand, if the deflection above the straight line is considered to be a measure of the pressure, this is a picture of the pressure wave.

We note that as the two waves approach one another closely, they begin to add up until they are perfectly superimposed and the amplitude doubles. Thereafter, they begin to depart in opposite directions. At the bottom of the page they are essentially separated again and racing apart. The two waves raced right through one another and; except for the brief moment when they were superimposed, they did not affect one another in the least.

An even stranger phenomenon is to be seen in Figure 9-3. Here we see the two waves with opposite amplitude (that is, one swings down and the other swings up). Here again the waves race toward one another. However, in this case the result is a complete cancellation. Note that the designated trace is perfectly flat.

It seems reasonable to ask how this could possibly represent physical reality. After all, at one point in the diagram the two pressure (or potential energy) waves completely annihilate one another; is it just a mathematical trick that makes them ressurect themselves from their own ashes like the phoenix?

The answer is no, this is not just a mathematical trick. The waves really do pass through one another freely. If you think about it, that is what we proved with the string experiment. The shocks passed freely through one another. But

```
100  REM   THIS PROGRAM SHOWS THE EFFECT OF WAVE INTERFERENCE WITH TWO GAUS
     S ERROR FUNCTION WAVES
110  HGR2
120  HCOLOR= 3: REM   WHITE
130  POKE  - 12524,0: REM   BLACK ON WHITE
140  POKE  - 12529,255: REM   PLOT UNIDIRECTIONAL
150  POKE  - 12525,64: REM   PLOT PAGE 2
160  LET X = 0
170  LET Y = 10
180  LET Q =   ABS ((X - Y - 70) / 10)
190  LET R =   ABS ((210 - X - Y) / 10)
200  LET Q = Q ^ 2
210  LET R = R ^ 2
220  LET D = Y + 10 *   EXP ( - Q) + 10 *   EXP ( - R)
230  LET Y% = Y + D
240  HPLOT X,Y%
250  LET X = X + 1
260  IF X <  = 279 THEN   GOTO 180
270  LET Y = Y + 4
275  LET X = 0
280  IF Y <  = 190 THEN   GOTO 180
285  END
```

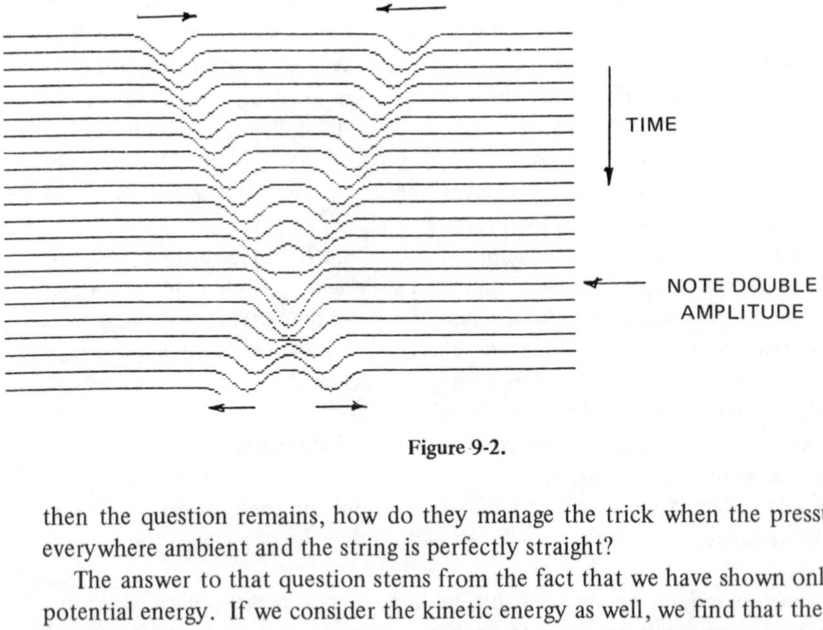

Figure 9-2.

then the question remains, how do they manage the trick when the pressure is everywhere ambient and the string is perfectly straight?

The answer to that question stems from the fact that we have shown only the potential energy. If we consider the kinetic energy as well, we find that the kinetic energy is doubled just when the potential energy cancels. As a matter of fact, if we consider Figure 9-3 to be a picture of the potential energy of the system, then Figure 9-2 is simultaneously a picture of the kinetic energy. The picture could also be reversed. If Figure 9-2 represented the potential energy, the Figure 9-3 would represent the kinetic energy. The waves do not annihilate one

```
JLIST 100,300

100  REM  THIS PROGRAM SHOWS THE EFFECT OF WAVE INTERFERENCE WITH TWO GAUS
     S ERROR FUNCTION WAVES
110  HGR2
120  HCOLOR= 3: REM  WHITE
130  POKE  - 12524,0: REM  BLACK ON WHITE
140  POKE  - 12529,255: REM  PLOT UNIDIRECTIONAL
150  POKE  - 12525,64: REM  PLOT PAGE 2
160  LET X = 0
170  LET Y = 10
180  LET Q =  ABS ((X - Y - 70) / 10)
190  LET R =  ABS ((210 - X - Y) / 10)
200  LET Q = Q ^ 2
210  LET R = R ^ 2
220  LET D = Y + 10 *  EXP ( - Q) - 10 *  EXP ( - R)
230  LET Y% = Y + D
240  HPLOT X,Y%
250  LET X = X + 1
260  IF X <  = 279 THEN  GOTO 180
270  LET Y = Y + 4
275  LET X = 0
280  IF Y <  = 190 THEN  GOTO 180
285  END
```

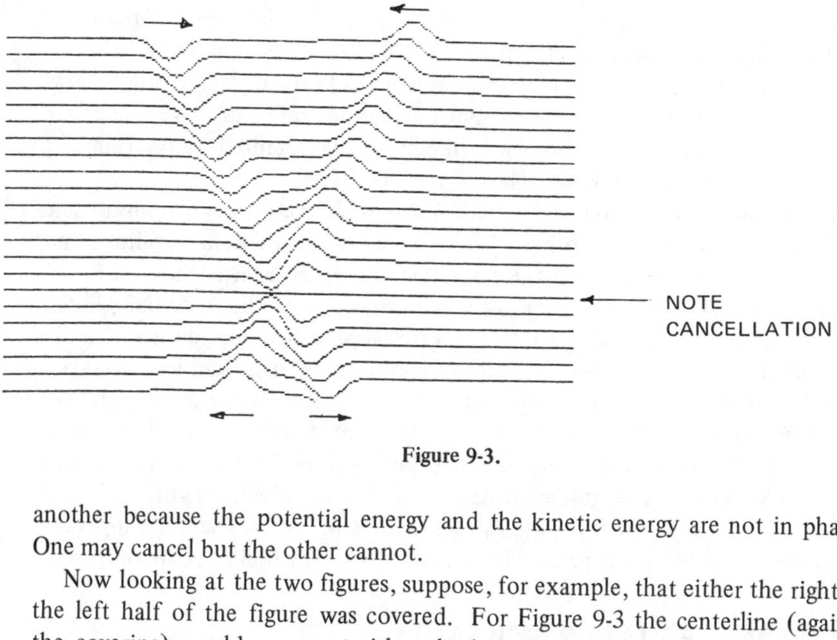

Figure 9-3.

another because the potential energy and the kinetic energy are not in phase!
One may cancel but the other cannot.

Now looking at the two figures, suppose, for example, that either the right or
the left half of the figure was covered. For Figure 9-3 the centerline (against
the covering) would represent either the boundary conditions for the string or
the open-ended tube. In the case of the string, the doorknob is essentially immovable so the string potential energy must be nearly identically zero at the attachment. In the case of the open-ended tube, the pressure at the far end must

be close to atmospheric since the tube no longer confines the wave. By the same token Figure 9-2 would represent the potential energy of a closed-end tube or a string being snapped like a bullwhip.

It is a general feature of wave equations that it is always necessary to represent two waves passing in opposite directions. If the waves were repetitive and of identical frequency, we would see standing-wave patterns as we did upon the string where some segments (the *nodes*) scarcely move and other segments (the *loops*) swing with large amplitude. For a sinusoidal wave the amplitude at a specific point X and a specific instant in time t is given by:

$$Y = A \sin (\omega t - x/V) + A \, \Gamma \sin (\omega t + x/V)$$

where: ω is the radian frequency
V is the velocity of propagation
Γ is the reflection coefficient

The term Γ deserves a little more explanation. This symbol is generally used to represent the reflection coefficient, assuming that the reflection is due to some discontinuity like the closed end of the tube or the loose end of the string or, alternatively, to the open end of the tube and the fixed end of the string. Γ will generally have some value less than but near unity for such situations. However, the value can be *either* plus or minus. When the reflected wave is opposite in sense to the initial wave, the sign is minus for the potential energy term but plus for the kinetic energy term. The converse is also true.

The computer simulation of Figure 9-4 shows, at the top, two trains of sine waves racing toward one another. These waves are identical in amplitude and phase; therefore $\Gamma = +1$. Below the centerline of the figure, after the collision of the two wavetrains, we see a series of standing-wave loops begin to build in the same triangular structure with which the waves approached one another. On the last (lowest) trace all but the last half-cycle at extreme right and left are taken up with standing waves. You will note that the spacing between the standing-wave loops is only a half-wavelength. The reason for this is that the leftward traveling wave and the rightward traveling wave accomplish a full wave of phase difference when each one travels a distance equal to a half-wavelength.

There are a great many physical resonators in which the traveling-wave phenomenon plays a great part. The string and panpipe oscillator are only two.

THE THERMAL AGITATION OSCILLATOR

Whenever one permits a gas at high pressure to escape into the atmosphere through a narrow jet, the gas molecules thus released are accelerated to very high velocities and can easily achieve near-sonic velocity. If the opening is uncon-

```
]LIST 100,270

100   REM   THIS PROGRAM PLOTS A PAIR OF INTERFERING SINEWAVES
110   HGR2
120   HCOLOR= 3: REM   WHITE
130   POKE   - 12524,0: REM   BLACK ON WHITE
140   POKE   - 12529,255: REM   PLOT UNIDIRECTIONAL
150   POKE   - 12525,64: REM   PLOT PAGE 2
160   LET X = 0
170   LET Y = 10
180   LET Q = (70 - X + Y) / 10
185   IF Q < = 0 THEN Q = 0
190   LET R = (X + Y - 210) / 10
195   IF R < = 0 THEN R = 0
200   LET D = (5 * SIN (Q) + 5 * SIN (R))
210   LET Y% = Y + D
220   HPLOT X,Y%
230   LET X = X + 1
240·  IF X < = 279 THEN   GOTO 180
245   LET X = 0
250   LET Y = Y + 10
260   IF Y < = 190 THEN   GOTO 180
270   END
```

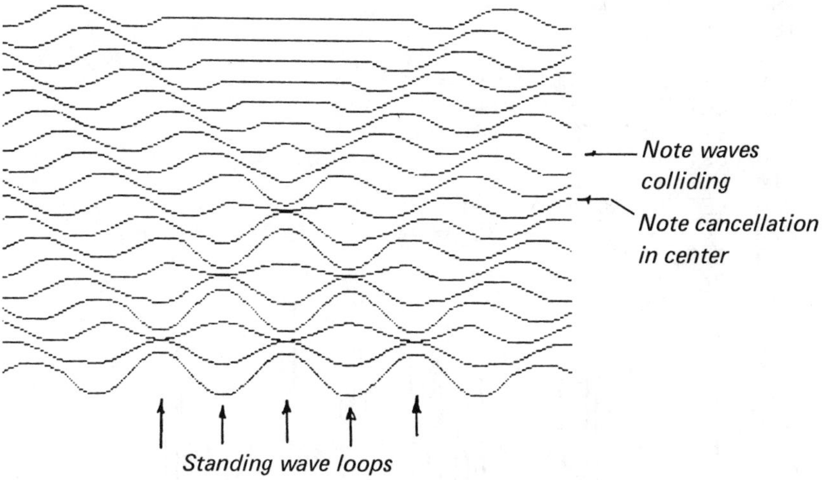

Note waves colliding

Note cancellation in center

Standing wave loops

Figure 9-4.

stricted, the expanding gases tend to form eddies and miscellaneous vortex and sinuous patterns in their haste to expand. This is termed a *thermal agitation oscillator.* In its grandest form this is the thunder of the space shuttle booster or the roar of a 747 takeoff. It is also the trailing *ss* of the word *hiss.* This is termed an *unvoiced sound;* that is, the vocal cords do not participate in its production. If you try to pronounce the word *hiss,* you will find that the tongue is arched against the roof of your mouth with a tiny opening through which the air issues, thereby producing the thermal agitation sound. Typically, the waveform of this sound tends to resemble the plot of Figure 9-5.

At first glance, this wavetrain appears to be entirely random in both amplitude and frequency. However, the appearance is a bit deceiving. On the figure, I have referred to it as a *pseudorandom* waveform. The reason for this is that it repeats. It might take a very large number of tries to make it repeat, say 10^{23} or so, but the fact that it is possible it *ever* make it repeat means that it is not truly random.

```
JLIST 100,300

100   REM   THIS PROGRAM PLOTS A PSEUDO-RANDOM WAVEFORM
110   HGR2
120   HCOLOR= 3: REM   WHITE
130   POKE  - 12524,0: REM   PLOT BLACK ON WHITE
140   POKE  - 12529,255: REM   PLOT UNIDIRECTIONAL
150   POKE  - 12525,64: REM   PLOT HGR2 PAGE
160   LET X = 0
162   LET M% = 0
164   LET N% = 85
170   LET Y% = ( RND (1)) * 190
180   LET X% = X + ( RND (1) * 4)
190   HPLOT X%,Y% TO M%,N%
200   LET M% = X%
210   LET N% = Y%
220   LET X = X% + 1
230   IF X < = 279 THEN   GOTO 170
240   END
```

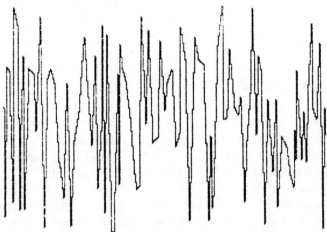

Figure 9-5.

A second feature of the wavetrain is that it is not random in either amplitude or wavelength. As a matter of fact, the wavelength has a median value of only two dot widths and the amplitude is restricted by the bottom and top capabilities of the plotter. The fact that there are many cycles on this single plot longer than 2 dot widths simply attests to the fact that a new plot command does not necessarily correspond to a large change in the $Y\%$, or vertical component. There is a finite, though very improbable, possibility (one in 10^{20}) that the plot could turn out to be a straight line across the paper from left to right.

THE HUMAN VOICE

The primary oscillator that powers the human voice consists of a pair of folds of tissue called the *glottis,* or vocal cords, working in conjunction with the lungs. The operation of this system is somewhat similar to the trick used by children to make a balloon whistle or squeal. If an inflated toy balloon is held so that the neck is pinched from opposite sides and stretched flat, it will make a squealing sound whose pitch can be varied upward by stretching the neck further. The sound is generated as follows:

The stretching of the neck tends to hold the two sides flat and sealed against one another. This tendency is counteracted by the pressure within the balloon, which attempts to pull the slit open. As the pressure and tension from the body of the balloon pull the slit open, a puff of air escapes. Because the pressure within the balloon is high, the escaping air rapidly expands and accelerates. Following Bernoulli's principle, the pressure of the accelerated air falls below atmospheric and the neck is pinched shut again. The air issues in a series of short puffs, which give rise to the high-pitched squeal.

Every breath of air that we take passes through the vocal cords. On intake these are open, presenting a triangular opening in the *larynx,* or voice box. The air passes through the larynx into the *trachea,* or windpipe. The trachea is a tube about 1 inch in diameter and 4.5 inches long. This is a flexible tube consisting of a series of rings of cartilage lined with tissue. The structure is similar to a vacuum cleaner hose, with rings to prevent collapse or blowout, and the tissue provides the necessary pressure-tight seal. The two primary bronchi split the airway and conduct air into the lungs, where each rapidly subdivides into a myriad of progressively smaller tubes finally terminating into grapelike clusters of *alveoli.* The structure is very similar to a tree, therefore it is difficult to assign any particular length to it. It is estimated that the lungs contain some 300,000,000 alveoli, and that their combined area, if spread out flat, would be equivalent to that of a tennis court.

When one inhales, muscles at the side of the chest pull the ribs, making the chest both wider and deeper from front to back. At the same time, the diaphragm descends; thus, the volume of the chest cavity increases. The interior of the *thoracic cavity,* or chest cavity, is lined with the *pleura.* There is a fluid between the outside of the lungs and the pleura that serves as a lubricant. The pressure in this fluid is maintained about 3 mm Hg below atmospheric, which helps keep the lungs inflated. As the chest expands, the pressure falls in the lungs and air is drawn through the trachea, larynx, pharynx, and the nose (or mouth) to equalize the pressure. This pressure dip is also about 3 mm Hg.

On exhaling, the process is reversed. The chest muscles relax, allowing the ribs to swing down. The diaphragm rises, reducing the volume of the chest cavity. This tends to raise the pressure by about 3 mm Hg, forcing air out of the lungs. If one is not attempting to speak at that moment, the glottis is open and the air passes freely out.

Under normal circumstances, the typical person will exhange about a half liter of air on each breathing cycle. As breathing becomes heavier due to exertion, the volume can increase to something like 3 liters per cycle. Since the chest does not completely flatten the lungs, there is always a volume of about 1.5 liters of air left in the lungs, which exchanges slowly from cycle to cycle. Such figures represent broad averages. Someone as small as Edith Piaf does not have the thoracic volume of a Dick Butkus.

The human vocal oscillator has the properties of both the string and the pan-pipe oscillator. When making a sound, the glottis closes. When the pressure from the lungs becomes sufficient, the vocal cords pop open, relieving the pressure behind them. This will initiate a negative pressure wave propagating down the larynx, the trachea, and into the bronchi and then the lungs. With the pressure reduced, the pull of the surrounding muscles can reseal the glottis. The trachea is certainly sufficiently tubelike to support such a wave without much attenuation.

Unfortunately, we come to a small technical problem at this juncture. It seems unlikely that one could alternate tense and relax the vocal cords by an act of will at the rate of 1,174.7 times per second (D^2). However, a soprano can easily sing this pitch. If we presume that a reinforcing wave were to arrive from the bottom of the lings, as in a quarter-wave resonator, we find that the length of the resonator should be one-fourth of 1,100 feet per sec divided by 1,147.7 Hz. And the length turns out to be 2.88 inches, which is less than the length of the trachea.

At the other end of the scale, to sing an F^2 or 87.31 Hz, the quarter-wave resonator would have to be 3.15 feet in length. This would place the bottom of the resonator somewhere below the kneecaps!

It seems likely that the vocal cords cannot oscillate at the frequencies they do and, in the case of voices trained with great precision, without a resonant reinforcement. Without such a reinforcing wave, it seems likely that the vocal cords would simply blow open and then stay that way. There must certainly be a negative pressure wave down the trachea, upon the opening of the vocal cords, which is reflected, causing them to reclose.

Unfortunately, there has been little written concerning this phenomenon. Singing teachers are not generally prone to speak in terms of pressure waves and resonant lengths. However, they do teach that the range and power of a voice can be extended by a proper management of the muscles of the chest and the upper abdomen. There is little doubt that a reach for a high note entails a "sucking in" of the abdominal viscera, which reduces the volume available for the lungs. Although an exact mechanism is not presently available, it would seem that the evidence supports the fact that a reinforcing wave from a chest resonance is used to reopen the glottis. The pitch is established not only by the tension and mass of the vocal cords, but also by the operation of the thoracic muscles and the abdominal muscles.

You can try this experiment for yourself. Sing three notes: one near the bottom of your range, one in mid-range and one near the top. At the end you will wind up with your lower ribs distended and your stomach sucked in to near minimum dimension. This is the reason that Italian tenors are forevermore having to pull their pants up!

On the basis of other measurements, which shall be discussed in due course, it would seem likely that the open period of the glottis represents only about 15% of the repetition period of the sound. In some cases the open period can diminish to as little as 3% of the total period.

The fact that the air is emitted in only short pulses is very significant from several points of view. From a physiological viewpoint,, it is significant because air is conserved. Normal respiration takes place at a rate of 14 to 16 cycles per minute, or about once every 4 to 6 seconds. In distinction, an ordinary sung or spoken passage will typically run 10 to 12 seconds, some three to four times the period of normal respiration. One cannot normally speak while inhaling air since it produces a gasping sound. (Note that in some forms of stammering people attempt to speak while inhaling.)

This serves to tell us something about the importance of air conservation in speech, and perhaps something about English sentence structure. A sentence composed of more than about 30 or 31 words without at least a comma or semicolon or colon cannot usually be red aloud without stopping for breath. Try reading the previous sentence aloud. It contains 31 words (if one counts the numerals "31" as two words) and should take something like 11 seconds to read aloud. Most people will be ready for a breath at the end of the sentence. In general, a good reader will breathe on the punctuation marks provided the writer had some respect for the reader's respiratory requirements. This writer has had occasion to see the notation "this sentence too long" (donated by the editor) on a number of occasions.

HARMONIC GENERATION

Short air puffs are also necessary to generate the harmonics that make intelligible speech possible. It has been noted earlier that the passband for a typical telephone or radio voice communication circuit has -6 db points at 260 and 3,000 Hz, and is approximately -24 db at 125 and 6,000 Hz. However, in normal male speech the vocal cord oscillating rate is generally on the order of 110 Hz, which is well below the cutoff frequency on the lower end. Despite this, male voices are regularly and easily understood through these circuits. Furthermore, the oscillograms or vowel sounds through the circuit will show spikes or peaks at the low frequency rate.

This transport is accomplished through the voice harmonics. The harmonics carry most of the intelligence in speech. There are several simple experiments that can convince one of this. If you have or have access to a hi-fi with the adjustable band-pass filters used for "room equalization," tune the radio to a station where people are talking and start to progressively cut off the high end of the modulation. At about 2,700 Hz, the speech is still intelligible but it sounds muffled. By the time the top cutoff reaches 1,500 Hz, it has become very difficult to understand anything that is being said and the speakers sound as though they have a mouthful of mashed potatoes.

If a single sideband radio is available to you, an even more dramatic and informative experiment is possible. It is the nature of single sideband radios that any error in tuning the receiver to the exact carrier frequency (which was originally used to generate the signal and is subsequently filtered out) results in an error in the frequency or frequencies that are subsequently output from the speaker. For example, if a single tone, say 1,000 Hz, is used to modulate the transmitter, and the receiver is mistuned by 15 Hz, the output of the receiver will be 1,015 Hz (or 985 Hz for mistuning to the other side). If two tones had been present, say 200 and 1,000 Hz, the output would be 215 and 1,015 Hz since the error is the same for all tones.

This is quite different from what happens when a tape recorder is caused to play a little fast or slow. Let us suppose that a tape recorder was used to record 200 and 1,000 Hz and that on playback it ran 7.5% faster than the tape did on record. In this case the unit would output tones of 215 and 1,075 Hz; the second tone would still be the fifth harmonic of the first.

Now the interesting thing is that speech, or, for that matter, even music, with such a frequency error would still be recognizable. As a matter of fact, in the absence of outside cues, a great many people would not recognize the fact that the machine was playing 1½ notes sharp!

In your single sideband experiment, however, the human speech is completely incomprehensible. You can probably not understand a single word. Music

played with a frequency error of this magnitude is so distorted that you probably cannot even recognize the piece! Furthermore, it would sound extremely
discordant.

The reason for this is the additive rather than multiplicative nature of the error.
The same error is added to all of the tones, thus destroying the harmony. In our
two-tone example, the higher tone, rather than being the fifth harmonic of the
first (215 × 5 = 1,075), is 50 Hz lower, or a full tone flat, and thereby very discordant, whereas the original tones were harmonious.

The conclusion to be drawn from this is that understandable human speech
relies not only upon the higher harmonics but also upon a strict preservation of
the harmonic relationship in a harmonious fashion.

The harmonics in the human voice are probably due to the shortness of the
pulses emitted from the vocal cords. It is difficult to measure these pulses
directly in the pharynx since the insertion of a tube through the mouth would
cause gagging and the sensation of something down the "Sunday throat." An
invasive surgical procedure would be little better since it would leave the patient
with a very sore throat that would prohibit talking. However, the shape of the
pulses can be inferred from the spectrum of the voice, with no discomfort
whatever.

THE FOURIER TRANSFORM

Around 1800 a French military engineer and mathematician, Jean B. J. Fourier,
showed that any single-valued function (or curve) can be created by assembling
a series of harmonically related sine waves having the proper amplitude and phase.
The sine waves take the form of a series of terms that are summed to achieve the
curve in the form shown below:

$$F(y) = \sum_{o}^{N} A_1 \sin(\omega t) + A_2 \sin(2\omega t) + A_3 \sin(3\omega t) + \ldots$$

$$+ B_1 \cos(\omega t) + B_2 \cos(2\omega t) + B_3 \sin(3\omega t) + \ldots$$

This expression is called a Fourier series. A and B are the amplitude coefficients. The sine and cosine terms are used to establish the phase angle, as well as
with the algebraic signs of A and B, which can have any value, including zero. If
the amplitudes, frequencies, and phases of all of the components in a complex
sound are measured, they may be added up to reestablish the shape of the waveform that generated them. Conversely, a given waveform can be decomposed
into a spectrum, giving amplitude and phase for a series of harmonically related
waves, thereby synthesizing the spectrum.

Figures 9-6 and 9-7 illustrate the latter procedure in a program running in Applesoft. The displayed spectrum shows the amplitude of the harmonics, and the curve below illustrates the assumed waveform for a single cycle from a train of many. It may be seen that the spectrum falls off very slowly for the narrow pulse.

As the pulse is broadened, the spectrum falls off very rapidly at the high end, as shown in Figure 9-8. Also, the rounding of the corners of the pulse reduces the amplitude of the higher harmonics.

```
100   REM   THIS PROGRAM PERFORMS A 32 STEP DISCRETE FOURIER TRANSFORM.   DAT
      A IS ENTERED IN LINES 170 THRU 177.
110   HGR2
120   HCOLOR= 3: REM   WHITE
125   GOTO 500: REM   CALCULATE AVERAGE
130   POKE  - 12524,0: REM   PLOT BLACK ON WHITE
140   POKE  - 12529,255: REM   PLOT UNIDIRECTIONAL
150   POKE  - 12525,64: REM   PLOT PAGE 2
151   LET M% = 0: REM   X AXIS SCALE FACTOR
152   LET B = 0
153   LET A = 0
154   LET X = 0
155   LET N = 1
160   REM   THE DATA STATEMENT CONTAINS A LIST OF 32 VOLTAGE READINGS
170   DATA   0,7,50,100
171   DATA   50,7,0,0
172   DATA   0,0,0,0
173   DATA   0,0,0,0
174   DATA   0,0,0,0
175   DATA   0,0,0,0
176   DATA   0,0,0,0
177   DATA   0,0,0,0
178   DATA   0,
180   LET P = (3.14159 / 16)
185   LET Q = P * X * N
190   READ D
195   LET D = D - DA
200   LET R = D *  SIN (Q)
210   LET A = A + R
220   LET S = D *  COS (Q)
230   LET B = B + S
240   LET X = X + 1
250   IF X < 33 THEN   GOTO 185
255   IF N = 1 THEN   GOTO 320
260   LET Y% = 100 - (100 *  SQR (A ^ 2 + B ^ 2) / C)
270   HPLOT M%,Y% TO M%,100
280   RESTORE
290   LET X = 0
295   M% = M% + 17
296   LET A = 0
297   LET B = 0
300   LET N = N + 1
310   IF N < 17 THEN   GOTO 170
312   HPLOT 0,100 TO M%,100
315   GOTO 340
320   LET C =  SQR (A ^ 2 + B ^ 2)
330   GOTO 260
```

Figure 9-6.

```
335  REM   THIS ROUTINE SORTS AND SCALES AND THEN PLOTS THE ORIGINAL DATA.
     VARIABLES ARE REASSIGNED.
340  LET M% = 0
345  LET A = 0
350  LET N = 0
360  RESTORE
370  READ D
380  IF D > N THEN N = D
390  LET A = A + 1
400  IF A < 33 THEN   GOTO 370
405  LET B% = 190
410  RESTORE
420  READ D
430  LET Y% = 190 - (D / N) * 80
440  HPLOT M%,Y% TO A%,B%
450  LET A% = M%
460  LET B% = Y%
470  LET M% = M% + 8
480  IF M% < = 247 THEN   GOTO 420
485  LET Y% = 190 - (DA / N) * 80
486  HPLOT 0,Y% TO 279,Y%
490  END
495  REM   THIS IS THE AVERAGE CALCULATION
500  READ D: REM   GET DATA
510  LET A = A + D
520  LET B = B + 1: REM   DO TALLY
530  IF B = < 33 THEN   GOTO 500
535  RESTORE
540  LET DA = A / 32
550  LET A = 0
560  LET B = 0
570  GOTO 130
```

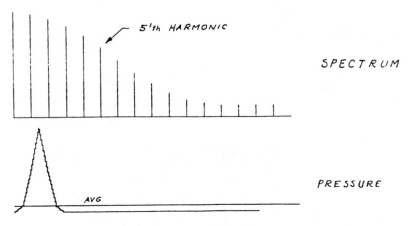

Figure 9-7.

```
170   DATA  0,7,14,24
171   DATA  37,52,70,85
172   DATA  96,96,85,70
173   DATA  52,37,24,14
174   DATA  7,0,0,0
175   DATA  0,0,0,0
176   DATA  0,0,0,0
177   DATA  0,0,0,0
178   DATA  0,
```

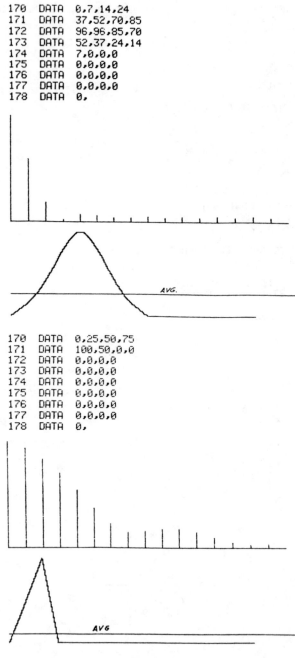

```
170   DATA  0,25,50,75
171   DATA  100,50,0,0
172   DATA  0,0,0,0
173   DATA  0,0,0,0
174   DATA  0,0,0,0
175   DATA  0,0,0,0
176   DATA  0,0,0,0
177   DATA  0,0,0,0
178   DATA  0,
```

Figure 9-8.

In this analysis, one cycle of the original pulse train is divided into 32 equal segments of time, and the amplitudes at these intervals form the data listed. The average is then calculated (lines 495 through 570). The reason for this is that it is easier to accommodate the baseline shift mathematically. The output of a tape recorder is not necessarily baseline adjusted and this can lead to errors in harmonic distribution. All of the amplitudes are normalized to the value of the amplitude of the fundamental frequency, which is the same as the pulse repetition frequency.

This process can be seen to be equivalent to a correlation function performed using a series of sine and cosine waves. As each of the samples is multiplied by either a sine or a cosine function, across the sample period (or window) the results are accumulated. Those with a high degree of correlation will show a higher sum than those with poor correlation.

Suppose, for example, that we are examining the sine function that completes 16 cycles across the window. Furthermore, let us suppose that the samples were a repeating sequence such that they ran 0, +1, 0, -1, 0, +1 . . . . It may be seen that the cosine series would have an amplitude summation of zero since it is zero when the sample is +1 or -1, and is +1 and -1 when the sample is zero. Conversely, the sine term would have an amplitude of 8 since +1 ∗ +1 = 1 and -1 ∗ -1 = +1, etc., so that the data would be highly correlated with the particular sine term and not correlated at all with the cosine term.

It should also be fairly obvious that the results for the fifteenth harmonic of the fourteenth harmonic would not produce totals as large as that for the sixteenth, for which the sine term is a perfect fit. This is the principle upon which the Fourier analysis operates. For an actual complex waveform, the sine and cosine terms are both liable to have a significant amplitude except under very special circumstances of symmetry. You will note that even a perfect sine wave with a frequency perfectly matching one of the harmonics of the analysis can have both sine and cosine terms if it is phased between the components.

THE FILTERS

The actual spectra of the various voice sounds are far more complex than the preceding figures show. While the vocal cords create a broad and slowly decaying spectrum made up of harmonics of the vocal cord frequencies, the actual tones are heavily filtered. In general, two or more higher pitched tones, called the *formant frequencies,* will be present. These are the tones that carry information.

During the 1920s, Dayton C. Miller showed that the vowel sounds could be synthesized by combining organ-pipe tones of suitable amplitude and frequency. Strict amplitude control prevented these sounds from simply being played on the keyboard.

By the 1930s, Dr. Harvey Fletcher of Bell Laboratories had measured the low and high formant frequencies for a variety of vowel sounds. Figure 9-9 shows a cutaway view of the human head, with the portions involving voice control flagged. It may be seen that there are several cavities, including the mouth, the nasal, the throat, and the esophagus or food pipe, which may be manipulated to shape the bandpass, or filtering, mechanisms. These filters shape the spectral comb formed by the vocal cords, helping to produce the final sounds for voiced sounds.

The table below lists the formant frequencies assigned by Fletcher. He attributed the lower frequency sounds to the mouth cavity and the higher frequencies to the throat:

SPEECH SOUND	LOW F	HIGH F
ū (pool)	400 Hz	800 Hz
u (put)	475	1,000
ō (tone)	500	850
a (talk)	600	950
o (ton)	700	1,150
a (father)	825	1,200
a (tap)	750	1,800
e (ten)	550	1,900
er (pert)	500	1,500
ā (tape)	550	2,100
i (tip)	450	2,200
ē (team)	375	2,400

In actual practice, these frequencies do not imply that only a single spectral line issues from the original spectrum. Instead, this filtering describes the centroid of the spectral group of harmonics in the vicinity of the filter. For example, at a 2,400 Hz high formant frequency, with a vocal cord excitation at 100 Hz, there would be considerable energy at 2,000, 2,100, 2,200, 2,300, ... to 2,700 Hz.

It should also be noted that these frequencies will not only vary from speaker to speaker, but also with the same speaker from day to day and perhaps even within the context of a single sentence. A "richer" sound to the voice is accompanied by a broader passband at the formant frequencies.

The complex manipulations required to produce human speech have been responsible for the relatively slow progress in its synthesis. At the San Francisco and the New York world's fairs, which ran in 1939, Bell Labs introduced a machine called the VODER. This machine was equipped with thirteen keys and, under the control of a skilled operator, could emit both voiced and unvoiced sounds to simulate human speech. A pedal was used to control the pitch. While

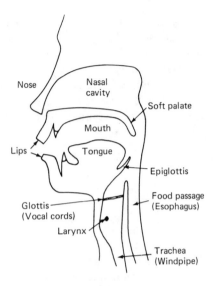

Figure 9-9. The human speech mechanism.

the advance was remarkable, the sounds were not very human. Over 40 years later, the ability to assemble natural sounding speech from "scratch" (that is, by not starting with an actual recording) has really not progressed very much.

THE UNVOICED SOUNDS

Some of the unvoiced sounds are formed using the thermal agitation oscillator. This is formed by blowing air through a constricted opening, as discussed earlier. The thermal agitation sounds, such as *s, th,* and *f,* are produced without using the vocal cords and have no characteristic pitch. A thermal agitation sound cannot be sung for this reason.

If you pronounce the word *hiss,* you will find at the end that your tongue nearly seals your mouth, allowing air to exit only in a narrow slit near the roots of your upper teeth, with the airstream bouncing off the lower lip. If you pronounce the word *stuff,* you will find that the tongue is drawn back and the upper teeth are resting upon the lower lip. For the word *thing,* you will find that the tongue is resting on the working edges of the upper teeth, nearly sealing the semicircle of the upper jaw, while pronouncing the *th.*

As noted in the text accompanying the pseudorandom waveform of Figure 9-5, the appearance of complete and utter chaos is a bit deceiving. There is some organization in the thermal agitation sounds, otherwise there would be only one sound.

One form of the organization is the absence of low-frequency components. Nearly all of the energy in these sounds is to be found between about 2,500 and 4,500 Hz. This brings up an interesting problem in connection with telephony. Since telephone circuits reject frequencies above 3 kHz, most of the information in the thermal agitation sounds is filtered out and does not appear at the far end of the circuit. This can lead to some difficulty in understanding. As an experiment, have a friend read over the telephone the following list of words several times in random order:

cat

sat

fat

hat

that

In most cases, people have difficulty scoring more than 30% correct interpretations, which is only slightly above random chance. The elimination of the upper three-fourths of the spectrum has largely destroyed the differences in the sounds. When spoken in the context of a sentence, the loss is scarcely noticeable since the mind of the hearer can correctly identify the word from the meaning of the sentence. However, out of context, as isolated words with no other cues, correct identification after telephone filtering becomes much more difficult.

The *s* sound is also interesting. Without changing the position of the tongue very much, if the lower lip is thinned and drawn over the lower teeth, a shrill whistle can result. It seems likely that the air impinging upon the lower lip is very significant in the production of the *s* sound.

The *th* sound (as in Ha*th*) is common to English and Greek but is not present in Polish, German, or Italian. People of these origins who learn English frequently have difficulty in learning the English *th*. In general, only the *t* is pronounced, as in one, two, *tree,* four.

The *h* in hat is pronounced with a sharp exhalation, with the mouth almost open, and the main stress of the sound actually exists in the following vowel, which the voice glides into.

We have attempted in this chapter to bring out some of the physiology of speech as it affects the construction of talking machines. In the following chapters we shall examine in more detail some of the other characteristics of speech. In the chapter on linear predictive coding, we shall see that this technique tends to model the vocal tract in order to more closely imitate normal speech.

10
Human Speech Characteristics

Having seen the mechanism by which the human voice is produced, we shall next begin to examine some of the characteristics of the output. We have seen from the previous work that the action of the glottis is to form a rich spectrum of harmonics of the vocal cords. The emerging sounds are formed by the filters that selectively attenuate or pass these harmonics. The characteristics of the filters are altered by the position of the tongue, lips, teeth, nasal cavity, and the distention of the throat.

To begin with, let us examine the spectrogram and oscillogram of Figure 10-1. The writer is indebted to Dr. George R. Doddington, Texas Instruments Fellow and Manager of the Speech Systems Research Group at Texas Instruments Corporation, for this and other spectrograms or Voicegrams that will be shown in this chapter and were supplied through the courtesy of Texas Instruments. The writer must comment upon the very high quality of these spectrograms. In the following chapters we shall see the difficulty of digitizing speech and will perhaps recognize the capability of the equipment required to produce such a display.

The phrase used in the spectrogram is "782." This is an example of what would be considered "connected speech," that is, words spoken in a conversational string. Judging from the spectrogram, the sounds produced were very likely something like s/eh/v/n/A-t/oo. The difference between the voiced and unvoiced sounds is relatively obvious in the illustration. The major marks reading from left to right represent 0.1 sec; therefore, the minor marks are 20 msec apart. Vertically, major divisions are 1 kHz. The *s* begins about 30 msec into the spectrogram and terminates at about 170 msec. Although the waveform of the amplitude at the bottom appears to be completely unstructured except for the crescendo to about 100 msec and the decrescendo thereafter, the spectrogram above shows that some structure exists in the form of a peak near 5,600 Hz. Note that the notch in the amplitude waveform near 115 msec is matched by a small peak near 2,400 Hz in the spectrogram. As noted in the preceding chapter, this single splotch is just about the only thing that would pass through a telephone filter at any volume.

Starting at about 170 msec, the *eh* begins and runs to about 260 msec. Obviously, the vocal cords are active during this period, oscillating with a frequency on the order of about 125 Hz. Of particular interest is the fact that the third, fourth, tenth, eleventh, eighteenth, twenty-fifth, and twenty-sixth harmonics are stronger than the rest. There are certainly three and perhaps four formant

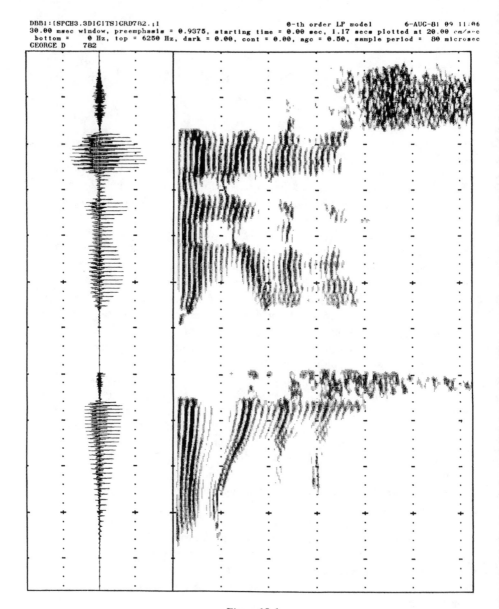

DBB1:[SPCH3.3DIGITS]GRD782.;1   0-th order LP model   6-AUG-81 09 11:06
30.00 msec window, preemphasis = 0.9375, starting time = 0.00 sec, 1.17 secs plotted at 20.00 cm/sec
   bottom =   0 Hz, top = 6250 Hz, dark = 0.00, cont = 0.00, agc = 0.50, sample period =   80 microsec
GEORGE D   782

Figure 10-1.

frequencies present. On the pressure waveform at the bottom, note that the base-line is shifted in the middle of the sound.

In an attempt to illustrate some of the fine details that can develop in such a waveform, the computer synthesized waveform of Figure 10-2 was developed using only the dominant harmonics. Note that it is not symmetrical about the zero axis and that it has two major positive and negative peaks before settling to a broader low-amplitude episode. There is evidence of a similar effect in the actual pressure oscillogram of Figure 10-1.

```
]LIST100,500

100  REM  THIS PROGRAM SYNTHESIZES A WAVEFORM CONTAINING HARMONICS 1,3,4,1
     0,11,18,25 AND 26.
110  HGR2
120  HCOLOR= 3: REM  WHITE
130  POKE  - 12524,0: REM  PLOT BLACK ON WHITE
140  POKE  - 12529,255: REM  PLOT UNIDIRECTIONAL
150  POKE  - 12525,64: REM  PLOT PAGE 2
155  X = 0
160  N = 85
170  FOR Q =  - 2 TO 21.56 STEP .084
180  LET A = 3 * Q:B = 4 * Q:C = 10 * Q:D = 11 * Q:E = 18 * QF = 25 * Q:G =
     26 * Q
190  LET Y = .2 *  COS (Q) + .33 *  COS (A) + .25 *  COS (B) + .1 *  COS (
     C) + .09 *  COS (D) + .055 *  COS (E) + .04 *  COS (F) + .038 *  COS
     (G)
200  LET Y% = ((Y / 1.2) * 95) + 95
205  IF X = 0 THEN N = Y%
210  HPLOT M,N TO X,Y%
218  M = X
220  X = X + 1
222   IF X = 279 THEN  GOTO 232
224  N = Y%
230   NEXT Q
232  X = X - 1
235   HPLOT 0,95 TO X,95
240  END
```

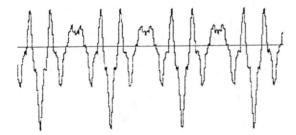

Figure 10-2.

Beginning at about 0.27 sec on the spectrogram and running to about 0.32 sec is the *v* sound. This is a relatively weak sound. However, from the striped pattern of the spectrogram we see that it is a voiced sound. If you say the *v* in *seven*, you will find that the vocal cords are active. However, the upper teeth are pressed lightly on the lower lip and the outer edges of the lower lip vibrate in sympathy with the vocal cords. Denture wearers with their dentures out will have difficulty with the *v* sound for this reason. Also note that the pitch rises about 20% during the duration of the sound. This is more easily seen by examining the ninth harmonic. On a logarithmic scale the stripes would be parallel and the shift in pitch less discernable. However, on the linear scale used, the strips tilt progressively since the absolute change in pitch is equal to the harmonic number times the change in the fundamental.

Another point of interest is that the *v* really has only two formant groups, the larger centered upon the second but including the third harmonic, and a smaller group near the ninth.

The *n* sound is made largely through the nose, with the tongue nearly sealing the upper mouth cavity. From about 0.32 to 0.37 sec, we find this sound has a pitch that decreases by about 10%. During this time, the amplitude increases then decreases, showing a minimum between 0.37 and 0.42 sec, as the *n* blends into the long *a* sound of the *eight*. During the blending period, the pitch is nearly constant. However, the formant around 1,300 Hz diminishes compared to the second harmonic, which actually strengthens somewhat. Note that the oscillogram shows considerably less detail between the peaks.

The loss of energy in the higher formant and the increase in the lower is probably caused by the movement of the tongue from the roof the mouth to a position against the back of the lower teeth at the start of the long *a* sound in *eight*.

The long *a* sound is particularly interesting. From about 0.42 to 0.53 sec, the pitch changes little except for a slight sag near 0.46 sec. However, the formant frequency in the middle moves from the tenth to the nineteenth harmonic, while those near the fifth and the twenty-second stay firmly in place! During this period the tongue is against the lower teeth and the lower jaw is moving downward, parting the teeth and lips. This would seem to present some evidence that this formant frequency is determined by the mouth cavity.

Beyond the 0.5 second point, the amplitude of the pressure wave decays more or less like a Gauss error function with the vocal cords giving a final pop at 0.55 sec. This pop it a bit late and more or less corresponds to a decrease in pitch. However, some portion of the drooping tail on the spectrum is an artifact of the spectrum-deriving process. This will be treated in detail later.

The trailing *t* on *eight* and the leading *t* on *two* are actually pronounced as one *t*. We shall see in a later spectrogram that even an *eight* that ends a phrase is characterized by a period of silence and an explosive thermal agitation sound. During the period between 0.57 sec and 0.7 sec, the tongue has to travel from its position against the lower teeth to the roof of the mouth, and some pressure must be accumulated within the mouth. The tip of the tongue then flips down to an *s* position (more or less). The silence and the sudden release of pressure give the *t* sound; compare the sharp leading edge at 0.7 sec with the gradual crescendo of the opening *s*. Note also that the general pitch is somewhat lower, with a significant amount of energy below 3 kHz.

The closing *oo* is drawn out for more than 0.3 sec. It is also distinguished by its decline to 60% of the starting pitch of 128 Hz, ending near 82 Hz. The amplitude tapers nearly linearly. Four formants are well established at the start. The highest is a carry-over from the *t* at 3,400 and 3,200 Hz. Another, which is somewhat longer lived, carries the seventeenth and eighteenth harmonics, and is centered about 2,300 Hz. The third bears the eleventh and twelfth harmonics near 1,500 Hz, and the lowest bears the second and third near 300 Hz.

There are a few other things which can be noted in summary from this spectrogram. First of all, we see that some of the sounds can have a duration as short as 60 msec (as in the *v*), whereas others may persist for as much 300 msec (as in the *oo*). A given sound may consist of as little as six repetitions of the (more or less) same waveshape (*v*), or as many as thirty (*oo*), and silent periods as long as 150 msec may form part of a given sound. The pitch can change at the rate of an octave in 250 msec, either rising or falling, and a single formant can move while others in the same sound are stationary.

The next spectrogram, shown Figure 10-3, gives the phrase "ZERO 98." In this spectrogram we see a very good example of what is meant by "connected speech." Except for the pause built into the terminating *t* of *eight*, the waves represent a continuous wavetrain. The *z* sound of *zero* is seen to be nearly identical to an *s* sound, except that it is voiced. If you try this sound, you will note that the mouth position is nearly identical and the voicing constitutes the only discernable difference. The rising middle formant of the long *a* in *eight* is nearly identical to the previous example (see 0.82 to 1.02 sec), and the amplitude tail-off is very similar.

THE PHONEMES

The basic sounds which make general american speech can be broken down into a relatively short list containing only thirty-four entries. These are classified ac-

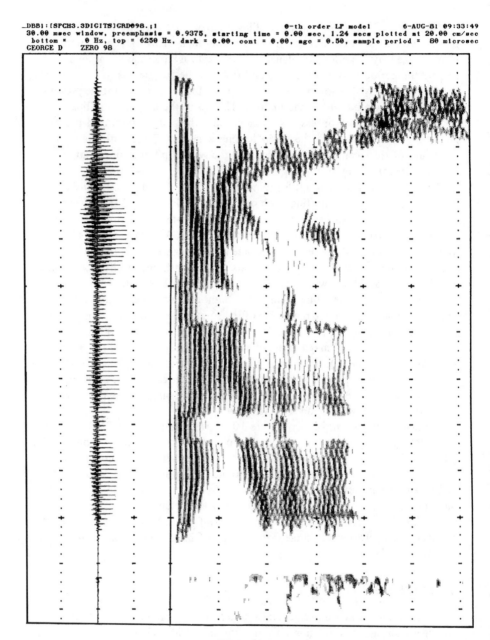

Figure 10-3.

cording to whether they are voiced, unvoiced, vowels, fricatives, nasal, or glides. The listing is as follows:

PHONEMES OF THE GENERAL DIALECT

VOWELS

/i/	(pronounced as *ee*)	as in thr*ee*
/il/		as in *i*t
/e/	(pronounced as a long *a*)	as in h*a*te
/ae/		as in *a*t
/a/		as in f*a*ther
/al/		as in *a*ll
/o/		as in *o*bey
/ol/		as in f*oo*d
/u/		as in *u*p
/ul/		as in b*oo*t
/u2/		as in b*i*rd

UNVOICED FRICATIVE CONSONANTS

/f/	as in *f*or
/th/	as in *th*in
/s/	as in *s*ee
/sl/	as in *sh*e
/h/	as in *h*e

VOICED FRICATIVE CONSONANTS

/v/	as in *v*ote
/th1/	as in *th*en
/z/	as in *z*oo
/z1/	as in a*z*ure

UNVOICED STOP CONSONANTS

/p/	as in *p*lay
/t/	as in *t*o
/k/	as in *k*ey

VOICED STOP CONSONANTS

/b/	as in *b*e
/d/	as in *d*ay
/g/	as in *g*o

NASAL CONSONANTS

/m/	as in *m*e
/n/	as in *n*o
/n1/	as in si*n*g

GLIDES AND SEMIVOWELS

/w/	as in *w*e
/y1/	as in *y*ou
/r/	as in *r*ead
/l/	as in *l*et

It should be observed that the notation used on the table is not the standard classical notation that involves either superscripts and subscripts or Greek characters not found in the type font of most typewriters or in the ASCII font, and therefore are difficult to produce in computer printouts or reports and correspondence. A widely used standard has not evolved to date; therefore, the notation is the writer's own.

The phoneme list of the general American dialect was evolved most by speech teachers for the purposes of teaching speech and permitting the phonetic spelling of words and phrases so that someone who did not know how to pronounce American sentences, either by reason of foreign origin or because of hearing impairment, could learn such pronounciation from a printed page. In this function the phonemes serve fairly well.

As work progressed in the development of artificial speech, it was first thought that artificial speech could be prepared simply by establishing a string of phonemes that would then produce the desired phrase. Unfortunately, this does not produce intelligible speech. (See Flanagan, *Speech Analysis, Synthesis and Perception.* Springer-Verlag, 1972.) As we have seen from the preceding spectrograms, the formant frequencies change continuously during transitions from one phoneme to another, and the pitch changes as well, as shown in the *v* sound of Figure 10-1 (/v/). This change can be independent of pitch or even of other formant frequencies, as in the *a* (/e/) sound of *eight*. Synthetic speech, which does not have the property of blending the formants during transitions, sounds very mechanical and is not highly intelligible to the untrained ear.

One of the first widely sold versions of a phoneme machine was produced under the name VOTRAX. In this machine, the phoneme list was expanded to 64 in an attempt to lick this phoneme-matching problem. The machine output was fixed in amplitude and the pitch was produced by a fixed clock. The speech would therefore be expected to sound flat and mechanical.

There is a surprising "learning curve" phenomenon to be found in this area. In a series of experiments, the writer produced a fairly large number of sentences for one of these machines. The programming of a simple phoneme machine is an acquired skill, like learning to play a violin, and as the number of sentences increased, the intelligibility increased as well, as noted both by the writer and his coworkers in the lab (who became used to hearing the machine).

This work was performed around 1977, before the introduction of "Speak and Spell"® by Texas Instruments. Very few people had heard a talking computer before. When these uninitiated people were exposed to some of the sentences that we felt were quite clear and intelligible, the reactions ranged from mild shock to wide-eyed, abject terror. People were actually frightened and shocked by the machine. Furthermore, the lack of understanding was nearly universal. On first contact hardly anyone could grasp even one or two words of a 15 to 20 word sentence. After a number of exposures these same subjects seemed to easily comprehend what the machine was saying. By the time of this writing nearly everyone in the country has been at least lightly exposed to talking computers in arcade games and toys. It is the writer's suspicion that arcade games and certain toys are understandable today because of the conditioning of the listeners.

VOCABULARY

The main attraction of the phoneme machine is the potential of creating a virtually unlimited vocabulary. Most of the other machines are fixed vocabulary types. The question frequently arises regarding the number of vocabulary words required to express nearly any thought in English. A number of people have analyzed this problem, and by the 1920s had arrived at an agreed-upon and standardized basic English (see C. K. Ogden *Learning Basic English,* 1929). A list of common ideas was made up and included 100 basic operations, such as come, get, little, tomorrow, etc. A 400-word general category covered words like: art, father, ink, profit, swim, etc. A 200-word list covered pictured items such as knee, library, moon, skirt, etc. A list of 100 qualities covered acid, full, electric, past, etc. A list of 50 opposites was also included, giving, awake, asleep, public, private, rough, smooth, etc. In all, the total list came to 850.

Other categories included 50 international words like automobile, piano, park, etc. There was also a list of 200 general science words, and 100-word lists for five specific sciences. In all, a total of about 1,600 words was deemed sufficient to express about 95% of one's thoughts in basic English, although, as Ogden points out, they require one to say " The fire is out" rather than " The conflagration has been extinguished."

Using either Linear Predictive Coding or Moser Coding, understandable speech can be encoded at about 150 bytes per word after a data compression of about

100:1. Our 1,600-word basic vocabulary would therefore require about 24 million bytes (or the capacity of a good-sized fixed disk system). The advantage of phoneme encoding is significant here. Presuming that we might enlarge the list to 256 phonemes, each requiring perhaps 8 bytes, the list itself would still occupy only 2K bytes. If we used 2 bytes to call up a phoneme, one to specify the phoneme and one to give pitch, amplitude, and duration, and assuming that the average word would have 6 phonemes, we find that we could specify our entire 1,600-word list with $12 \times 1,600 = 19.2$K bytes. In addition, we would have to store the phoneme itself. If the phoneme required 64 bytes, the phoneme table would have $64 \times 256 = 16$K bytes. A total of 35K bytes would therefore suffice for the entire basic English vocabulary. This is of course exclusive of an algorithm capable of producing connected speech from the phoneme library. The latter program is not in any sense trivial and, in the experience of the writer, is not even close to a solution at this writing.

Phoneme blending can take place in a variety of ways. Both Moser encoding and Texas Instruments expand the basic phoneme list. In the TI approach, the added sounds are termed *alonemes* and serve to perform the transitions. Dr. Moser observes that /s/ and /n/ will blend intelligibly with nearly any other phoneme and are represented singly in some of the Moser machines (to the neglect of /s1/ and /n1/ for maximum compression).

As a counterexample, Moser points out that /r/ and /i/ used in the word *three* require considerable blending to produce the word in any intelligible fashion. He notes that this is because /r/ has relatively low-frequency formants, whereas /i/ has high-frequency formants. Since the original Moser product was a pocket calculator for the blind, the word *three* was required along with the other numerals; therefore, a blended /r/i/ phoneme was included in the library.

Moser cites another example. The number 5 was produced by blending /a/ (as in father) and /i/ (as in three) to obtain the compound phoneme /ai/, giving the word /f/ai/v/. We shall see some other examples of the Moser technique in the next chapter.

There are a number of other techniques for blending phonemes when sufficient computer processing power is available. U.S. Patents 3,575,555 and 3,588,353 contain descriptions of such techniques.

THE VOCODER

One of the earliest techniques for speech synthesis consisted of an apparatus that analyzed speech into a spectrum and made a voiced/unvoiced decision. Suppose we had a machine that contained a filter bank, as illustrated in Figure 10-4, consisting of a bank of bandpass filters (with only a few of the passbands shown). Provided that one had a large enough filter bank, one could sample the filter

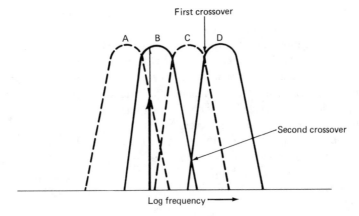

Figure 10-4. Model filter bank response.

outputs at the relatively slow rates at which the formants change and simply record which filters had energy in their passbands and how much. The speech could then be reconstructed by the inverse process, generating only a tone or a thermal agitation source and controlling the signal strength through a matched filter bank with controllable attenuators. Such a machine is termed a *vocoder* and can produce very intelligible and realistic speech. U.S. Patents 3,102,165 and 3,318,002 describe machines of this type.

The advantage of the vocoder is that it need not sample too rapidly. If we refer to Figure 10-1 and examine the traveling middle formant at 0.48 sec, we see that two harmonics are present at any time, and a reasonable reconstruction could be obtained with perhaps four steps to carry this formant from 1,400 Hz to about 2,000 Hz. Since the shift takes place in about 0.12 sec, we could get by with a sample every 40 msec at the maximum, although a somewhat faster sampling might be desirable.

The vocoder was the first practical mechanism for digitizing speech with good intelligibility because it is relatively undemanding of the digitizing equipment. Successful vocoders were operated by Bell Labs in the 1950s. Unfortunately, it is also somewhat hardware-intensive. From our same example, let us presume that we have filters with a constant percentage bandwidth. We find that four steps would require a frequency step ratio of 1:126, and we require a string of 20 filters to cover the range from 300 Hz to 3,000 Hz. Presuming that we sampled on a 10 msec time base and used an 8-bit level descriptor along with an 8-bit pitch descriptor for the fundamental, we find that the total rate would be 168 bits/10 msec or 16.8K bits/sec. Unfortunately, the system would have an awful lot of parts, including a pitch locator, which might consist of additional filters of a phase-locked loop tracker, 20 filters, 20 electronically controlled attenuators, etc. In addition to this, the bit rate is such that the signal could not be sent in digital format through an ordinary 3-kHz voice channel.

One of the earliest uses for the vocoder was in military "secure voice" applications. Once a word has been digitized by the vocoder, it can be scrambled by adding to it a pseudorandom number generated by a long shift register with multiple feedback connections. A similar shift register running at the same part of its pseudorandom cycle can then subtract the scrambling function and the speech can be reconstructed. However, even if you had an identical shift register but did not have "the code for the day" (or the correct step on which to start the shift register), you would get only garbage out. If the message was recorded, you could try different synchronizations but this would take a very large number of tries and the news would be "stale" by the time you had the message decoded.

Vocoders operating with an 8-filter sort and five levels have been constructed. At the encoding rates these produce, the signal can be sent through a voice channel by using narrow phase-shift modulation techniques on the resulting 4,800 bit/sec signal.

Instead of using the large number of filters required for the direct vocoder approach, it is possible to use a single bandpass filter and transpose the voice frequency signal so that it is swept through the speech passband. This has an advantage over the filter bank arrangement not only in reducing the amount of hardware but also in resolution. If we examine Figure 10-4, we see that a single signal in filter B would be indistinguishable from the addition of two smaller signals indicated by the heavy arrow centered in A and the light arrow centered in B. The swept filter approach will produce an output that is a tracing of the frequency response of the bandpass filter centered on the single frequency line. However, two signals separated by the passband cannot be resolved.

Figure 10-5 shows a basic block diagram of a spectrum analyzer. This device is also known nowadays as an "analog" spectrum analyzer. The output of a voltage controlled oscillator (VCO) is added to the incoming voiceband signal in a mixer. The sum signal is then passed through the bandpass filter. As F_h is swept in frequency, different portions of the input signal are passed through the bandpass filter. These are detected and displayed as vertical deflections on the oscilloscope. The horizontal deflection comes from the sweep generator and can be calibrated in frequency.

There are some relatively stern restrictions upon the rate at which the filter can be swept. Let us suppose that the bandpass filter is centered at 50 kHz and has a passband width of 50 Hz. This would give it an effective Q of 1,000. Now, it is a natural characteristic of filters that it takes about 3Q cycles for the filter output to rise (ring up) to 95% of the final output value when a tone is suddenly

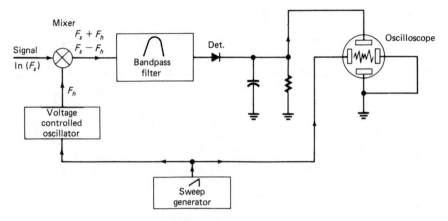

Figure 10-5. The spectrum analyzer.

turned on. A similar period is required to ring down to 5%. This says that the tone must stay within the passband for approximately 5Q cycles for a full response, with any faster transit yielding an erroneous amplitude reading. The period is 5Q rather than 6Q since the filter response is not zero outside of the passband. This tells us that approximately 5,000 cycles at 50 kHz are required to sweep a 50-Hz band, for a sweep rate of 50 Hz/0.001 sec = 50 kHz/sec. A sweep from 0 to 3 kHz would require 60 msec. As we have seen earlier, the various phonemes can come and go faster than this; therefore, the rate is too slow for speech processing. If we doubled the filter passband, we could double the sweep speed, but the passband would now be too broad to resolve the harmonics of a male voice, which tend to be on the order of 100 Hz apart.

As a second approach, one could consider moving the frequency of the filter down. With the arrangement shown, the VCO would sweep from 47,000 to perhaps 49,950 Hz. Unfortunately, it is the property of mixers that they not only output the sum of the two frequencies but also the difference, as well as many smaller terms such as $F_h + 2F_v$, etc. It is therefore necessary to keep the VCO frequency well separated from the top limit of the signal to be analyzed, particularly when the signal is very rich in harmonics. The sweeping oscillator has been used as a pitch finder in vocoders. However, it tends to suffer in comparison to the filter bank for the phoneme characterization.

As the art of large-scale integration grows, certain techniques for active-filters-on-silicon are being developed. It is likely that these developments will lead to integrated filter banks on a single chip, which will make the vocoder a more economical and miniaturized device competitive with the digital techniques now in vogue.

DIGITAL SPECTRAL ANALYSIS

Today, the largest amount of speech processing for speech synthesis is performed by digital computers utilizing the Fourier transform. Unless a very large and fast computer is used, the processing does not take place in real time. For example, it takes six to seven seconds to compute each harmonic term of the discrete Fourier transform shown in Figure 9-6. This routine was not particularly set up for fast run time, but was intended instead for illustrative clarity. For example, the main loop between 170 and 310 has a number of LET'S that were included for clarity. Each time the Apple encounters a LET, it takes some time for it to decide to ignore it. The program works just as well without the LET, but it is not read as easily by humans.

Similarly, the use of APPLESOFT to write the program slows the execution by a factor of 10 to 100 compared to a machine language routine in which the sine and cosine terms were simply taken from a look-up table that was precalculated outside of the loop. Also, the statement of line 260, which sets $Y\%$ (an integer number) equal to the expression of several floating-point numbers, wastes time on every pass of the loop because it forces the machine to consider $Y\%$ as a floating-point number first, and then converts it to an integer number. This happens only once for every harmonic rather than n times for the inner loop running from statement 185 to statement 250, where n is the number of samples.

Enough respect was maintained for running time to keep the number of REMs (remarks) inside the main loop to zero. The use of REM inside of a repetitive loop is to be avoided since the machine has to consider and reject the REM on every pass (thereby wasting a good deal of running time). The calculation of D-DA on every pass is also a time waster since this could have been adjusted on a single pass subroutine.

However, even with a fast machine language subroutine, it is still out of the grasp of the 6502 processor to calculate the spectrum in real time (that is between samples) by at least an order of magnitude.

The discrete Fourier transform takes the amplitude of each of the n samples and multiplies it by a superimposed sine wave and cosine wave and adds the products separately. It then combines the sine and cosine sums using the Pythagorean theorem (line 260). It could have calculated the phase angle of the harmonic; however, this was omitted for reasons that will be subsequently described.

We see that the routine requires $2n$ multiplications in the small loop, half for the sine and half for the cosine, to calculate the amplitude of a single harmonic. If we wish to calculate $n/2$ harmonics, we see that n^2 multiplications are required.

In reality, the routine as shown is too coarse-grained for practical speech synthesis work. The spectrum of Figure 10-1 was calculated with an 80 usec sampling time and a 30 msec "window." This means that there were 375 samples per "frame." If we assume that the running time is mainly concentrated in the minor loop, this program would run $(375/32)^2$ = 137 times as long. Instead of 7 seconds per harmonic it would take 16 minutes!

There is a very interesting and noticeable difference between the analysis of Figure 9-6 and the spectrograms of Figure 10-1 (and the other TI spectrograms) beside the coarseness. Whereas the spectrum of Figure 9-1 is made up of a series of single lines, the spectrum of the TI spectrographs are definite bands with considerable width. Why are these broad whereas the simulated ones are mathematical points? This leads us to the concept of the "window."

In the calculation of Figure 9-6, we had 32 points describing the shape of the pressure wave. The manipulation assumed that this was the exact mathematical length of the wave, that is, any other equal "window" along the wave would have produced an identical picture with exactly one pressure peak.

In the more nearly "real world" analysis applied in the TI spectrogram, the arbitrary voice wave was sampled every 80 usec, and 375 such samples were applied to make up a "window." Now, at a 125-Hz pitch frequency, the window would contain 3.75 repetitions of the wave. This means that if we were to take a 30-msec window and slide it along a wavetrain, such as the synthesized one of Figure 10-2, we would sometimes have the low-amplitude end showing at both edges and would sometimes have four of the double-peak complexes within the window. Figure 10-6 shows these two cases. The Fourier transform has the property that it assumes that each window is exactly representative of the entire time-history of the wave. It would therefore interpret the two cases as shown in Figure 10-6. It is not unreasonable to suppose that the two different waveforms will have a somewhat different fundamental frequency and harmonic structure, thereby smearing out the response into broader bands. As the window slides along the trace of the pressure wave, the picture changes cyclically.

As a matter of fact, the DFT assumes that the fundamental frequency is equal to the sampling frequency divided by the number of samples in the window. For the TI spectrograms, this would work out to 12,500 Hz/375 = 33.33 Hz. The transform actually shows a response curve similar to that of a bank of filters with each having a 33.33-Hz bandwidth with a 33.33-Hz spacing.

The shape of the individual filter response is determined by the weighting attached to the samples. In the program of Figure 9-6, all of the samples had equal weighting and it can be shown that the response curve of the virtual filter would be a sin X/X function with –13 db sidelobes as shown in Figure 10-7.

To understand this figure, a few words of explanation are in order. First of all, the graphics technique has plotted the response envelopes as black on gray and white on gray in order to make the "busy" parts of the sidelobes visible. For clarity of the presentation, only two harmonics of the sampling frequency were calculated: $n = 8$ and $n = 9$. The input excitation was taken in steps from

100 REM THIS PROGRAM SYNTHESIZES A WAVEFORM CONTAINING HARMONICS 1,3,4,1
    0,11,18,25 AND 26.

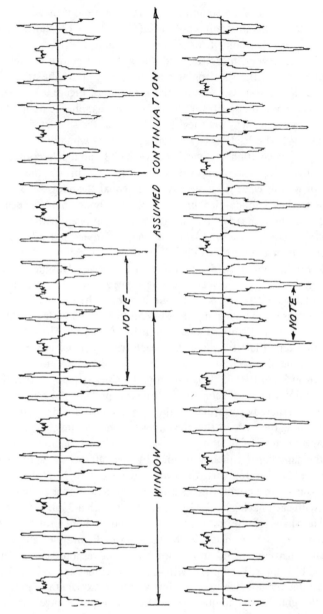

Figure 10-6. Windowing errors.

```
]LIST

100  REM   THIS IS AN ANALYSIS OF THE RESPONSE OF THE FOURIER TRANSFORM WIT
     H A UNIFORM WINDOW.
110  HGR2
120  HCOLOR= 3: REM   WHITE
130  POKE  - 12524,0: REM  PLOT BLACK ON WHITE
140  POKE  - 12529,255: REM  PLOT UNIDIRECTIONAL
150  POKE  - 12525,64: REM  PLOT PAGE 2
152  M% = 0: REM  X AXIS SCALE FACTOR
154  A = 0:B = 0:X = 0
156  N = 8
157  D = 6
158  P = (3.14159 / 16)
160  C = P * X * D
170  E = 10 *  SIN (C)
175  Q = P * X * N
180  R = E *  SIN (Q)
190  A = A + R
200  S = E *  COS (Q)
210  B = B + S
220  X = X + 1
230  IF X < 33 THEN  GOTO 160
240  Y% = 190 -  SQR (A ^ 2 + B ^ 2)
245  IF N = 9 THEN  GOTO 370
250  HPLOT M%,Y% TO M%,190
260  X = 0
270  M% = M% + 4
275  IF M% > 279 THEN  GOTO 320
280  A = 0:B = 0
290  D = D + .1
310  IF D < 11 THEN  GOTO 160
320  D = 6
322  A = 0:B = 0:X = 0
330  M% = 2
340  N = N + 1
350  IF N < 10 THEN  GOTO 160
360  END
370  HPLOT M%,Y% TO M%,0
380  GOTO 260
```

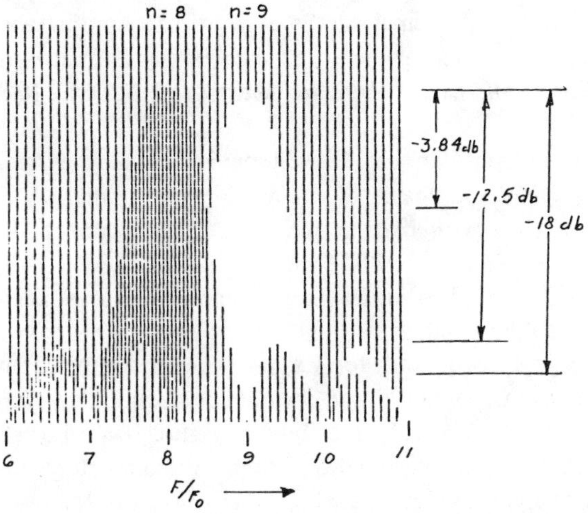

Figure 10-7.

a value well below the design center of the two filter sections to a point well above the design center. The black-and-white envelopes represent the locus of the tip of the response as it passes through the filter. The number, F_o, represents the sampling frequency divided by the number of samples in the window, which in this case is 32. In this case all samples are treated with equal importance.

We see that the virtual filters cross over somewhat below the half-power point (at –3.84 db) at $F/F_o = 8.5$. When the frequency is centered at 8, we see that the response in filter 9 is essentially zero. However, on either side it rises quite rapidly. The first sidelobe is –12.5 db, and the second is –18 db. The filters, of course, are merely the mathematical output of the Fourier analysis. However, they have some of the same limitations as the hardware filters of the vocoder. Note that when the value of F/F_o is 10.5, the output of 10 and 11 would be down –3.84 db and the outputs of 9 and 8 would be down by only –12.5 and –18 db, respectively. The filtering is far from perfect. A strong signal in one channel can produce significant outputs in adjacent channels both in a real hardware filter and in the Fourier analysis.

One approach to this problem has long been used for antenna applications and in optics. More recently, this approach has been applied to the field of digital spectroscopy. In the antenna field, the technique is termed "illumination tapering," and in optics it is called "apodizing." In digital spectroscopy, the technique is termed "windowing," or "Hamming Windowing." In all three processes, the mathematics are nearly identical and the function is applied in the same manner: the importance of the samples at the edge of the aperture or window is reduced. In optics, this is done by darkening the outside of the lens or by using a star-shaped mask. In antenna work, it is done by reducing the power fed to the outside elements. In digital spectroscopy, it is done by multiplying the samples by a function that is small at the edges of the window and large in the center. (A detailed treatment of the effect and examples of patterns may be obtained from S. Silver, *Microwave Antenna Theory and Design.* Rad Lab, Vol. XII, McGraw-Hill, 1949).

To accomplish this weighting, consider that the window is pi radians across, and then multiply the samples by the cosine of the angle Pi∗n/N, where N is the number of samples and n is the particular sample number. In Figure 10-8, this windowing function is to be seen in line 170 of the program.

On examination of the envelopes, it is obvious that the windowing has reduced the spurious responses considerably, but at the expense of some broadening. The first crossover is now up to 2.18 db and, for a signal precisely centered on the eighth harmonic, the signals in channels 7 and 9 would be down only –10.6 db. The system has a high second crossover, as defined in Figure 10-4. For all intents and purposes, the heavy windowing function has nearly completely discarded the outside readings, thereby making the window narrower and the resolution (the ability to separate two closely spaced signals) much poorer.

```
100  REM  THIS IS AN ANALYSIS OF A FOURIER TRANSFORM WITH COSINE WINDOWING

110  HGR2
120  HCOLOR= 3: REM  WHITE
130  POKE  - 12524,0: REM  PLOT BLACK ON WHITE
140  POKE  - 12529,255: REM  PLOT UNIDIRECTIONAL
150  POKE  - 12525,64: REM  PLOT PAGE 2
152  M% = 0: REM  X AXIS SCALE FACTOR
154  A = 0:B = 0:X = 0
156  N = 8
157  D = 6
158  P = (3.14159 / 16)
160  C = P * X * D
165  T = (P * X / 2)
170  E = 10 *  SIN (C) *  SIN (T)
175  Q = P * X * N
180  R = E *  SIN (Q)
190  A = A + R
200  S = E *  COS (Q)
210  B = B + S
220  X = X + 1
230  IF X < 33 THEN  GOTO 160
240  Y% = 190 -  SQR (A ^ 2 + B ^ 2)
245  IF N = 9 THEN  GOTO 370
250  HPLOT M%,Y% TO M%,190
260  X = 0
270  M% = M% + 4
275  IF M% > 279 THEN  GOTO 320
280  A = 0:B = 0
290  D = D + .1
310  IF D < 11 THEN  GOTO 160
320  D = 6
322  A = 0:B = 0:X = 0
330  M% = 2
340  N = N + 1
350  IF N < 10 THEN  GOTO 160
360  END
370  HPLOT M%,Y% TO M%,0
380  GOTO 260
```

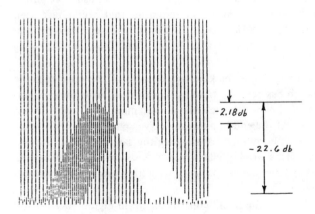

Figure 10-8.

A very beneficial effect is to be noted with regard to the "window edge" jitter described in Figure 10-6. Since the importance of the edges is diminished, the jitter effect would be much smaller with cosine windowing.

There are a large number of different windowing choices that can be used. Tschebyscheff windowing has the property that all of the sidelobes can be made equal. With the Taylor distribution, it is possible to have the first three sidelobes (or the first n) all equal, and then fall off. In theory, the Gauss error function window has no sidelobes at all!

The Gauss error function is the only function that is its own Fourier transform. However, in practice, the Gauss error function cannot be used completely since it extends from minus to plus infinity and would require an infinite window width. When used with a finite number of samples of a finite antenna width, it must be truncated at some point. The two illustrations of Figure 10-9 show the Gauss error function window performance with the function terminated so that the edge excitation is 25% and 5%, respectively. It may be seen that the top one has the advantage of a fairly rapid descent so that the second crossover is down –12 db, which is slightly better than the cosine weighting.

In speech spectroscopy, the use of a weighting function is relatively important because of the inherent window edge noise. There is always some jitter in the basic pitch. The fact that the pitch varies makes it impossible to have an even number of cycles in the window at all times with one window fixed. For the sampling rate used in Figure 10-1, at 33.33-Hz harmonic spacing it may be seen that the frequency bands of the pitch harmonics are always about 100-Hz wide; therefore, it seems likely that each of the heavier stripes represents about three filter outputs. This is the result that would be obtained if a windowing function like that of the top illustration of Figure 10-9 or a cosine weighting were used. This obviously destroys some of the resolution that would have been obtained with uniform weighting. However, this would have been destroyed in actual practice by window edge jitter. The selection of an optimum windowing function is a bit tricky.

An alternative solution is possible, making use of some of the powers of the computer. Once the speech has been digitized, it is possible to have the computer constantly adjust the window width such that a fixed number of whole cycles is present in each window. At the end of a run for a given phoneme, the computer could fill in additional "phony" cycles, showing the same trend established by the previous history. This would yield a higher resolution than either uniform distribution with windowing noise or heavy weighting with the consequent higher second crossovers.

All of this brings us back to the final "pop" of the /e/ in Figure 10-1. It was mentioned that this was to some extent an artifact of the measuring system. Any window sliding along that train would eventually come to the point where

```
100  REM   THIS PLOTS THE RESPONSE OF A FOURIER TRANSFORM WITH GAUSS ERROR
     FUNCTION WINDOWING. EDGE AMPLITUDE IS 25%

160 C = P * X * D
165 T = ((16 - X) / 13.589) ^ 2
170 E = 7.5 *  SIN (C) *  EXP ( - T)
```

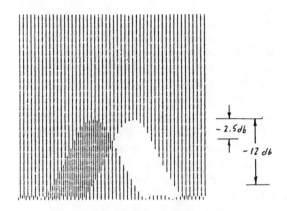

$-2.5 db$

$-12 db$

```
100  REM   THIS PLOTS THE RESPONSE OF A FOURIER TRANSFORM WITH GAUSS ERROR
     FUNCTION WINDOWING. EDGE AMPLITUDE IS 5%.

160 C = P * X * D
165 T = ((16 - X) / 9.24) ^ 2
170 E = 7.5 *  SIN (C) *  EXP ( - T)
```

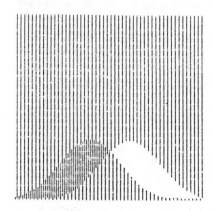

Figure 10-9.

there was only one pulse left in the window. At a 12.5-kHz sampling rate with a 375 sample window, this will be interpreted as a 33.33-Hz pitch. On the original, this "pitch crash" was clearly visible, and is noted in the hole in the low formant in the reproduction.

THE FAST FOURIER TRANSFORM

In a practical sense, the Fourier transform simply amounts (in the discrete or digital format) to the sum of the product of the various samples of the voltage waveform and a series of harmonically related sine waves. Obviously, a sine wave that is highly positive when the samples are highly positive and highly negative when the samples are highly negative will produce a large output (or sum) compared to a sine wave (or cosine wave) that does not vary in step with the samples. These are the steps performed in lines 200 through 230 of Figure 9-6.

In a similar situation, the inverse Fourier transform amounts simply to the addition of a series of sine and cosine waves, as illustrated in Figure 8-2. In a digital computer manipulation, one simply adds the product of an amplitude and the sine or cosine of an angle to the product of another amplitude and the sine or cosine of twice the angle, etc., to obtain the final waveshape.

As noted earlier, this is a calculation-intensive problem. If we have N samples we would like to test for $N/2$ harmonics, then we must perform $N^2/2$ multiplications times the sine of an angle and $N^2/2$ multiplications times the cosine of the angle, for a total of N^2 multiplications. In addition, we must perform N^2 additions and $N/2$ solutions to the Pythagorean theorem if we intend to obtain absolute magnitude, and $N/2$ tangent determinations if we wish to preserve the phase data, with the information presented in magnitude/angle form. For some small number of samples, the restrictions are not too onerous. However, as one approaches speech or music processing, the run time begins to increase very dramatically. Obviously, some technique for decreasing the run time would be significantly appreciated in speech and music processing where long sample strings and high resolution are required.

THE FFT/IFT PROGRAM

An algorithm to make the Fourier transform run faster on a computer was introduced by J. W. Cooley and associates. (See W. T. Cochran and J. W. Cooley, *What Is a Fast Fourier Transform?* IEEE Transactions on Audio and Electroacoustics, Vol. AU-15, June 1967, pp 45–55). It should be noted that this is not actually a departure from the process of the Fourier transform, but rather, simply, a mechanism for organizing the operation of the computer in handling the transform that results in two factors of improvement. First of all, the number of operations is reduced from N^2 to something approaching $2N$. Secondly, the computer memory storage requirements are reduced by a process termed "multiplication in place," whereby the final data appear in place of the original data.

(A detailed operational discussion of the FFT is beyond the scope of this text and the reader is referred to the earlier Cooley reference).

Fundamentally, the basic reduction achieved in running time stems from a technique of breaking up the problem. Let us suppose that we have to perform a Fourier analysis on a window containing 1,024 samples. As we have noted, this would require 1,048,575 multiplications (i.e., $A_i*\sin(\emptyset)$, $A_i*\cos(\emptyset)$, ...). Now, let us suppose that instead we were to neglect every other sample so that only 512 samples were present. The manipulations would be reduced to 262,144, or 1/4 of the original. A second transform performed on the samples neglected in the first would still only bring us up to 524,288 manipulations, thereby cutting the effort in half. Of course, there would be some overhead manipulations required to combine the two individual transforms, provided that this could be done. Presuming that this "decimation" process were to continue, we see that we could arrive at a situation where only $4N/2$ manipulations are required, plus, of course, the overhead calculations. This is, in essence, the key to the reduction of effort required by the FFT.

The FFT/IFT routine that follows was designed to run on an Apple II+. Being written in Applesoft, it is not nearly as fast as a routine written for the machine language of the 6502, but it does offer the reader some basis for comprehension of what is going on (which the native machine language routine makes much more difficult).

As written, the program is a third cousin to one originally written by G. Waggener, which appears in his article in *Electronic Design News* magazine: *Basic Subroutine Runs a Slow* FFT. EDN, Oct. 5, 1978, p. 82. This program was modified by R. H. Cushman and presented in an article in *Electronic Design News* magazine. The Cushman article also presented another FFT/IFT program modeled after Hal Chamberlin (*Musical Applications of Microprocessors*. Hayden Book Co., Inc., Rochelle Pk., N. J., 1980).

Cushman was at pains to minimally alter the notation in the interest of reducing the possibility of error. His program was written to run on an AIM-65 and required some modification for the Apple. The writer has similarly attempted to keep as much of the original as possible, while adding a print/plot/both option. Compared to the discrete Fourier transform of Figure 9-6, this routine is much faster. As a matter of fact, the transform itself takes less time than the printer takes to print the results if the Apple Silentype is used.

The plotting routine scales the results and plots the data on HGR2. The largest term will always represent a full-scale deflection in the vertical direction.

It also combines the real and imaginary terms to obtain the magnitude by using the Pythagorean theorem. If the print option is used, the real and imaginary components are preserved separately.

To demonstrate some of the versatility of this routine, Wegener developed it for use in evaluating the properties of instrumentation amplifiers. He first applies an impulse of known properties (say a transition from 0 to 1 V) and known duty cycle (say 1 V from 0 to 10 msec and 0 V from 10 to 30 msec), and then proceeds to digitize the output of the amplifier. The FFT is then applied to the digitized output of the amplifier and the frequency and phase of the harmonics of the impulse are determined. Then they are compared with the known properties of the input signal. In this single step, the passband amplitude and phase characteristics of the amplifier are completely determined.

In a somewhat different approach, Chamberlin applies the FFT to the generation of music. In this case, the IFT is actually used. One or more fundamental pitches can be inserted into the program (akin to striking keys on a piano) along with harmonics and the program run in the R (reverse or inverse Fourier) direction to develop the waveshape in digital format. This can then be applied to a D/A converter, which drives a loudspeaker to produce the music. The relationship between the fundamental (or basic note) and the harmonics can be made to simulate either a known instrument, such as a clarinet, oboe, violin, etc., or to "create" an entirely new instrument with tone characteristics (relation between fundamental and harmonics) unlike any existing instrument. In essence, this is a digital version of the Moog Synthesizer, which is an analog instrument.

It should be noted that the sound of various instruments, such as the piano and the organ, are not time-stationary; that is, the pitch and the pitch/harmonic relationships change with time. With enough knowledge and skill, even such sophisticated relationships can be synthesized using this technique. The principal limitations of this technique stem from the fact that it is very memory-intensive. It seems likely that digitally synthesized music with a whole "orchestra" of nonphysical instruments is waiting in the offing and shall be heard widely before long.

One of the advantages of the "multiplication-in-place" technique is that the operation can be repeated in reverse after some processing of the data. For example, a waveshape can be entered in the forward direction (F) and transformed to the frequency domain. A filtering action can then be applied (mathematically) to the resulting spectrum, and the data then transformed in the reverse direction (R) to obtain the resulting waveshape.

An example of this is shown in Figures 10-13 and 10-14.

In the example you will note that lines 6 through 70 of Figure 10-10 have been replaced with lines 6 through 44, which describe two sine waves of different frequency. As a matter of fact, the description covers the 2,025 and 2,250

```
1    PRINT "++++++++++++++++++++++++++++++++"
2    PRINT '          FFT/IFT            "
3    PRINT "AFTER WAGGENER/CUSHMAN/KUECKEN "
4    PRINT "   WITH PRINT & PLOT OPTIONS   "
5    PRINT "&&&&&&&&&&&&&&&&&&&&&&&&&&&&&&&&"
6    PRINT "FOR PRINT ENTER 1"
7    PRINT "FOR PLOT ENTER 2"
8    PRINT "FOR BOTH ENTER 3
9    INPUT PR
11   PRINT "    ENTER FWD OR REV (F/R)     "
13   INPUT AN$
14   IF AN$ = "F" THEN D = 0: GOTO 20
15   IF AN$ = "R" THEN D = 1: GOTO 20
16   PRINT "IT HAS TO BE F OR R DUMMY!"
17   GOTO 11
20   PRINT "ENTER M"
21   INPUT M
22 N = 2 ^ M
23   PRINT "N=",N
24   DIM X(N,2)
25   IF D = 0 THEN  PRINT "INPUT TIME DOMAIN DATA"
26   IF D = 1 THEN  PRINT "INPUT FREQ DOMAIN DATA
30   FOR I = 1 TO N
31   PRINT "############################"
32   PRINT "INPUT X'("I",0) X("I","1)"
33   INPUT X(I,0),X(I,1)
34   NEXT I
35   IF PR = 2 THEN  GOTO 40
36   IF PR = 1 THEN  GOTO 39
37   IF PR = 3 THEN  GOTO 39
38   GOTO 40
39   PR# 1
40   PRINT "=============================="
41   IF D = 0 THEN  PRINT "TIME DOMAIN DATA IS"
42   IF D = 1 THEN  PRINT "FREQUENCY DOMAIN DATA IS"
45   PRINT "POINT","REAL       IMAGINARY"
50   FOR I = 1 TO N
55   PRINT I,X(I,0),X(I,1)
60   NEXT I
65   PR# 0
70   GOSUB 500
75   IF PR = 2 THEN   GOTO 100
80   IF PR = 1 THEN   GOTO 95
85   IF PR = 3 THEN   GOTO 95
90   GOTO 100
95   PR# 1
100  PRINT "////////////////////////////"
110  IF D = 0 THEN  PRINT "NOW IN FREQ DOMAIN
111  IF D = 1 THEN  PRINT "NOW IN THE TIME DOMAIN"
112  PRINT "XFRMD DATA IS"
114  PRINT "POINT","REAL       IMAGINARY"
116  FOR I = 1 TO N
118  PRINT I,X(I,0),X(I,1)
120  NEXT I
122  PRINT "=============================="
124  PRINT "DATE = 09/22/81"
125  PR# 0:
126  IF PR = 2 THEN  GOTO 1100
127  IF PR = 3 THEN  GOTO 1100
128  END
500  REM    :::::::::::::::::::::::::::::
```

Figure 10-10.

```
500  REM    ::::::::::::::::::::::: .:::::::
501  REM    FFT/IFT SUBROUTINE
502  REM    :::::::::::::::::::::::::::::::::
550 N = 2 ^ M
552  REM  *****DO BIT SHUFFLE******
570 N2 = N / 2
580 N1 = N - 1
590 J = 1
600  FOR I = 1 TO N1
610  IF I > = J THEN  GOTO 680
630 T1 = X(J,0)
640 T2 = X(J,1)
650 X(J,0) = X(I,0)
655 X(J,1) = X(I,1)
660 X(I,0) = T1
670 X(I,1) = T2
680 K = N2
690  IF K > = J THEN 730
700 J = J - K
710 K = K / 2
720  GOTO 690
730 J = J + K
740  NEXT I
750  REM  *****END OF SHUFFLE***********
760 S1 =  - 1
770  IF D = 0 THEN  GOTO 790
780 S1 = 1
790 PI = 3.1415926
800  FOR L = 1 TO M
810 L1 = 2 ^ L
820 L2 = L1 / 2
830 U1 = 1
840 U2 = 0
850 W1 =  COS (PI / L2)
860 W2 = S1 *  SIN (PI / L2)
870  FOR J = 1 TO L2
880  FOR I = J TO N STEP L1
890 I1 = I + L2
895  REM  ******DO BUTTERFLY************
900 V1 = (X(I1,0) * U1 - X(I1,1) * U2)
910 V2 = (X(I1,1) * U1 + X(I1,0) * U2)
920 X(I1,0) = X(I,0) - V1
930 X(I1,1) = X(I,1) - V2
940 X(I,0) = X(I,0) + V1
950 X(I,1) = X(I,1) + V2
960  NEXT I
970  REM  *****DO TWIDL FACTOR**********
975 U3 = U1
976 U4 = U2
980 U1 = (U3 * W1 - U4 * W2)
990 U2 = (U4 * W1 + U3 * W2)
1000  NEXT J
1010  NEXT L
1020  IF D = 1 THEN  GOTO 1060
1030  FOR I = 1 TO N
1040 X(I,0) = X(I,0) / N
1045 X(I,1) = X(I,1) / N
1050  NEXT I
1060  RETURN
```

Figure 10-11.

```
1075   PRINT "#############################"
1080   PRINT "   START OF PLOT ROUTINE"
1085   PRINT "PLOTS BLACK ON WHITE ON HGR2"
1090   PRINT ">>>>>>>>>>><<<<<<<<<<<<<<<<<<"
1100   DIM Y(N,1)
1110 X% = 558 / N
1120   REM   CALC. HORIZONTAL SCALE
1130   HGR2
1140   HCOLOR= 3
1150   POKE   - 12524,0
1160   POKE   - 12525,64
1170   POKE   - 12529,255
1180   REM   SETS TO PLOT B/W ON HGR2
1190   IF D = 1 THEN   GOTO 1400
1200   FOR I = 1 TO N
1210 H = I
1220 Y(H,0) =   SQR (X(I,0) ^ 2 + X(I,1) ^ 2)
1230   IF Y(H,0) > Y1 THEN Y1 = Y(H,0)
1240   IF Y(H,0) < Y2 THEN Y2 = Y(H,0)
1250   NEXT I
1260 N4 = 190 / (Y1 - Y2)
1270   REM   THIS SETS VERTICAL SCALE
1280 M4 = 0
1290 M5 = (N / 2) + 1
1300   FOR H = 1 TO M5
1310 Y% = 190 - (Y(H,0) * N4)
1320   HPLOT M4,190 TO M4,Y%
1330 M4 = M4 + X%
1340   NEXT H
1345 M4 = M4 - X%
1350   HPLOT 0,190 TO M4,190
1360   END
1400   FOR I = 1 TO N
1410 H = I
1420 Y(H,0) =   SQR (X(I,0) ^ 2 + X(I,1) ^ 2)
1430   IF X(I,0) < 0 THEN Y(H,0) = Y(H,0) *  - 1
1440   IF Y(H,0) > Y1 THEN Y1 = Y(H,0)
1450   IF Y(H,0) < Y2 THEN Y2 = Y(H,0)
1455   NEXT I
1460 N4 = 190 / (Y1 - Y2)
1470   REM   CALC. VERTICAL SCALE
1480 N5 = N4 * Y2
1490   REM   LOCATE AXIS
1495   FOR H = 1 TO N
1500 Y% = 190 + N5 - (Y(H,0) * N4)
1510   IF H = 1 THEN M6 = 0:N6 = Y%
1520   HPLOT M6,N6 TO M4,Y%
1530 M6 = M4
1540 M4 = M4 + (X% / 2)
1550 N6 = Y%
1560   NEXT H
1570 Y% = 190 + N5
1575 M4 = M4 - (X% / 2)
1580   HPLOT 0,Y% TO M4,Y%
1590   END
```

Figure 10-12.

Hz signals that represent, respectively, the ANSWER frequencies of a 300 BPS modem by the Bell 301 STD. As may be seen, the higher of the frequencies has slightly more power in the spectrum since it represents 7.416 cycles (this is the MARK state), compared to the 6.375 cycles of the SPACE state. The rewriting of the program simply relieved the author of having to make 512 real and 512 imaginary entries for the original waveform!

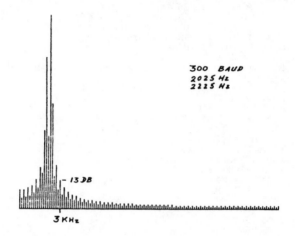

```
1   PRINT "*****************************"
2   PRINT "          FFT/IFT           "
3   PRINT "AFTER WAGGENER/CUSHMAN/KUECKEN "
4   PRINT "   WITH PRINT & PLOT OPTIONS   "
5   PRINT "&&&&&&&&&&&&&&&&&&&&&&&&&&&&&&&"
6 PR = 2
8 D = 0
10 M = 8
12 N = 2 ^ M
14   DIM X(N,2)
16 Q1 = (3.14159 / 128) * 14.832
18 Q2 = (3.14159 / 128) * 13.5
20   FOR I = 1 TO 128
22 I1 = I - 1
24 A =  SIN (I1 * Q1)
26 X(I,0) = A
28 X(I,1) = 0
30   NEXT I
32   FOR I = 129 TO 256
34 I1 = I - 1
36 A =  SIN (I1 * Q2)
38 X(I,0) = A
40 X(I,1) = 0
42   NEXT I
44   GOSUB 500
```

Figure 10-13.

It should be noted that in a digitized wave form there really are no imaginary entries. The real and imaginary components are used only to make the FFT/IFT analysis symmetrical. Unless the waveshape chosen satisfies certain very restrictive laws of symmetry, the frequency analysis of a waveshape will contain both real (or sine) and imaginary (or cosine) terms (see J. A. Kuecken, *Solid State Motor Control*. Tab Books # 929, Ch. 13, 1978). Conversely, the phase terms in the resolved spectrum cannot be neglected if the waveform is to be reconstructed accurately (as will be shown in Chapter 12).

Figure 10-14 shows the alteration of the program to represent the "filtering" due to passage through a telephone circuit. Both the low and the high frequencies of the spectrum have been truncated or attenuated. No phase manipulation is included in this analysis; however, it could easily have been.

Cushman notes in his article that certain effects are best handled in the amplitude-time regime, such as clipping and the addition of noise and the effects of nonlinear amplification. On the other hand, effects such as filtering and the addition of harmonics are most easily handled in the frequency-amplitude regime. Cushman cites a study in which Stuart Perelman of RCA, using an FFT/IFT technique, analyzes the complete path from the light and image in a studio to the presentation on a home TV receiver. In this operation the FFT and IFT are applied 11 times to permit an assessment of the overall processing degradation (see Stuart S. Perelman, *Computer Tool Evaluates Horizontal Transient Response of the NTSC Color TV System*. RCA Engineer, May/June 1981).

In the filtering procedure, it should be noted that the bandpass characteristic of the filter must be folded about the center of the response. Due to the requirement (the NYQUIST limit of 2 samples per wave form) for multiple samples per wave, the spectral analysis is always mirrored about the center. For this reason, the spectrum plot covers only half as many frequencies as the sample. When using the filtering routine, it is necessary to make the filter response symmetrical about the center, as shown in the program if correct results are to be obtained.

A FINAL WORD

In summary, concerning the FFT/DFT discussion, it should be noted that a faithful reproduction of a waveform usually requires a large number of samples; however, the system does not necessarily transmit all of the harmonics. One of the advantages of the DFT is that it is easily truncated to calculate only the harmonics of interest. This advantage does not obtain with the FFT. Therefore, under some circumstances, the DFT can be made to run at competitive speeds compared to the FFT, if the upper harmonics can be neglected in the system.

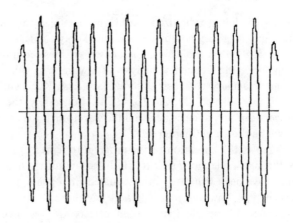

```
]LIST 1980,3000

1980   REM   )))))))))))))))((((((((((((((((((
1985   REM      THIS IS THE FILTER ROUTINE
1990   REM   $$$$$$$$$$$$$$$$$$$$$$$$$$$$$$$$$$$
2000   IF D = 1 THEN  GOTO 1100
2010   D = 1
2020   X(1,0) = 0
2021   X(2,0) = .5 * X(2,0)
2022   X(255,0) = .5 * X(255,0)
2023   X(255,1) = .5 * X(255,1)
2024   X(2,1) = .5 * X(2,1)
2025   X(255,0) = 0
2030   X(1,1) = 0
2035   X(255,1) = 0
2040   X(20,0) = .5 * X(20,0)
2045   X(237,0) = .5 * X(237,0)
2050   X(20,1) = .5 * X(20,1)
2055   X(237,1) = .5 * X(237,1)
2060   FOR I = 21 TO 236
2070   X(I,0) = 0
2080   X(I,1) = 0
2090   NEXT I
3000   GOTO 44

]

?SYNTAX ERROR
```

Figure 10-14.

11
Speech Digitization

One of the prime requirements for computer treatment of human speech or, for that matter, music, is the rendering of the continuously varying (or analog) form of the signal into a digital format characterized as a series of discrete steps. This function is generally performed with some form of analog-to-digital converter. In this chapter we shall treat some of the various forms of A/D conversion that are suitable for music or speech encoding.

In actual practice, there are a fairly large number of techniques in popular use for converting an analog voltage into a digital format. Some of these have very fine properties when the task does not require a fast conversion. For example, it is not too difficult to construct a voltage or current controlled oscillator that will produce an output frequency linearly proportional to the control voltage. An ordinary astable multivibrator has this property over a limited range. Also, a number of the silicon houses offer function generators and V/F converters into which this voltage-to-frequency function has been carefully built and temperature compensated.

For most such devices the problem is one of time. Suppose that we had a device that had an output frequency of 1 kHz at 1 V and an output of 10 kHz at 10 V. Assuming that the device was perfectly linear in its voltage response, we could, by counting the frequency over a 1 sec period, resolve the input voltage to one millivolt. For example, 3.765 V would provide 3,765 cycles over a period of a second. Obviously, this is great for precision; a voltage measurement with four significant figures is not to be sneezed at. However, for anything to do with speech or music it is useless.

In a history-making paper, Claude Shannon showed that not less than two samples per wave period must be taken to define a wave (C. E. Shannon, *A Mathematical Theory of Communication.* Bell System Tech. Journal, Vol. 27, pp. 379 to 623, 1948). This makes a good deal of sense if one thinks about it for a moment. The illustration of Figure 11-1 shows, at the top, a wave being sampled just two times per period. This is called a "lucky" sampling since the triangular wave shown dotted is a reasonable approximation of the original sine wave.

In the middle example we have an "unlucky" sampling. In this case the sample is taken at the same rate as before. However, we happened to catch the wave precisely at the zero crossing every time. The two-sample-per-wave rate can completely lie to us and tell us that the amplitude of the wave is zero.

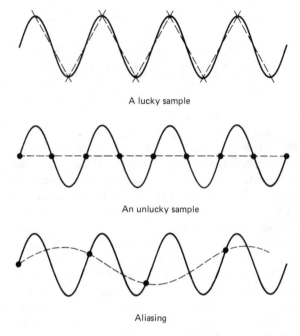

A lucky sample

An unlucky sample

Aliasing

Figure 11-1. Sampling Theory.

When the sampling rate is less than a half-wave period, we can obtain "alias-ing," as shown in the bottom illustration. In this case, what is actually a high-frequency wave is interpreted as a low-frequency wave. As a matter of fact, the "aliased" wave is precisely as far below the two-sample-per-wave point as the actual wave is above it. In general, any digital technique must incorporate an anti-aliasing filter that cuts off somewhat below the two-sample-per-wave point to prevent this effect.

With the cutoff frequency of the telephone system set at 3 kHz, we see that a digital sampling scheme must operate at something in excess of 6 kHz. Obviously, it is economically desirable to operate at the lowest possible digitization rate since the sending of the digital information uses up the capabilities of the system. After some extensive and very exhaustive studies, the Bell System came to the conclusion that the most economic rate at which to digitize voice is 8 kHz. Fig-ure 11-2 shows a 3-kHz wave sampled at an 8-kHz rate. It may be seen that the dotted waveform is not too good a representation of the original wave. Further-more, it may be seen that the error pattern repeats itself every four cycles of the 3-kHz wave. This means that a 3,000/4 = 750-Hz error component is introduced by the sampling process.

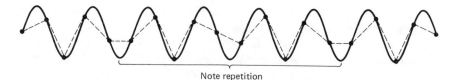

Note repetition

Figure 11-2.

It should be noted in this regard that the 3-KHz energy is attenuated 6 db by the telephone system (typically) and, furthermore, that the energy in the human voice is typically low at the 3-kHz level (except on the unvoiced sounds). The unvoiced sounds are noise anyway; therefore, the distortion introduced by such digitization is considered acceptable. As a matter of fact, most of the time that one talks over a long distance circuit, the voices are digitized. You can judge for yourself whether the degradation is acceptable.

Obviously, one of the next questions that arises regarding the digitization of speech is the question of how many discrete steps are required. If the data is to be sent in serial format, the number of bits to be sent for any given sample period is a product of the sampling rate times the number of bits in the sample. An 8-bit binary word can describe any number between 0 and 255; therefore, the 8-bit word has a *dynamic range* of 255:1 in voltage, or 48 db, assuming that the steps are linear. Sent in serial format and without the overhead of start and stop and parity bits, an 8-bit sample combined with an 8-kHz sampling rate amounts to 8 X 8,000 = 64,000 bits per second.

Presuming that the necessary circuitry can be provided with sufficient stability for the conversion, the fidelity of the conversion that can be attained is unlimited. At 16 bits, for example, the binary word can represent any of 65,535 numbers. In this case the dynamic range is 96.33 db. Nowadays the very finest studio recording is done by digitizing the sound on tape at a 50-kHz rate and at a 16-bit word level. This is the current state of the art in high fidelity, and the tapes sound absolutely beautiful. The tapes can go from a deafening roar to absolute silence, and the recordings do not deteriorate with playing until the wear proceeds to the point where a 0 is mistaken for a 1.

The extreme fidelity of digital recording will probably see this product emerge as *the* form of hi-fi in the next few years. However, it carries a penalty if the digital data is to be placed in semiconductor memory. The sad truth is that the system is producing 16 X 50,000 = 800,000 bits/second. A typical 8-bit microprocessor can address only about 65,536 bytes (8-bit words) directly. If we assume that 32 K bytes were available for storage, then the unit would be able to store about 1/3 of a second of hi-fi.

With a recording medium such as magnetic tape the huge bit count is no significant problem on either streaming tape or a cassette or one of the disks in which a laser is used to blast a tiny pit for a 1 and a zero is the absence of a pit. Unfortunately, these are serial access devices. Now music is typically played in a serial access mode; we seldom want to hear a particular passage without the music that preceded it. However, in the case of a digitized speech machine, the announcement we would like to output may be at the far end of the tape and we would not particularly care to wait for 3.5 minutes while the tape spools through fast forward to get to our desired passage.

If we back off from the hi-fi levels and use an 8-bit word for speech and an 8-kHz sampling rate, we find that our 32 kbytes would hold 4 seconds of speech, or about 10 words. A 1-megabyte bubble memory would hold 125 seconds of speech, or about 400 words. It is obvious that if a random access medium is required, then a certain amount of data processing and compression is necessary. It is precisely in the area of data processing that digital computers shine. For this reason, the analog-to-digital conversion is usually performed fairly early in the process. This has several advantages. First of all, unlike analog log op amps, digital converters are relatively insensitive to such factors as temperature and supply voltage. Secondly, once the A/D conversion has been accomplished, no further errors are introduced into the system, except for those that are a designed-in part of the process.

In actual practice, most of the A/D converters actually function by using a D/A converter and comparing the output with the signal to be digitized. We shall therefore treat this form of converter first.

THE D/A CONVERTER

There are a number of formats that can be used to assemble a D/A converter. We shall first show a pair of the more common types to illustrate the operation and to give us an opportunity to discuss some of the fabrication problems. The types discussed are the types generally used in the audio frequency range. The superfast "flash" types used for video conversion are usually too expensive for this type of application if they have sufficient resolution.

Figure 11-3 shows one of the simplest forms of D/A converters. The op amp U1 is configured as a current-to-voltage converter that also provides a stable low-impedance voltage output. A series of transistors are provided with resistive loads between the V+ reference and the summing junction of U1. The transistors act purely as switches, with the current supplied being determined by the resistance value of the collector load resistor. R is the scaling resistor that establishes the ratio of the current-to-voltage conversion.

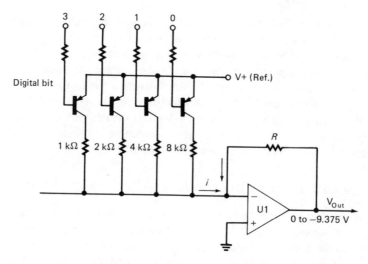

Figure 11-3. A simple D/A converter.

It may be seen that the resistors are arranged in descending binary sequence; therefore, the value for bit 4 would be 500 Ω. If we assume that V+ = 10 V and the transistor has a 1-V forward drop, we see that this would put a current of (10 – 1)/500 Ω = 0.018 A on the summing junction. If we wished to have this provide an output of –10 V, we see that R = 555.6 Ω would be required. The unit would then be capable of providing an output of 0.000 to –9.375 V in –0.625 V steps, according to the binary code present on bits zero through 3. Note that the input would be inverted or active-low since the PNP transistor switches turn ON when the base is taken low.

One of the problems with this type of structure is that the transistors draw widely differing currents. In the zero bit, the transistor will draw only something like 1.156 mA and the forward drop of the transistor will be considerably lower than 1 V, whereas the bit 3 transistor will be drawing 9 mA and the forward drop could be 1 V (note that with good switching transistors the forward drops would actually be lower than this, but the principle remains). These differences mean that the resistors in the chain would have to be tweaked away from the theoretical values in order to make the steps even. This helps. However, with changing temperature the accuracy still remains a problem since the higher current-drawing transistors will get hotter.

Converters of this type are sometimes fabricated in monolithic form with the individual transistor emitter and collector area proportioned in binary sequence to equalize the forward drop and temperature response. However, something like 6 bits, where the highest current (and therefore the highest transistor area) would be 32 times as great as the smallest, represents about the maximum practical resolution that would be achievable with this form of construction.

The unit as configured will output a negative voltage. If a positive output is required, this can be obtained by following U1 with a unity gain inverting amplifier. As another alternative, the feed network could be reconfigured to operate from the negative voltage reference and U1 would then output a positive voltage. In this configuration, however, each of the switching transistors would have to be level shifted to operate from conventional positive logic levels.

THE LADDER NETWORK D/A CONVERTER

One mechanism that will free the device from some of the natural limitations of the graded current device is the ladder network D/A, illustrated in Figure 11-4. In this circuit, a ladder attenuator is used for regulating the contributions from subsequent stages so that all of the transistors can operate at the same level. This greatly alleviates the problem of equalizing the forward drops. A second and somewhat less obvious advantage is that all of the resistors have small and rather modest values. This is of great advantage in monolithic device construction since it is difficult to place either very large or very small resistors on the same silicon chip. In order to understand the operation of this device, let us first examine the nature of the ladder network.

As shown in the figure, the main body of the ladder consists of 5-K resistors in the ladder leg and 10-K resistors in the ladder rungs. You will note that the extreme right end and left end are somewhat different, as shall be explained shortly.

Starting at the inverting input of U1, we note a 10-K resistor. The action of U1 will keep the end of this resistor at ground potential through the feedback current. This 10 K is therefore electrically in parallel with the 10 K that descends vertically from A. The two resistors in parallel represent 5 K, and this added in series to the 5-K resistor between A and B adds up to 10 K. This 10 K is of course in parallel with the 10 K vertically below B, which of course adds up again to 5 K. This resistance taken in series with the 5 K between B and C adds up again to 10 K, and so forth.

If we consider any "rung" on the ladder, we see that the sum of the resistances to the right is 10 K and the sum of the resistances to the left is also 10 K no matter which rung we choose. The ends of the ladder have to be modified so that they will look like the central rungs. At the right-hand end, this was done by using two resistors essentially in parallel. At the left-hand end, this was done by simply reducing the 10 K to 5 K. The extra 10 K is called the *termination*.

Next let us consider the overall system operation. It can be seen that each of the ladder rungs has been fitted with a constant current generator and a switch.

This generator could be in the form of a voltage-to-current converter. In our example, the current generator always supplies either 3×10^{-4} A or zero current. At the bottom of the illustration we observe that with A closed the op amp will receive 1/3 of the generator current. One-third flows in the "rung" and the other third flows in the left-hand portion of the network.

In the next lowest example, B is closed and A is open (the resistor symbols have been left off for clarity). We note that the current divides again in thirds on rung B and divides symmetrically to the right-hand side of rung A. Therefore,

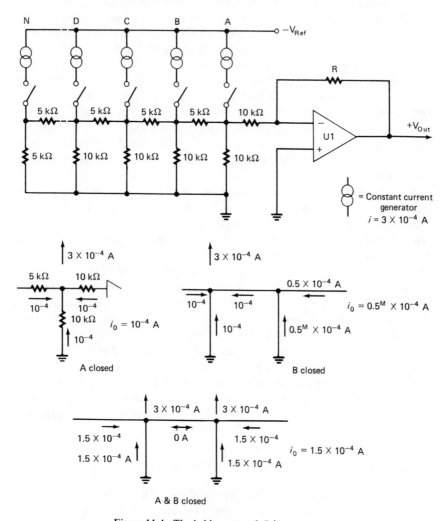

Figure 11-4. The ladder network D/A converter.

generator B delivers exactly half as much current to U1 as A does. This tells us that the most significant bit is adjacent to the op amp and least significant bit is the most remote.

It is fairly easy to see that the circuit will provide currents in binary sequence from any one generator. However, it is not so obvious that it will provide the binary sequency when more than one switch is closed. In the bottom illustration, we see the results when switches A and B are closed. Here we see that the current through the 5-K resistor is canceled and the output is in fact 1.5 times as great as would be obtained from A alone. Without belaboring the point, it can be shown that the closing of switches down the line does in fact increase the current in binary sequence, depending upon which switches are closed. The reason for this is that the voltage across the rung increases with distance from the output and with respect to the more significant switches that are closed.

Let us suppose that all of the switches are closed. The output current from the network will be lower than twice the current from rung A alone by the current of one least significant bit. If we assume that the LSB is negligibly small, then for the values in our example the current into U1 will be 2×10^{-4} A. Thus the voltage across A will be 2 V. The voltage at the LSB end of the ladder will be half again as great, or 3 V. This represents the compliance range of the constant current generators.

It can be seen that the construction of a D/A of this type from discrete components or even from op amps and transistors would not be a trivial task particularly if great temperature stability was required. However, converters of this type have become available in single chip monolithic form for prices less than $10. At that rate it is both impractical and uneconomical to actually construct a device of this type rather than using a commercially available unit.

The advantages of this type unit are considerable when compared to the simple D/A of Figure 11-3. For one thing, there is no compelling influence to limit the resolution that is attainable, except for problems of size and economics. Another factor is that all of the elements are relatively modest in proportion. The resistors are all in easily attainable values and the repetition makes it possible to obtain a high level of reproducibility.

With regard to speed, either of the two types of D/A can be made to be relatively fast. The switches can all be set simultaneously and the limits on speed are principally set by the slow rate of the op amp since the switches are generally much faster.

ACCURACY

The errors found in a D/A converter can be classified in several ways, as shown in Figure 11-5. The first and most obvious limitation is the resolution error. When one wishes to present a given voltage, the degree of the approximation is

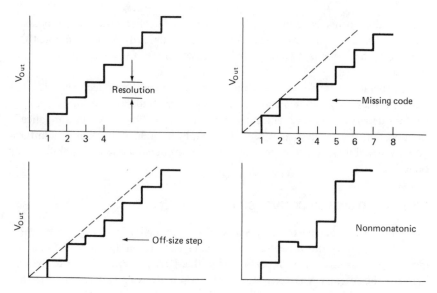

Figure 11-5. Types of D/A errors.

limited by the resolution or the least significant bit size. This varies in the manner shown:

Bits	Min Step
4	0.0625 V/V_{max}
5	0.03125
6	0.015625
7	0.0078125
8	0.00390625
9	0.00195312
10	0.000976562
11	0.000488281
12	0.00024414

Commercial units are available with resolutions down to 16 bits. However, it may be seen that as the resolution rises above 8 bits, the device is rapidly becoming a high-precision instrument and is therefore more expensive. Low-cost monolithic single-chip D/A's are available in 6-, 8- and 10-bit resolutions. The higher resolution units are generally hybrid types that are larger and considerably more expensive. The accuracy of the monolithic types is generally enhanced by automatic laser trimming of the resistors prior to packaging.

The other forms of errors are shown in the lower illustrations. It is possible that the device can have missing codes, off-size steps, and may be nonmonatonic in performance, that is, a commanded increase can result in an actual decrease in the output.

In general, most modern D/A units are guaranteed to an accuracy of ± 1/2 LSB, meaning that they will have no errors in monotonicity. Furthermore, they will not depart from the design slope by more than 1/2 bit. Such performance is so good that it scarcely makes sense to attempt to build a "homebrew" unit, especially if stability over temperature range is considered along with stability over time.

DIGITAL-TO-SPEECH CONVERSION

Obviously, once the speech has been converted to digital format, it is eventually desired to convert the processed digital data back to an analog waveform. In most cases, this conversion is performed with a D/A converter similar to the one used for the original A/D conversion. This is not always precisely true since the speech processing can, on occasion, entail a change in number of bits. However, the more usual case is that the same number of bits is used in reconstructing the speech as was employed in the original digitization. Obviously, the D/A can be used to drive an audio amplifier to accomplish this task. A low-pass filter is usually interposed between the D/A and the audio amplifier to remove the sharp corners of the steps in the output waveform. This stepping action is similar to that shown for the digital DTMF generator of Figure 4-7.

THE A/D CONVERTER

As noted earlier, most of the A/D converters used for audio frequency conversion really consist primarily of a D/A converter and a comparator that compares the input voltage with the output of the D/A. Figure 11-6 shows such an arrange-

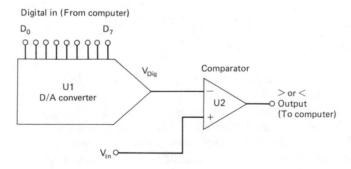

Figure 11-6. The basic A/D.

ment. In this illustration, we have assumed that a computer can output digital data to the D/A and can input the one bit that tells it whether the D/A output is greater than or less than the value of V_{in}. For the moment, we shall consider that the logic required to operate the A/D function is contained in the computer software. In actual practice, we shall see eventually that it is generally necessary to contain the operating program in hardware for voice digitization.

There are a variety of strategies that can be used to make such an A/D track an input voltage that is varying with time. From a programming standpoint, the simplest and also the slowest is simply to increment the input data in steps of one LSB from zero and to test after each increment whether the D/A output had exceeded the value of V_{in}. For an 8-bit converter, this could occupy as many as 255 tries if the value of V_{in} was equal to the maximum. On the average, it would require 128 tries.

Let us presume that we are using a Motorola 6800 processor and that we are driving the D/A through a PIA (Peripheral Interface Adapter). If the address of the PIA requires extended addressing (as it usually will), it would require 5 usec to output each new increment to the PIA, assuming a 1-MHz clock. Next, it is necessary to load the accumulator from another PIA port to determine whether the comparator has flipped (for another 4 usec). If the comparator is not exclusively in command of the PIA, we may have to complement (2 usec) OR with a mask (2 usec), recomplement (2 usec), and compare (2 usec). If the result was not attained we would increment (2 usec) and branch back (4 usec). The total takes 25 usec per step and 128 steps would require 3.2 msec. This would suffice for 2 samples/wave, digitizing a 117-Hz signal. Obviously, a full-scale swing would reduce the frequency to about 59 Hz, which is far too slow for anything like speech.

As a matter of fact, there are a number of steps left out of this example, which tend to slow the process further. It should be noted that the assumed example represents a machine language program. If the micro had had to stop and interpret the language in each line of a program in Basic or Fortran, the program would have run slower by a factor of at least 10 and perhaps as much as a hundred. Speech digitization requires compact machine language coding if one is going to attempt to run on an ordinary 8-bit microprocessor. Even with the fastest running program, these machines have little speed left to spare for speech digitization.

THE SUCCESSIVE APPROXIMATION STRATEGY

Counting up from the bottom in least significant bit steps is obviously not a winning strategy. A considerably better one is presented in flow chart form in Figure 11-7. In this technique we try the largest step first and then determine whether the D/A voltage is higher than the V_{in}. If it is we subtract out the last addition. If it is not we leave it in place and try the next smallest bit. Even though the run time through the loop 2-3-2 is longer than the simple increment this routine saves a considerable amount of time because one tries each bit in the D/A only once, that is, it takes only eight tries on any conversion.

The particular program shown in nitty-gritty detail on Figure 11-7 has been used by the writer with great success on a Motorola 6802 processor. It takes advantage of both the powerful indexed addressing of the chip and the presence of two accumulators. The routine is fast enough to work up to about 1 kHz with reasonable fidelity if a sample-and-hold is employed. This is a great speed for capturing one-shot transients and servo responses, but you can see that it is too slow by nearly an order of magniude to be really useful for speech digitizing.

Figures 11-8 and 11-9 show several of the output waveforms of the D/A in homing in on the value of V_{in}. The Applesoft program is similar to an actual A/D program; however, it runs much too slow for speech.

The nitty-gritty detail of this type of program is dependent upon the detailed architecture of the specific microprocessor. For example, the 6502 does not have two accumulators so the trick of keeping track of which bit is being tested must be done with a RAM (random access memory) address. Secondly, the 6502 does not have the powerful index addressing scheme possessed by the 6800 family; that is, any location in memory cannot be accessed directly from the index register. Probably the fastest way for storing in a long string of memory on the 6502 is via indirect addressing with the current addressed stored in RAM.

On this subject, it is very difficult to guess apriori how fast a given microprocessor will run this scheme. The fact that the 8080 uses an 8-MHz crystal whereas the 6800 and the 6500 families use 4 MHz does not mean that the program would run faster on an 8080. Only the actual benchmark will prove this and the benchmark is subject to the imagination and programming skills of the programmer.

Obviously, the 6802B version, which uses a 10-MHz crystal and operates at a 2.5-MHz clock, will run it 2.5 times as fast as a 6802 system with a 1-MHz clock. However, this means that the entire system must be constructed with 200-nsec memories (or perhaps 150 nsec) and these are premium price parts. For speech digitization, a large memory is required; 32K bits is insufficient. The premium processor and memory (including EPROM) make the unit rather expensive. You will not find modestly priced units such as the Apple II+ thus equipped.

THE TRACKING A/D

A further improved strategy stems from the fact that in human speech, the amplitude decreases with increasing frequency; as a matter of fact, it falls off just about as the reciprocal of frequency. The time rate of change of voltage on a sine wave is given by:

$$d\,(A \sin \omega t) = A\,(\cos \omega t)\,dt * \omega \qquad (11\text{-}1)$$

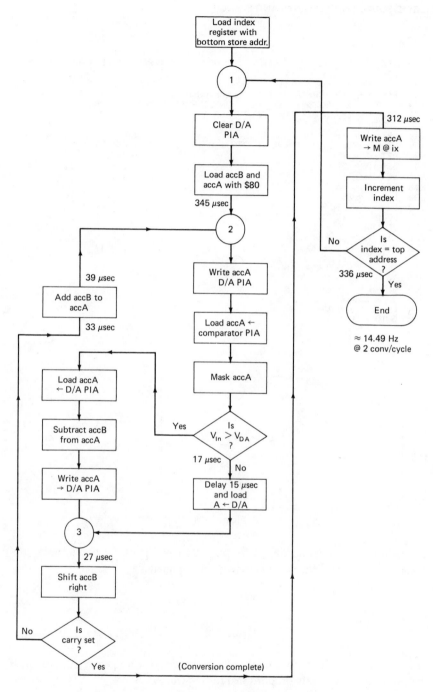

Figure 11-7. An A/D conversion routine (8-bit timing).

175

```
JLIST 100,350

100  REM  THIS PROGRAM SIMULATES A SUCCESSIVE APPROXIMATION A/D CONVERTER
110  HGR2
120  HCOLOR= 3: REM  WHITE
130  POKE  - 12524,0: REM  PLOT BLACK ON WHITE
140  POKE  - 12529,255: REM  PLOT UNIDIRECTIONAL
150  POKE  - 12525,64: REM  PLOT PAGE 2
160  INPUT V
170  LET Y% = 190 - V
180  HPLOT 270,Y% TO 279,Y% TO 279,190 TO 0,190 TO 0,Y% TO 9,Y%
190  LET M% = 25
200  LET N% = 50
205  LET P% = 190
210  LET VA = 85
220  LET X = 85
230  LET Y% = 190 - X
240  HPLOT N%,Y% TO M%,Y% TO M%,P%
250  LET VA = VA / 2
260  LET M% = M% + 25
270  LET N% = N% + 25
275  LET P% = Y%
280  IF N% > 225 THEN  END
290  IF X > V THEN  GOTO 320
300  LET X = X + VA
310  GOTO 230
320  LET X = X - VA
330  GOTO 230
```

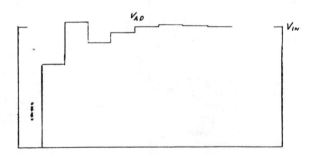

Figure 11-8.

The right-hand term is maximum for $\omega t = 0$ or pi. Thus, for two different frequencies whose amplitudes fall inversely with frequency:

$$A_1\,\omega_1 = A_1\,\frac{\omega_1}{\omega_2} * \omega_2 \qquad (11\text{-}2)$$

$$A_1\,\omega_1 = A_1\,\omega_1 \qquad (11\text{-}3)$$

Thus we see that the time rate of voltage change with frequency is constant if the amplitude is inversely proportional to frequency.

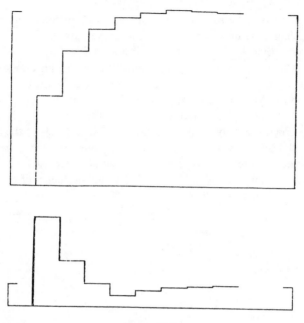

Figure 11-9.

Now, let us suppose that we have a signal that is 10 V peak to peak; that is, $A = 5$ V. Then, at 300 Hz,

$$\frac{dA}{dt} = 5 \text{ V} * 300 * 2 * \text{pi} \tag{11-4}$$

$$= 9{,}425 \text{ V/sec}$$

If this seems a little fast, consider the fact that if the voltage passed linearly from 0 to 5 volts in a time equal to a quarter of a cycle, the rate of change would be

$$5 \text{ V} \div (1/4 \times 1/300 \text{ sec})$$

or 6,000 V/sec. Obviously, the sine wave must cross the axis faster because it slows to zero at the top.

If we are sampling at a rate of 8,000 times per second, the result of equation 11-4 tells us that between samples, the voltage could not have changed by more than 9,425/8,000 = 1.18 V. An 8-bit D/A operating on a 10-V peak-to-peak range has minimum steps of 10 V/256 = 0.039 V. Thus, we need only search through 1.18 V/0.039 V = 31 steps, or 5 bits, to find the value of V_{in}.

The strategy would be to read the comparator first to determine whether the value of V_{in} had gone up or down. The successive approximation always ends with V_{ad} higher than V_{in} so that if V_{in} had not changed at all, the comparator would read "down." If the voltage had gone up, one would then read the current contents of the D/A and add 31 (hex $1F) and write to the D/A. Thereafter, one would begin a 6-step successive approximation from the top down with the contents of the B accumulator initially set at $20 (decimal 32). It can be seen that the top-down successive approximation is a mirror image of the one on Figures 11-8 and 11-9 and would wind up with V_{ad} one half step lower than V_{in}.

This routine requires that one have two distinct successive approximation routines, one that operates from the top down and another that operates from the bottom up. We have substituted a sequence of:

Operation	μsec
Read comparator	4
Mask	2
Conditional branch	4
Load B	2
Read D/A	4
Subtr./Add	2
Total time	18 μsec

This takes the place of two circuits of the 2-3-2 loop, which take 39 μsec each, for a saving of 60 μsec. This would boost the speed up to 1,811 Hz.

It may be seen that the loop does not close on this calculation. The algorithm is capable of sampling in 276-μsec intervals, with a 1.18-V span. However, the voltage could change by 9,425 V/sec $*$ 276 $*$ 10^{-6} sec = 2.60 V. Although we have speeded up the conversion by 21%, it is still a long way from the required speed.

If one considers the possibility of reducing the number of passes through the loop even further, say to 4 loops, the loop would run in something like 206 μsec, during which time the voltage could change by 1.94 V, compared to a D/A range of 0.585 V.

Although the tracking program can be made somewhat faster than the successive approximation routine, it can be seen that it is still a long way from being able to do the trick.

DELTA MODULATION

In the limit when only 1 step up or down is searched, the tracking scheme becomes a form of *delta modulation*. As a matter of fact, any of the tracking schemes can be considered to be a form of delta modulation. In the least of these schemes, we have the overhead associated with advancing the storage address and testing for end of memory, which amounts to 24 μsec. If we reduce the routine to read/mask/branch (13 μsec) and then read the D/A and add or subtract 1 bit, this works out to another 13 μsec or so, for a total of 50 μsec. During this period, the voltage can change by 0.471 V, or roughly ten times a single step. This is still not an answer; as a matter of fact, it is less close than the answer; given by the successive approximation method.

The nature of the problem of speech digitization is such that it is very sensitive to the detailed operation of the particular processor and the ingenuity of the programmer. Therefore, an actual proof that a software-driven A/D for speech digitization is beyond the capabilities of existing microprocessors cannot be given. However, it seems likely, on the face of the preceding analysis, that existing processors are 5 to 8 times too slow for software-driven real-time speech digitization.

HARDWARE A/D

If the A/D conversion is carried out in a hardware-driven device, the picture changes somewhat. The cycle then reduces to reading the A/D, writing to memory, and incrementing and testing the memory address. This runs to a total of about 36 μsec. If the A/D can perform a conversion during the increment between the end of a read and the beginning of the next read, the time to be added for the conversion goes to zero and a 6800-family unit could operate at 27,777 conversions per sec. In actual practice, conversions on the order of 18,000/sec have been achieved with a 6502 machine language program in an Apple II+.

Commercially available chips, such as the Analog Device AD7574, feature an average A/D conversion time of 15 μsec. This is faster than the increment and test memory address routine, thereby ensuring that the next reading will be ready when the computer asks for it. The chip is equipped to go across the computer data bus directly since its outputs are tristate devices activated by a chip enable signal that can be derived from the address decoding AND'ed with VMA (in the 6800).

The AD7574 has two lines, labeled $\overline{CS}$ and $\overline{RD}$, which control all operations of the chip. The converter reads these lines as commands. During a conversion, the converter outputs a $\overline{BUSY}$ signal that can be used to inform the computer that a conversion is in process and that data will not be valid until $\overline{BUSY}$ goes high again. Internally, the chip is a successive approximation device that contains its own clock and successive approximation register to permit operation in excess of the data bus speeds.

In terms of addressing, the device can be used in a static RAM mode, a ROM mode, or a slow memory mode. The slow memory mode will work with an 8080,

8085, or an SC/MP, where the $\overline{\text{BUSY}}$ signal is used as a memory ready signal. The 6800 and 6502 have the memory ready control. However, neither will tolerate a wait state of 12 to 15 μsec without losing data; therefore, this mode cannot be used on these processors.

In the ROM interface mode, $\overline{\text{CS}}$ is tied low and the address decoding AND'ed with VMA can be used to generate $\overline{\text{RD}}$. In this case the processor can simply stooge around until $\overline{\text{BUSY}}$ goes high again. In a speech digitizing application, the time can be used to increment and test the new memory address. Any $\overline{\text{RD}}$ initiates a new conversion. In this mode, in effect, the converter and the processor operate in parallel and the conversion speed is limited only by the slowest of the two. In the case of the 6802, this would be the processor:

Operation	μsec
Read A/D	4
Indexed store	6
Increment IX	4
Compare IX	5
Conditional Br	4
Total time	23 μsec

CONCLUSION

At the time of this writing, the state-of-the-art of monolithic A/D converters and microprocessors is about even; the processor is not held up waiting for the A/D, and the A/D does not outrun the processor. A moderately fast A/D will just suffice for digitizing speech, and the processor will be hard pressed to do anything but the housekeeping and data storage operations. No processing in real time is available.

12
Moser Encoding

One of the leading contenders for speech synthesis equipment at the time of this writing is the Moser encoding technique. This system has been licensed to a number of vendors and is found in calculators for the blind (the initial commercial product), arcade games, and and talking chess sets. The voice that emerges in the "heaviest" encoded examples is an extreme monotone and completely expressionless; however, it is very clear and intelligible. First-time listeners will understand numbers and words precisely, although they may deplore the "R2D2" or "martian" sound.

It should be promptly noted that this system is covered by U. S. Patent 4,214,125, issued to Forrest S. Moser* and Richard P. Staudahar of Berkeley, with Staudahar assigning his rights to Moser. The patent is dated July 22, 1980. An initial application was made on January 14, 1974, with continuations filed November 20, 1974 and November 14, 1975. In this text, I have and shall be discussing the Moser technique as presented in the patent. However, no licence to use the technique is implied. The material presented here represents only the writer's interpretation and comments upon the Moser technique with *no authorization* from Dr. Moser.

Dr. Moser became interested in the encoding of speech and "decided to see what could be done." He has accomplished a great deal in terms of compacting data. His output was the first product capable of miniaturization on a single chip and proved to be a powerful spark for the entire market. Unlike the LPC technique developed by TI, Moser encoding is a collage of items with each carried to new extremes. There is something old (differentiation for pre-emphasis, and pitch-period repetition), something new (Moser zero-phase encoding), something borrowed and improved upon (floating-zero two-bit delta modulation), and something blue (X-period zeroing). We shall deal with each of these techniques separately.

Because of the ease of copying computer-based systems (which often are merely running programs for a general-purpose processor chip), many of the originators of such programs lack confidence in the ability of the patent system to adequately protect their investment. The result is the inclusion of some little "hooks" in the software. A more significant level of protection is obtained

---

*38 Somerset Pl., Berkeley, CA 94707.

when the system is reduced to a single custom chip. Usually, several advantages accrue to this approach. The custom hardware is generally smaller and more convenient to use and it can often yield performance advantages compared to general purpose hardware. Furthermore, the software generated for the custom chip will generally not run on general purpose hardware without some alteration. It would not make economic sense to attempt to duplicate the custom hardware; therefore, any small to medium-size user will usually simply buy the chip. The cost of the development is "bundled" in the package.

Chips employing the Moser technique are available from TSI (Telesensory Systems Incorporated) and the National Semiconductor Corp. The TSI Moser chip is a PMOS device with heavy encoding. It operates at a rate of about 1,100 bps and requires minimal memory for a given vocabulary. A single 2K byte EPROM will produce more than 36 seconds of speech. This device is used in a calculator for the blind and a number of telephone response systems, including several developed by the writer. The speech sound is mechanical but very intelligible.

The National Semiconductor Digitalker® operates on a somewhat different philosophy. It would seem that National Semiconductor decided that it is best for the "shoemaker to stick to his last." Since they are a silicon house, they decided to handle the speech quality problem with silicon. The Digitalker is far less heavily encoded than the TSI offering and, as a result, it requires a great deal more memory. National Semiconductor solved this problem by coming up with a very large masked ROM, 128K bytes, which will yield about 2 minutes of speech. The speech is realistic and pleasing and can reproduce recognizable mens, womens or childrens voices.

For the large user this solution poses little problem since the masked ROM is not expensive in large quantity. Unfortunately for the small user, that amount of EPROM is expensive and bulky. Worse still, the masking charge (currently $5,000 or so) and the minimum order (currently 1,000 units) place any sort of custom vocabulary out of reach. National does offer a standard vocabulary suited for control applications with words including a complete number set, a complete alphabet, and items like pounds, degrees, volts, amperes, kilo, etc. Several people have incorporated this relatively inexpensive set into talking controllers or instruments. In some cases, the device spells out words it cannot pronounce.

In both the TSI and the National system, the unit is built of two separate devices, a memory chip (or chips) and a custom processor. The operation of the system is simplicity itself. One simply sends the processor a byte that defines the word or phrase desired. The processor then addresses a look-up table in its memory to find the starting address and length of the phrase. It then generates the string of addresses required for the word or phrase and performs the inverse of the manipulations, which will be described shortly, to derive the code to be sent to an internal D/A converter. An external filter to remove switching noise is required and an external amplifier is generally required.

When one outputs the word-specifying byte and the strobe, the processor takes over and toggles a signal that is maintained as long as the speech processor is busy. Release of this signal can be interpreted as meaning that the speech processor is ready to talk again. Pauses between words or phrases can either be written into the vocabulary or accomplished with a software timing loop. The writer has driven these chips using a 6821 PIA (only half is required). The synthesizer does not occupy the main computer memory bus and operates independently. In between the word commands, which come 2 to 4 times per second (less frequently for phrases), the main computer is free to perform other functions. The Moser machines require less attention and less programming from the main computer than any other type.

THE ENCODING TECHNIQUE

As noted earlier, effective speech digitization had been accomplished as early as the 1950s. However, these were large, cumbersome machines not suited to miniaturization. As the digital computer developed and techniques for sufficiently rapid A/D conversion developed, people began to digitize speech and store the results in a computer with a large memory. Landmark patents in this area are due to Martin (U. S. Pat. 3,588,353) and Ichikawa (U. S. Pat. 3,892,919).

It had long been known that human speech contains redundant information, as witness the restriction of the telephone band to 300 to 3,000 Hz, whereas the human voice normally contains significant energy to 100 Hz (male) and 6,500 Hz (unvoiced sounds). In addition to this, an examination of the spectrograms will show that there are many instances when a given phoneme is generated by repetition of essentially the same pressure wave, either without change or with some simple amplitude shaping. A landmark patent in this area is due to Martin (U. S. Pat. 3,588,353, cited earlier). Dr. Moser set about to develop new techniques for reducing the redundancy in speech even further, using techniques suitable for LSI implementation.

DIFFERENTIATION

The process of speech synthesis, in all of the currently used techniques, begins with someone speaking a word or phrase into a microphone. This is true of even the phoneme techniques. The art has simply not yet progressed to the point where intelligible connected speech can be constructed mathematically; without someone first saying the word, phrase, or sound.

Working on the basis that the majority of the intelligence in speech is carried in the higher-pitched phonemes, Moser differentiates the incoming sound through a conventional RC network. The network shown in Figure 12-1 shows the circuit of a differentiator above and a conventionalized response below. U1 serves to provide a low impedance drive to the differentiator, $R_1 C_1$, and U2 provides an essentially infinite impedance to the filter output. The response does not acutally have a sharp corner at 2.8 kHz, but blends smoothly from the slope to the level section.

The waveform thus derived has a much flatter power spectrum than the original spectrum of the speech. This process is sometimes referred to as *preemphasis*. A similar technique is used in FM mobile radio and in disk recording. In the case of disk recording, it reduces the amplitude of the needle swing on low frequencies so that the needle does not cut into the adjacent groove on a loud low-frequency passage. Of course an inverse filter of low-pass design is required to restore the balance to the sound.

Moser states that the advantage to the differentiation is that a 4-bit digitization after differentiation is just as effective as a 6-bit differentiation of the original voice signal. The 4-bit digitization, of course, describes only 16 levels, and the 6-bit describes 64. This is a significant savings in storage, reducing the stored data to 2/3 of the original value. Stated another way, this represents a compression factor of 1.5.

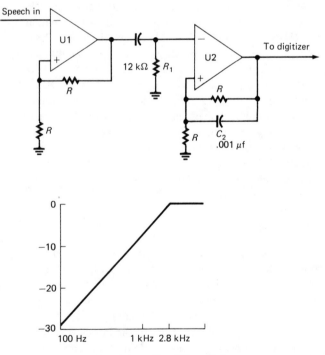

Figure 12-1. The differentiation.

The differentiation can also be done digitally simply by subtracting the first reading from the second and the second from the third, etc. Figure 12-2 shows the synthesized speech waveform of Figure 10-2 (above) and the first difference waveform (below). From the earlier discussion of digitization, it can be seen that this process, when performed digitally, actually is identical to the simplest form of delta modulation.

It was noted that the differentiation should be replaced by integration on reconstruction of the speech; however, this need not require a filter. If the second reading output to the D/A converter is the sum of the first and second and the third is the sum of the first, second, and third, etc., it is readily seen that the process is reversed and the integration is performed simply by adding the delta to the previous sum. Note that this will generally require that the output D/A have more bits than the digitizer used.

In his studies of this technique, Moser examined the possibility that other derivatives, perhaps of higher power, might produce greater compression factors.

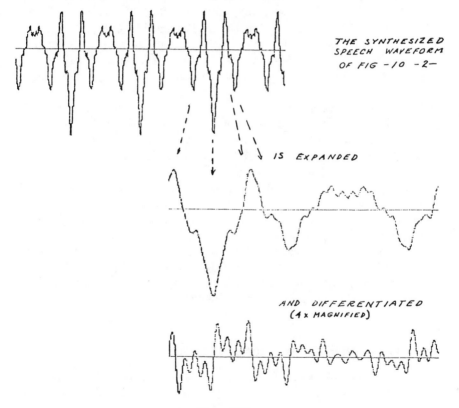

Figure 12-2.

His results were negative and he attributes this to the fact that the normal voice spectrum decreases in power roughly inversely with frequency, thus making the first derivative the flattest in power spectrum.

DIGITIZATION

In his patent, Moser describes his digitization method as proceeding at 10,000 Hz, noting that either faster or slower rates are possible. There is a certain amount of trade-off possible between the number of bits or work width and the digitization rate. For example, an 8-bit word need not be done quite as often as a 6-bit word for the same total harmonic distortion. This is particularly true of a delta modulation scheme. When digitizing a differentiated wave form, increased fidelity tends to go in the direction of the shorter word and the higher sampling rate.

It should be noted that the Moser patent was initially applied for in 1974. Dr. Moser was probably employing instruments with technology dating circa 1970 in the initial work. High-speed, wide-word (8-, 10-, or 12-bit) A/D converters were not very readily available at this time, and have only been on the market at reasonable prices since about 1979. The descriptions and techniques used in the patent reflect the technology available at the time the initial work was performed and are not necessarily representative of what is being done today.

Using currently available high-speed A/D chips, it is not difficult to obtain 8-bit sampling at speech rates. The minimum sampling rate is probably about 8 kHz if a telephone bandwidth is to be considered. Once this data has been stored, it can be mathematically manipulated at the leisure of the operator to transform it into four-level delta modulation.

It should be noted that 16-bit A/D's compatible with the data bus on high-speed wide-word processors, such as the Motorola 68000, are now avaliable. Unfortunately, such setups are terribly expensive at present because the memory is not only twice as wide as an 8-bit machine but also must be made up of premium memory chips with access times of 150 nsec or better if full use is to be made of the processor speed and width. This situation will probably be remedied by "learning curve" price reductions by the mid or late 1980s, and the flexibility of the 16-bit precision (and higher) sampling rates will become available at a lower price.

MULTIPLE PHONEME AND SYLLABLE USAGE

As noted in chapter 10, Moser makes use of phonemes and multiple phonemes in his encoding scheme. And, as a matter of fact, these phonemes are used multiple times in the control vocabulary chip offered by TSI. For example, /p/ is used in *plus, point, amp, up, per,* and *pound.* In this particular vocabulary, Moser used a total of 35 phonemes in 140 different places, thus accounting for a compression factor of 4:1.

Moser states that "depending upon the amount of compression required . . . voiced and unvoiced fricatives, voiced and unvoiced stop consonants and nasal consonants may be stored as phonemes with minimal degradation of the intelligibility of the generated speech."

Through the discussion, Moser stresses the fact that a certain amount of subjective judgment is supplied by the operator in the use of compression techniques. This remains a "fit and file" operation on the part of the operator in both the Moser and the LPC techniques. The result is a function of the skill and artistry of the operator.

The technique also makes use of the words or partial words, which Moser terms "syllables" in a special definition. In this group, for example, "teen" is used in the numbers thirteen to nineteen. "Over" is used in over and overflow, etc. On the control vocabulary chip, the average syllable is used 2.4 times, corresponding approximately to a compression factor of 2.4:1.

It is worthy to note that the amount of compression attainable from these techniques is considerable. But it is also a function of the detailed content of the vocabulary. It is not immediately evident just how much compression can be obtained on a given phrase or word. A skilled operator does acquire an ability to estimate the compression available. However, the user also sometimes has to compromise.

In a machine developed by the writer, the initial try at the custom vocabulary was satisfactory except for the words *code,* which came over the telephone as "toad," *three* which came over as "rhee." Faced with space limitations in the EPROM, we were able to correct *code* but not *three.* We probably could have used a "thuree," "fiuve," and "niyun," (as telephone operators used to be trained), but we found that the "rhee" was regularly copied by users as "3," and we had few objections about intelligibility. In developing a product such as this, everyone involved becomes an art, music, and diction critic and tends to be more demanding than the eventual user.

PITCH-PERIOD REPETITION

We earlier touched upon the fact that voiced sounds will sometimes have a fairly repetitive waveform characterized by a nonmoving formant spectrum. The fact that a single pitch period could be repeated through the entire phoneme or a part of it without loss of intelligibility was first reported by A. E. Rosenburg in the Journal of the Acoustical Society of America (Vol. 44, 1968).

Figure 10-3 shows a spectrum in which most of the sounds are candidates for this sort of treatment. The /e/ of the final *eight* would obviously require some change because of the moving middle formant. Moser points out that ideally, the number of repetitions should be as large as possible. As a practical matter, no significant degradation is generally found for three or less repetitions, and sometimes as many as ten repetitions are possible.

The large compression obtainable is very attractive when n exceeds three. One simply stores the detailed waveform with the instruction that it is to be repeated n times. The compression factor approaches n but does not quite reach it because of the overhead required for repetition period and possible amplitude shaping.

In this connection, it is noteworthy that Moser's instructions for the initial recording specify that the speaker read the initial message "in a nearly monotone voice." The monotone actually serves several purposes. First of all, it enlarges the possible value of n; secondly, it reduces the amplitude shaping.

As a practical matter, looking at Figure 10-1, we find that the /eh/ runs only 11 cycles, the /v/ runs 7, and the /n1/ only 10 in this sample of connected speech. All three are heavily shaped in this nonmonotone utterance. The /o1/ in the final *two* has the pitch droop 40% because the word is used to terminate the sentence. Had the word been used in the middle of the sentence pitch would have been approximately constant. If the speech is not connected, the absence of the trail-off on pitch is not particularly noticeable. However, in connected speech, the final *two* has to trail in pitch or a distinctly monotone effect is produced.

Pitch is used in a variety of ways to allocate emphasis, and can change the entire meaning of a sentence. Try reading the following sentences with the italic word slightly elevated in pitch:

> Did you push *that* button?
> Did *you* push that button?
> Did you *push* that button?

You can see that the mere change in pitch can change the entire meaning of the sentence. If you read aloud, you would also note that the underlined word was also slightly louder. If read in a monotone, and there is more than one button or more than one person or more than one level of force, the sentence is ambiguous if it is out of the context of additional speech.

Sometimes a rising or falling pitch can turn a declaration into an interrogation. For example, the statement "You did" can have two entirely different meanings.

> Husband: I got my bonus today!
> Wife: You did?

> Husband: I quit that darn job!
> Wife: You did!

In the first case the response terminates with a rising pitch; the second with a falling pitch. A still different meaning can also come:

> Husband: Who ate the last donut?
> Wife: You did!

In the latter case the pitch and volume is elevated on "You."

Moser notes that the pitch can be changed about 10% without appreciably affecting the sound quality or intelligibility. This corresponds to about a whole tone sharp or flat. You might want to try the following exercise to get a feel for the range. The writer has found that a two-tone range (± 26%) seems closer to the limit.

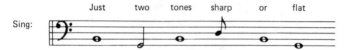

This range is adequate for a limited amount of expression. It is consonant with the trailing two, but would certainly not suffice for an exasperated: "You did what?" A clearly intelligible bass utterance becomes "the singing chipmunk" when raised a full octave.

In the original TSI offering, Moser opted for the monotone without pitch control. Instead, he attempted to take the curse off the monotone by supplying a 2% pitch variation (or tremolo) at a 3-Hz rate. Moser says: ". . . this oscillation is not intelligible as such in the output sound but it results in the *disappearance* of the annoying monotone quality of the speech that would be present if the clock frequency were constant." Had Moser said "reduction" rather than "disappearance" the writer would be a bit more in agreement. The principal criticism of the Moser encoded device used by the writer has been with regard to the mechanical monotone of the speech, not the intelligibility.

The National Digitalker does include pitch variation and control, and produces very realistic speech. However, this is accomplished at a considerable cost in storage space. First of all, the value of n is generally reduced because of use of the phoneme with changing pitch. Secondly, the same phoneme may have to be included twice to accommodate pitch ranges separated by more than 25%.

In the generation of the model waveforms, rather than to simply select one pitch period to represent the phoneme, Moser actually used a more sophisticated routine in which the wavetrain was broken into parts three pitch periods long. These were overlaid in some manner that is not too clearly described in the patent. However, the result is a compression factor of three (or so) in the practical case.

There are several mechanisms that can be employed to obtain a filtering effect for noisy waveforms. If each digital sample corresponding to a particular time slot in a pitch period is multiplied by the identical digital sample in successive pitch periods until N multiplications have been performed, and then one extracts the Nth root of the result, those features of the waveform that are consistent and regular will rapidly emerge and those that are irregular will rapidly shrink. This is termed *autocorrelation,* a process commonly employed to extract repetitive signals buried in noise. It has the problem that, like the Fourier transform, it requires a lot of multiplication. It also requires a lot of root extraction. It is therefore very time consuming.

Another problem with autocorrelation is that it works best when one has a precise knowledge of the repetition period or at least knows that the repetition period is precisely constant. When the task is to dig the radar or sonar data out of the noise, this is generally the case. With human speech, however, the problem becomes something different since the pitch generally has phase noise that causes the pitch period to "jitter." If one synchronizes on the major spike for each pitch period in the sample processing, the data immediately following will overlay quite well. However, features toward the end of the period will become progressively more jittery. The technique that follows gives an alternative that is perhaps superior.

MOSER ZERO-PHASE ENCODING

In our discussion of the Fourier transform, it was noted that we had neglected to calculate the phase angle. In order to really fit together the harmonics to reproduce the original waveshape, the phase angle must be known. The sine and cosine functions are actually identical except for a phase difference of $90°$. The phase angle could have been calculated in Figure 9-6 with the statement:

   165 PH = ATN (A/B)   (This would not run in Applesoft)
       or:
   163 AN = A/B
   165 PH = ATN (AN)   (This would)
(Applesoft does not accept transcendentals in which the argument requires calculation.)

In our discussion of the operation of the human ear, we noted that, at least for well-separated tones, the ear does not seem to mix. It behaves instead more like an array of separate receivers on a one-receiver-per-tone basis. As a result, the ear is not particularly sensitive to phase relationships. This property was used to advantage by Dr. Moser for data compaction.

In Figure 12-3 we see two very different waveshapes overlaid. The interesting thing about this is that both are made up of exactly the same components, just as one could use a set of toy blocks to build either a garage or a tower. In both cases, the constituents are the first seven components of a square wave.

If one performs a Fourier analysis of a square wave, which is mirror symmetrical about the zero axis and crosses the zero axis in the positive-going direction at $Q = 0°$, one finds that the resulting data has no even-order harmonics, and the odd-order harmonics will all calculate with all of the cosine terms equal to zero. If one then reassembles the first seven terms by adding only the sine terms, one obtains the dotted curve shown. This is a reasonable approximation of the original square wave.

On the other hand, if one uses the very same coefficients but reassembles them using a cosine series, one obtains the odd-looking peaky curve shown solid in the figure. Since the cosine of zero is one, we see that the summation at zero is equal to the sum of all the coefficients. Therefore, this curve gets much taller than the sine curve in which the coefficients never all add up. In the example, the peaky curve is 1.778 times as tall as the square form. As harmonics are added, the square form gets squarer and the peaky form evolves into a triangle.

Interestingly, if these two waves were played through a good loudspeaker, you would hear no difference since the ear hears the components separately and not the summation. Of course, this would not be true of the loudspeaker itself, which would have to be capable of responding to the higher peaks which, in the limit, would be twice as high in voltage as the square wave. As a matter of fact, loudspeakers being the devices they are, possessed of mechanical inertia, the actual motion of the speaker cone as a function of time with a square wave applied is a triangular wave; however, the launched pressure wave in the air is a square wave.

Now, if we return to our synthesized speech waveform of Figure 12-2 and elsewhere (the /eh/ of "782"), and look at the manipulation performed to obtain this waveform on Figure 10-2, we see that the waveform was assembled using the cosine series without regard to the actual phase angles of the components (which were not given in the spectrum of Figure 10-1 and are therefore unknown). This waveform was therefore approximately Moser *zero-phase encoded.*

Now, since the cosine is symmetrical about the zero point, the waveforms thus encoded will also be symmetrical about the zero point. Moser points out that this makes possible a compression factor of two in the data since any symmetrical shape can be produced by encoding only one-half. A data table for the first half of the wave could be read from bottom to top and then top to bottom to reproduce the entire wave with only half the data.

If the spectrum contained only odd harmonics (3, 5, 7 . . .), the resulting waveform would be possessed of fourfold symmetry and only one-quarter of the waveform would have to be encoded. Even-order harmonics tend to destroy

```
JLIST 100,400

100  REM  THIS PROGRAM PLOTS THE ADDITION OF THE FIRST  THRU SEVENTH HARMO
     NICS OF A SQUAREWAVE.
110  HGR2
120  HCOLOR= 3: REM  WHITE
130  POKE  - 12524,0: REM  PLOT BLACK ON WHITE
140  POKE  - 12529,255: REM  PLOT UNIDIRECTIONAL
150  POKE  - 12525,64: REM  PLOT PAGE 2
155 X = 0
160 Q = .0450407 * X
165 A = 3 * Q:B = 5 * QC = 7 * Q
170 Y = .63662 *  SIN (Q) + .21221 *  SIN (A) + .12732 *  SIN (B) + .0909 *
      SIN (C)
180 Y% = (Y * 85) + 95
190  HPLOT X,Y%
200 X = X + 1
210  IF X < 280 THEN  GOTO 160
220 X = 0
230 Q = .0450407 * X
235 A = 3 * Q:B = 5 * Q:C = 7 * Q
240 Y = .63662 *  COS (Q) + .21221 *  COS (A) + .12732 *  COS (B) + .0909 *
      COS (C)
245 Y% = (Y * 85) + 95
247  IF X = 0 THEN  GOTO 255
250  HPLOT M,N TO X,Y%
255 M = X:N = Y%
260 X = X + 1
270  IF X < 280 THEN  GOTO 230
280  HPLOT 0,95 TO 279,95
290  END
```

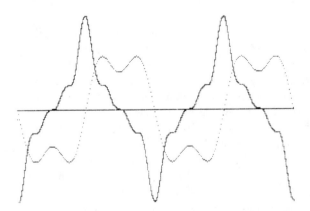

Figure 12-3.

the fourfold symmetry; therefore, this reduction is not feasible in speech digitization. In the actual Moser technique, the algorithm is arranged to place the maximum in the center of the window with minimal energy at the edges to maximize the effectiveness of the last two techniques.

X-PERIOD ZEROING

With the phase-adjusted waveform arranged to have the peak in the center of the window, it may be seen that the beginning and end of the window contain very little energy and therefore contribute little to the overall sound. Moser experimented with setting these low-amplitude portions to zero. This was done on the basis of holding the output D/A at a constant level for a fraction (X) of the pitch period. Moser experimented with a range of X from 0.25 to 0.75, and concluded that X less than 0.6 gave results indistinguishable from the original. Above 0.75 he notes that the speech sound "mushy" but is still intelligible. In the original product, X was arbitrarily selected at 0.5 for a compression factor of 2. Of all of the characteristics of the output oscillograms of a Moser-encoded (TSI) machine, this is one of the most evident. The output voltage comes in bursts, with flat spots in between.

Moser also notes that a mechanism for "rests" is useful in that normal speech is characterized by periods of silence. Note that the /t/ of Figure 10-1 runs a full 140 msec if the tail on the /e/ is zeroed, and at least 100 msec without other zeroing. The /t/ is more than 66% silence and the instruction to stall for 100 msec can be written with far fewer bits than are required for a table of zeros.

Moser notes that X-period zeroing does not apply to unvoiced sounds since it would introduce a pitch-period component. This would, for example, turn an /s/ into a /z/. However, some of these sounds are frequently associated with pauses. Moser notes that in his control vocabulary, about 80% of the phonemes are half-period zeroed, thus resulting in a compression factor of 1.8. In addition, the stop consonants used to terminate a word will all have a pause on the order of 100 msec. Even more lengthy pauses are found between words and sentences. Therefore, an "idle for n msec" command is an important part of the data compression operation.

DELTA MODULATION

We have noted earlier that delta modulation is an important technique for data compression since even differentiated speech waveforms tend to undergo relatively smooth changes between levels. However, not all forms of delta modulation are created equal. After experimenting, Moser concluded that a form called *floating-zero, two-bit delta modulation* produces little or no degradation of speech quality or intelligibility. In this type of modulation or encoding, small changes (less than 2 levels) are reproduced exactly, and large changes are accomodated by slewing three levels per digitization. The technique was implemented in computer software on the differentiated, zero-phase-adjusted and X-period-zeroed data.

Moser began by digitizing with a differentiated wave, and the wave was digitized at 4 bits, describing 16 binary levels. These 4-bit words are eventually replaced by a set of 2-bit words describing the delta modulation. The 2-bit words, of course, can describe only four levels. However, Moser uses both the current value and the preceding value to cause a level change. The values are determined from the following table (values are shown in decimal for clarity):

MODULATION LOOK-UP

Previous change (required)	Current Change (required)	Output Action change (actual)
3	3	3
3	2	1
3	1	0
3	0	-1
2	3	3
2	2	1
2	1	0
2	0	-1
1	3	1
1	2	0
1	1	-1
1	0	-3
0	3	1
0	2	0
0	1	-1
0	0	-3

It may be seen that this function is very easy to implement in either hardware or software. The binary code for the previous change is shifted left two places and the binary code for the current required change is shifted into the least significant bits. The output can be obtained from a look-up table with 16 entries, using the 4-bit word as the address. This procedure is a prime example of a case where the machine language implementation is much easier to write than a high-level program.

The output can be seen to take on the values -3, -1, 0, 1, and 3. Because of the five levels, it is necessary to use both the previous 2-bit word and the current

2-bit word. It is interesting to note that both $3N$ and $2N$ describe the same sequence; as do $1N$ and $0N$, whose entries are a mirror image. Using this address scheme Moser could have used sixteen different entries in the output table rather than the five he elected to use. The example given by Moser in the patent shows very good tracking, as in Figure 12-4, and Moser notes that the limited slew rate of the delta modulation effectively performs the integration needed to compensate for the differentiation done on the original input. A slightly less complemen-

```
100   REM   THIS PROGRAM SOLVES FOR  CODE FOR FLOATING-ZERO TWO-BIT DELTA MO
      DULATION AND PLOTS DATA AND RESPONSE.
110   HGR2
120   HCOLOR= 3
130   POKE  - 12524,0
140   POKE  - 12529,255
150   POKE  - 12525,64
151   PR# 1
152   PRINT "D","M","B","A","C"
155   REM   PLOT UNIDIRECTIONAL B/W PAGE 2
156   M = 7
157   A = 3
158   X = 2
160   DATA  10,13,14,15,15
170   DATA  13,9,7,5,4
180   DATA  5,7,10,13,10
190   DATA  8,5,3,2,2
210   READ D
220   B = D - M
230   IF B = 3 THEN   GOTO 300
240   IF B = 2 THEN   GOTO 350
250   IF B = 1 THEN   GOTO 400
255   IF B =  - 1 THEN   GOTO 450
257   IF B = 0 THEN   GOTO 1000
260   IF B =  - 2 THEN   GOTO 500
270   IF B =  - 3 THEN   GOTO 550
280   IF B > 3 THEN   GOTO 600
290   IF B < 3 THEN   GOTO 650
300   IF A = 3 THEN C = 3: GOTO 700
310   IF A = 2 THEN C = 3: GOTO 700
320   GOTO 800
350   IF A >  = 2 THEN C = 2:B = 1: GOTO 700
360   C = 1:B = 1: GOTO 700
400   IF A = 3 THEN C = 2: GOTO 700
410   IF A = 2 THEN C = 2: GOTO 700
420   IF A = 1 THEN C = 3: GOTO 700
430   IF A = 0 THEN C = 3: GOTO 700
450   IF A = 3 THEN C = 0: GOTO 700
460   IF A = 2 THEN C = 0: GOTO 700
470   IF A = 1 THEN C = 1: GOTO 700
480   IF A = 0 THEN C = 1: GOTO 700
500   IF A >  = 2 THEN C = 0:B =  - 1: GOTO 700
510   :C = 1:B =  - 1: GOTO 700
550   C = 0: GOTO 700
600   C = 3:B = 3: GOTO 700
650   C = 0:B =  - 3: GOTO 700
660   IF A = 0 THEN C = 0: GOTO 700
670   GOTO 900
```

Figure 12-4.

```
700  GOTO 920
702 X1 = X + 10
710 Y1 = 170 - (M * 10)
720 Y2 = 170 - ((M + B) * 10)
730  HPLOT X,Y1 TO X1,Y1 TO X1,Y2
740 P1 = 168 - (D * 10):P2 = P1 + 4:P3 = X + 8:P4 = X + 14
750  HPLOT P3,P1 TO P3,P2 TO P4,P2 TO P4,P1 TO P3,P1
760 X = X1
770 A = C
780 M = M + B
790  GOTO 160
800 C = 3:B = 1: GOTO 700
900 C = 0:B = - 1: GOTO 700
920  PR# 1
930  PRINT D,M,B,A,C
940  PR# 0
950  GOTO 702
1000  IF A > = 2 THEN C = 0: GOTO 700
1010 C = 2: GOTO 700
```

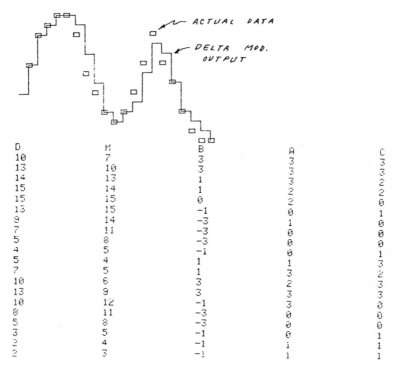

D	M	B	A	C
10	7	3	3	3
13	10	3	3	3
14	13	1	3	2
15	14	1	2	2
15	15	0	2	0
13	15	-1	0	1
9	14	-3	1	0
7	11	-3	0	0
5	8	-3	0	0
4	5	-1	0	1
5	4	1	1	3
7	5	1	3	2
10	6	3	2	3
13	9	3	3	3
10	12	-1	3	0
8	11	-3	0	0
5	8	-3	0	0
3	5	-1	0	1
2	4	-1	1	1
2	3	-1	1	1

Figure 12-4. (Continued).

tary example is given in Figure 12-5. This example roughly follows a Moser zero-phase encoded wave and was selected to have a number of steps of amplitude -2.

There are, of course, many many different delta modulation schemes and it is difficult to determine which is optimum in a given situation. In this particular scheme, if the data is to start at zero (as it might in an X-period-zero'd waveform which had been phase adjusted for minimum energy at the window edges), we find that the two initial zeros would slew the output to -3. The subsequent 0, 3 would send the value to -2, which would begin a pattern -2, -1, -1, -2, ... Since a 1-bit oscillation is characteristic of most delta modulation schemes, the sequence is not bad except for the initial transient. It is difficult to say whether another scheme offering equal compression would do better.

```
160  DATA  5,5,5,5,7
170  DATA  9,13,15,13,8
180  DATA  8,13,15,13,9
190  DATA  7,5,5,5,5
```

D	M	B	A	C
5	5	0	0	2
5	5	0	2	0
5	5	0	0	2
5	5	0	2	0
7	5	1	0	1
9	6	1	1	3
13	7	3	3	3
15	10	3	3	3
13	13	0	3	0
8	13	-3	0	0
8	10	-1	0	1
13	9	3	1	3
15	12	3	3	3
13	15	-1	3	0
9	14	-3	0	0
7	11	-3	0	0
5	8	-3	0	0
5	5	0	0	2
5	5	0	2	0
5	5	0	0	2

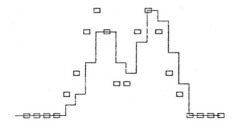

Figure 12-5.

SUMMARY

We have seen that the Moser encoding technique can accomplish the remarkable feat of compressing 6-bit (equivalent) data from 10,000 samples per second down to about 1,100 bits per second, while preserving a remarkable degree of intelligibility. The basic process is reminiscent of the design of an airplane in which an engineer is assigned the responsibility of weight and balance. He goes over every piece of the airplane to make sure that there is not a single ounce left that does not contribute in some functional way. In the hard-coded TSI version of the Moser technique, it seems likely that there is not a single ounce of "fat" left that does not contribute to intelligibility.

Whereas the TSI version is a stripped-down high-performance vehicle with no frills whatever, the National Digitalker bears more resemblance to a jet airliner with upholstered seats, rugs on the floor, and decorative wall paneling. It provides the luxury of natural-sounding speech at the cost of less efficiency.

To the communications man, Moser encoding would seem at first glance to offer hope of the dream of narrow-band secure-voice communication. Just the bandwidth compression alone is enticing. The economic advantages of being able to double the capacity of a satellite or to double the number of available radio channels need little amplification. Unfortunately, the system encounters something of a stumbling block in the matter of time.

Voice communication is generally employed these days when one would like to have an immediate answer (excluding broadcasting) or when the party at the far end does not have a terminal capable of receiving and decoding data. Any significant delay is not particularly tolerable. Unfortunately, the delay involved in Moser encoding a given phrase is measured in hours.

The part that requires the most time is the zero-phase encoding. The differentiation, the delta modulation, and even the X-period zeroing can be done by computer in milliseconds. However, the zero-phase technique requires that a Fourier analysis be performed on nearly every pitch period. The resulting spectra must then be compared to determine the number of permissible repetitions. Next, the waveform is reconstructed in the zero-phase pattern. Only after this is the X-period zeroing performed.

At present, the process is more or less manual, requiring a great deal of subjective judgment on the part of the operator. This facet will eventually diminish with the development of suitable algorithms or hardware to automate the process. However, the very large amount of mathematical manipulation involved in the Fourier transforms remains. A number of people are working on high-speed hardware for this purpose. However, it seems likely that real-time Moser encoding is not likely in the immediate future.

13
Linear Predictive Coding

At the time of this writing, the *linear predictive coding* technique is probably the leader in terms of the "naturalness" that can be achieved with a given level of compression. Male speech compressed down to an average rate of 1,200 bps sounds very much like a mediocre quality tape recording. Over the telephone it is sufficiently realistic to cause a number of people to guess that they are speaking to a human being. There is no "martian" monotone or mechanical sound to the speech.

As is the case with the Moser technique, this procedure is protected with patents (assigned to the Texas Instruments Company), and the writer does not either assert or imply any rights to the use of the subject patents that TI notes as "the intellectual property of the Texas Instruments Company." The license to use the devices covered is included in the purchase price of the pieces from TI. This chapter presents only the writer's concept of the method by which the inventions work.

The patents in question are:

U. S. Patent 4,209,781, issued June 24, 1980 to Ajay K. Puri, Michael J. Caruso, Stanley M. Dennison, and Jay Brown; all assignors to TI. Title: *MOS Digital To Analog Converter Employing Scaled Field Effect Devices.*

U. S. Patent 4,209,836, issued June 24, 1980 to Richard H. Wiggins and George L. Brantingham, assignors to TI. Title: *Speech Synthesis Integrated Circuit Device.*

U. S. Patent 4,209,844, issued to George L. Brantingham and Richard H. Wiggins, Jr., assignors to TI. Title: *Lattice Filter for Waveform or Speech Synthesis Circuits Using Digital Logic.*

Also of interest is the work by Markel and Gray — *Linear Prediction of Speech* — Springer Verlag, NY, 1976.

Whereas the writer has described Moser encoding as a collage of items, each carried to new extremes, the LPC technique, as developed by TI and others, is a great deal more monolithic. LPC represents a more unified approach to the encoding of speech and is describable by computer algorithm. It requires a great deal less judgment and artistic skill on the part of the operator than Moser encoding and is much closer to being an automatable process. It also requires a large amount of computer capability and power.

The TI advertisements are fond of saying that LPC works by modeling the vocal tract, however the model is somewhat different from the more traditional vocal tract model which consists of a pair of filters to model the throat and the mouth with a branch to model the nasal cavity. The LPC filter is rather more like a transmission-line affair. If you imagine a length of pipe with a pair of irises which partially close it at two points, it is not hard to see that this would act like a bandpass filter with resonances wherever the distance between the obstructions was an integral number of half wavelengths. The LPC acts in more or less this fashion with ten adjustable obstructions to model the portions of the vocal tract. The obstructions most distant from the input model the lips and those closest to the input model the throat close to the glottis.

As in the Moser technique, the TI encoding process begins with someone speaking into a microphone. The digital recording made from this utterance is then processed by computer in the linear predictive coding technique for reproduction by the processor. The processor itself represents a very sophisticated and specialized microcomputer, which includes the D/A converter. A current version is the TMS 5220.

The TMS 5220 can be used either with the speech data stored in the host computer memory or with a specialized ROM, the TMS 6100. This unit is a 128K-bit serial device. In large-volume applications, where the masking charge can be justified, this ROM represents a good solution since it frees the host computer from a majority of the service requirements. The 5220 has the capability of addressing up to 16 of the 6100's and yielding up to 30 minutes of speech. A standard control vocabulary version of the 6100, the VM61002, offers 206 words, including numbers, the alphabet in both normal and phonetic (Alpha, Bravo, Charlie, . . .) form. It also includes volts, motor, electrician, check, etc., in a pleasing male voice. The sixteen-chip ensemble would be capable of making up a pretty comprehensive representation of the basic English word list, thereby yielding a very powerful, general purpose talking machine. The available word list grows daily, and perhaps, this set may eventually be offered.

If a custom vocabulary is required and the economics of the situation preclude the use of a custom ROM, the 5220 VSP (Voice Synthesis Processor) can be operated by delivering the data from the host computer memory to the VSP via the host data bus. In this case the host computer assumes a great deal more responsibility for control of the VSP, however, it makes it possible to store the speech data in EPROM or any other nonvolatile memory the host has available. This is very significant economically since it cannot be done practically with the National Digitalker.

When one is developing a new product, the exact choice of vocabulary is critical. The very first thing that generally happens when a new product hits the market is that the user would like some changes. This is particularly true in an expensive professional or industrial product. With a consumer item, game, or appliance, the customer will generally not directly request a change. However, if he does not like something about the product he may not buy it. On the other hand, when someone expects to spend $185,000 on an automated blood gas chromatograph and wants the machine to say "sample" instead of "specimen," "marketing" is very liable to listen. The problem is that any change, no matter how slight, in a ROM means a new mask, a new mask charge, and a new minimum quantity order. It is very comforting to know that a small change in vocabulary can be made in EPROM for only the cost of encoding.

On the other side of the coin, in any significant volume, the cost of the masked ROM is so much lower than an equivalent volume of EPROM that the loss of flexibility is small compared to the price advantage. In principle, there is no reason that the Digitalker could not be used with EPROM except that the compression is so much smaller than the LPC that a prohibitive amount of memory EPROM would be required.

THE CONTROLS

The 5220 interfaces with the host processor with four lines and an 8-bit data bus. The controls are: $\overline{RS}$ — Read Select Not; $\overline{WS}$ — Write Select Not; $\overline{INT}$ — Interrupt Not; and $\overline{READY}$. $\overline{RS}$ and $\overline{WS}$ are supplied by the host computer to the VSP. The conditions are (H = high, L = low):

$\overline{RS}$	$\overline{WS}$	VSP ACTION
H	H	Data lines in a high-impedance state. The VSP is not selected by the host.
H	L	The VSP data lines are in a receive condition, ready to accept the contents of the host data bus. The host writes to the VSP.
L	H	The VSP is writing on the host data bus. For the host, this is a "read memory" condition.
L	L	Forbidden command — results not predictable.

The 5220 is a PMOS chip and acts as a very slow memory. If used with a dynamic host processor, such as the 6800 family or the 6500 family, it is far too slow to be written into or read as a normal memory location. $\overline{RS}$ and $\overline{WS}$ are normally derived in the host by some address decoding scheme AND'ed with $R/\overline{W}$ and VMA or a $\emptyset 2$ clock, just as a normal memory chip. The output from the VSP on the data bus is not valid until $\overline{READY}$ goes low again. In a maximum of 100 nsec after $\overline{RS}$ goes low, $\overline{READY}$ goes high. Some 6 to 11 μsec later,

$\overline{READY}$ will return low, indicating that the data on the data bus of the VSP is valid, and the data, in this case the status register, can be read. $\overline{RS}$ must be held low for at least 6 μsec and a 12-μsec delay is required before another command, either $\overline{RS}$ or $\overline{WS}$, is asserted.

Although it would be possible, through the addition of tristate buffers and some latches, to place the VSP directly on the data bus of the host, it can be seen that it is much easier to work the VSP through a PIA (peripheral interface adapter, such as the 6821), which will take care of the latching of the commands and keep the unstable data off the host data bus.

In the case of writing data into the VSP, $\overline{WS}$ is pulled low by the host and $\overline{READY}$ is asserted high by the VSP 100 nsec later. The data is read by the VSP and must be held stable. $\overline{WS}$ must be held low at least 6 μsec and cannot go low again for a new write command for at least 10 μsec. Data input must be valid no later than 7 μsec after $\overline{WS}$ goes low.

The importance of the PIA stems from the fact that a processor like the 6800 or 6502 cannot easily be made to hold even the chip select steady for a period of 7 μsec since the devices are dynamic and can tolerate a memory hold state for only about 10 μsec without losing data. The chips are equipped with a memory ready signal to permit interfacing to slow memory chips, but the use of this line to delay for as much as 7 μsec is not to be recommended.

LOADING THE DATA

The following technique has been used successfully to operate a 5200 VSP on a product based on a Motorola 6802 microprocessor that interacts with the 5200 through a 6821 PIA. The system has a limited vocabulary and operates over the telephone, acting as an unattended telephone directory. The product is manufactured by Radionics Inc., in Webster, N.Y., and sells under the name TEL-TRAK.®

When the machine initializes on RESET, the PIA is set up with all of the A bank in the WRITE condition. The A bank is connected to the data lines of the 5200 VSP. It is worthy to note that TI has elected to call their most significant bit DBUS $\emptyset$, and the least significant data bit DBUS 7. This is the reverse of the terminology used in the Motorola system, in which the MSB is D 7 and the LSB is D $\emptyset$. In an attempt to minimize confusion, we shall henceforth refer only to MSB and LSB.

After initializing bank A of the PIA, the B bank is initialized with the lines attached to $\overline{WS}$ and $\overline{RS}$ in the WRITE condition, and the line attached to $\overline{READY}$ in the read condition. In the mode of operation used, no other lines are employed. The unit operates with the vocabulary stored in a 4K-byte EPROM, which is directly on the microprocessor data and address bus.

Each utterance must first be identified. The microprocessor then goes to the look-up table in the EPROM and finds the starting address and calculates the length of the utterance in bytes. The starting address is then stored in the index register and the loading process is ready to commence.

In this ROM'less mode of operation, each utterance must be preceded by a SPEAK EXTERNAL command to the VSP. This command is:

MSB   LSB

XII∅XXXX

Where the Xs are don't cares. The actual command used is $6F. The transfer is effected by setting $\overline{WS}$ = ∅, $\overline{RS}$ = I, and writing $6F to the A bank of the PIA. The microprocessor then commences to read $\overline{READY}$ from the VSP. Immediately after the receipt of the write command, the VSP sets $\overline{READY}$ high; when it returns to the low state, the VSP is telling the microprocessor that it has accepted the data and is ready to be loaded.

In the initial load, the VSP will accept a set of 16 bytes, which it stores in an internal FIFO (first-in-first-out memory). The loading procedure is identical to the procedure for the SPEAK EXTERNAL command. The microprocessor goes to the index address and obtains the byte. It asserts the write command to the VSP and writes the byte. During the waiting interval the microprocessor could increment the index and test the index address to determine whether the end of the utterance has arrived. When $\overline{READY}$ returns low it waits the required 10 μsec and gets the next byte for transfer. During this interval, the index register can be incremented and tested for end of utterance. Either of the delays is useful for this purpose.

After the initial transfer of 16 bytes, the VSP sets the $\overline{READY}$ line high and holds it until 8 bytes have been consumed in the speech process. $\overline{READY}$ will then become active again and an 8-byte transfer can be accomplished. When the microprocessor senses that the end of the utterance has arrived, it ceases to send data.

Now you may question how the microprocessor knows whether the VSP has finished speaking before starting another utterance, as in the case where a string of numbers are to be read out or words and phrases concatenated. The answer is that in this case it doesn't. For a relatively small vocabulary, and especially one where the machine is reading a string of telephone numbers the listener is presumably copying, some delay between numbers is desirable. In practice we have found that a normal 240 msec, delay enhances the accuracy with which the listener can copy a long string of numbers. In general, by the time that the delay is over the VSP has finished talking anyway. In the particular machine it was found that only on the utterances /call/, /message/, and

/"beep"/ was it necessary to extend the delay to 360 msec. Since this delay is generated by a software loop, every time these utterances are called for, the delay loop is loaded with a larger constant and the requirement for testing for end of speech is eliminated.

This is a workable but not elegant routine. In the case where the VSP is being used in a phoneme or aloneme (extended phoneme) stringing routine, you may not want a preceptible delay between successive utterances, therefore, it becomes necessary to closely monitor the VSP to determine whether it is still speaking. For this it is necessary for the microprocessor to access the VSP STATUS REGISTER.

When the VSP receives $\overline{WS}$ high and $\overline{RS}$ low it places the STATUS REGISTER on the data bus in a talking condition. The STATUS REGISTER contains three lines significant to the microprocessor:

TS — Talk Status is active (high) when the VSP is processing speech data. This is the MSB on the data lines. TS goes high after the initiation of a SPEAK command when using the ROM or after nine bytes of data have been loaded in SPEAK EXTERNAL. It goes inactive (low) after receiving a STOP CODE (ENERGY = IIII) or after a buffer empty condition or a RESET. The audio energy is interpolated to zero during this frame.

BL — Buffer Low is active (high) when the buffer is half empty (has eight bits or less). Upon starting a refill of the FIFO, BL becomes low when the ninth byte is loaded.

BE — Buffer Empty is active (high) when the FIFO buffer has run out of data to process. This should never happen during a SPEAK EXTERNAL run since it indicates that the VSP was not properly serviced by the microprocessor.

TS is the most significant bit on the data line, BL is the next most, and BE is the next most.

It may be seen that the microprocessor can determine whether the VSP is talking at any instant by first issuing a read command ($\overline{WS}$ = high, $\overline{RS}$ = low) and then, after a 6 μsec reading, the output of the VSP. The data on the data bus can be masked by OR'ing with $7F. If the result is $FF, then TS is high and the VSP is still talking.

Now, one of the things about using a PIA to address the VSP is that the PIA has to be reset to read the data lines rather than write on the data lines. In order to do this, one has to write to the PIA control register in order to access the data direction register. A control word is then written into the data direction register (a $\emptyset$ sets the bit to read and a I to write), whereupon the control register must again be written to, to deselect the data direction register. This process takes about 30 μsec on a machine running at 1-MHz clock.

The delay is really not so terrible in view of the fact that the VSP should not be accessed for at least 10 μsec after a previous read or write; thus, the business with the PIA wastes probably only about 15 μsec, presuming that some allowance for good engineering practice is allowed.

It can be seen that BL could be used to signal the next data batch load to the microprocessor. However, this is actually slower than testing $\overline{\text{READY}}$, and the latter has the advantage of providing all of the housekeeping. Using BL, it becomes the responsibility of the microprocessor to determine that eight, and only eight, bytes are loaded after BL goes high. OR'ing the data with $BF and testing for $FF would indicate BL is high.

The BE signal seems to the writer to be of very limited utility in SPEAK EXTERNAL mode. If this signal ever arises during an utterance, it means that your program did not run and that something is wrong with either the hardware or the software. When an utterance is finished, this can be determined just as easily on TS since it sets TS low.

The rules for operating the chip under ROM control are somewhat different and rather lengthy to describe. Development programs being what they are, you will most likely be very familiar with the operation of the VSM before you ever purchase a custom ROM. In any event, the TI instructions concerning the use of the VSM with ROM are quite explicit and detailed and will not be repeated here.

One item that appears to be a good idea in either mode is to initialize the VSP at start-up with a RESET. A somewhat disquieting line appears in the TI data for the 5220 under the heading POWER-UP CLEAR. "The VSP contains internal circuitry to ensure a clear condition 95% of the time on power-up, provided . . . ." The reset after power-up will take care of the other 5%. This is accomplished by writing a RESET which is:

MSB   LSB

XIIIXXXX

followed by nine bytes of all ones.

THE WORD FRAME

In the next section we shall be discussing the basic unit of the encoding, the word frame. This is a reasonably complex structure and is somewhat oddly divided for reasons of economy of memory. We shall take the parts of the word frame one at a time. When operating in the SPEAK EXTERNAL mode, the portions of the word frame are not apparent to the microprocessor, which simply passes 8-bit bytes from the EPROM to the VSP. The VSP, however, interprets and resegments the bytes according to its own rules.

PITCH AND ENERGY CONTROL

The basic principle upon which the VSP operates is that an initial command gives the directions first for energy and then for pitch, with a repeat bit interspersed. The VSP then receives a series of words that describe the coefficients of the linear predictive filter in a total word frame of 50 bits (in most cases). The LPF serves to shape the spectrum formed by the pitch to correspond to the formants that were present in the original utterance. The output of the LPF is fed to a slightly specialized D/A that drives an external power amplifier from which the speech is output. The 50-bit (or less) control frame is updated at a 40-Hz rate. We shall tackle the individual components separately in the following discussion.

ENERGY CONTROL

The first 4 bits of the control frame represent the energy control. Basically, there are 16 levels available; however, energy 1111 is the stop code that signals the VSP that the utterance is concluded; therefore, it is not available as an energy level and only 15 levels remain.

A second word is more or less reserved as well. The energy code 0000 describes zero energy or silence. The VSP recognizes this and requires no other parameters. Energy = 0000 during interword or intersyllable pauses. For example, the 60 msec pause of /t/ would be represented by a series of two zero-energy frames and then an unvoiced frame. The presence of this zero-energy situation is used to reduce the data storage requirements. Upon receipt of a zero-energy frame, the VSP does not ask for data from memory until the next frame time.

All utterances conclude with a stop code. When the VSP receives this energy code, it shuts off the output and "sweeps out the kitchen."

THE REPEAT BIT

The repeat bit is used as another mechanism for economizing on memory. The fifth bit sent is the repeat bit. When the repeat bit = 1, the VSP asks only for energy and pitch and leaves the filter coefficients unchanged. It is possible to change the pitch and energy during a repeat frame. The repeat frame is useful because the vocal tract changes relatively slowly compared to pitch and energy change, therefore it is not necessary to change the filter parameters as often as pitch and energy. A repeat frame requires only 11 bits compared to the full frame of 50.

THE PITCH WORD

The pitch word is a 6-bit word and is therefore capable of changing pitch through 64 levels. Actually, one pitch level is reserved. When pitch = 00000, the VSP recognizes this as an unvoiced sound and switches to a digital random generator, which outputs a relatively high pitched but random output for filtering into the fricatives.

With the unvoiced sounds, another economy measure is used. In this case, only the first four coefficients are sent, with coefficients 5 through 10 arbitrarily set to zero. In this case, the word frame is reduced to 29 bits. The statement is made that coefficients 5 through 10 are less important.

As we have seen earlier in the spectrograms, the structure in the unvoiced spectra is not too organized, and a great deal of the nature of the phoneme is carried in the amplitude shaping as in crescendo, decrescendo of the /s/, and the pause-explosive onset of /t/. In any event, the combination of economies serves to reduce the data rate from 40 Hz $*$ 50 bits = 2,000 bps, to an average rate on the order of 1,100 to 1,200 bps in normal speech. The actual rate is a function of the content of the utterance. Note that a sung passage would benefit only from the breathing or punctuation pauses and would thus have approximately twice the data rate of a spoken passage.

It is noteworthy that these economies are effected only by a considerable degree of sophistication in the handling of the data by the VSP. It must have a decision point at the energy word, deciding whether silence, a given energy level, or an end of the utterance is required. Next it must decide whether a repeat is requested and either prepare to pass on new filter coefficients or repeat the previous coefficients. When the pitch word arrives, it must decide whether a voiced or an unvoiced sound is required and adjust its response to the coefficients accordingly. We shall see shortly that this is only the beginning of the sophistication.

THE CHIRP ROM

The principal source of sound in human speech is the output of the glottis, as discussed earlier in chapter 9. It would probably be possible to use nearly any impulse with a small enough duty cycle to simulate the sound of the glottis, provided only that the harmonic content was adequate to permit the subsequent filtering to output the formants. However, this is not the way the 5220 operates. Instead of a simple, shaped impulse, the output is simulated with a device called a *chirp* ROM.

Suppose that we wish to generate some arbitrary waveform, for example, an electrocardiogram form. Using a D/A converter, we could take a memory device such as a ROM (or a read/write memory for that matter) and write into successive addresses the data that would force the D/A output to the closest possible simulation of each of the EKG sample voltages taken at some constant time base. A counter attached to the address lines of the ROM would then cycle the

ROM through the successive addresses, and our desired output would be achieved. If we wanted the EKG form to repeat more rapidly, we could simply speed up the clock driving the counter. Note that there is no necessary restriction between input and output, that is, a 9-bit-wide ROM could be driven with only five address lines. In this case the output voltage could assume any of 512 levels (9 bits) on any one of 32 stored readings (5 bits). Obviously, the errors due to not sampling often enough are just as bad as the errors due to not having enough levels. Therefore, the output width is frequently selected to be approximately equal to the address width.

A special case exists when an impulse or short duty cycle wave is to be modeled. In this case, without some hardware aid, most of the ROM readings will wind up being zero. This is obviously not a very efficient use of the ROM. However, when one is designing hardware to go on an LSI chip, certain of the hardware tricks can be incorporated, trading off logic complexity for ROM cells. This was done on the 5220.

The basic scheme employed in the 5220 consists of a digital comparator, an add-one circuit, and a counter. The counter is used to drive address lines A_0 through A_5 of the chirp ROM, which has an 8-bit output. The data is stored in the ROM in twos-complement form.

In voiced speech operation, the contents of the counter is updated by the add-one circuit on each circuit or cycle of the LPC filter. The counter is actually an 8-bit counter. However, logic is provided so that any address in excess of 00110010 (decimal 50) gives a zero output from the ROM. The output of the counter is also compared to the 8-bit pitch word which has been expanded from the supplied 6-bit word. When the pitch word matches the counter contents, the counter is zeroed and the cycle begins anew.

The update of the counter takes place every 100 μsec. Therefore, a pitch word of 11111100 (decimal 253) will result in a pitch period of 253 * 100 * 10^{-6} = 0.0253 sec, or a pitch of 40 Hz.

A parameter-decoding ROM is used to derive the 8-bit pitch word used by the comparator. Obviously, from the previous discussion, the pitch can have only 63 discreet levels.

The contents of the chirp ROM are very interesting. While the ROM was able to contain 50 discrete entries (each 8-bits wide), the original SPEAK AND SPELL® unit (the one described in the patents) actually contained only 41, with entries 42 through 50 set equal to zero. The form of the data is also interesting. Figure 13-1 shows a graph of the data. It may be seen that the chirp would seem to be made up of a 5-kHz tone at the start, which rapidly diminishes as a 770-Hz tone grows with time. Other components are also present.

It is noteworthy that the spectrum of the voiced sound will be a function of the pitch word since the chirp always occupies 41 cycles of a variable repetition

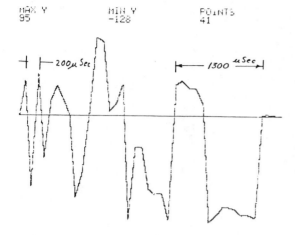

```
LIST

?SYNTAX ERROR
JLIST 100,600

100  REM  THIS PROGRAM READS DECIMAL DATA IN LINES 110 THRU 160 AS Y AXIS
     VALUES. IT THEN SCALES THE VALUES AND COUNTS THE POINTS TO SCALE THE X
     AXIS AND PLOTS ON HGR2 SCREEN.
110  DATA  0,42,212,50,178,18,37,20,2,225
111  DATA  197,2,95,90,5,15,38,252,165,165
112  DATA  214,221,220,252,37,43,34,33,15,255
113  DATA  248,238,237,239,247,246,250,0,3,2,1
200  READ D
202  IF D > 127 THEN D =  - (D - 127)
205  ONERR  GOTO 250
210  IF D > M THEN M = D
220  IF D < N THEN N = D
230  D = D + 1
```

Figure 13-1. The chirp.

period. The spectrum of Figure 13-2 was calculated from the chirp data on the assumption that the chirp occupied half of the pitch period. In this case the pitch would be 8.2 msec and the frequency 122 Hz. It may be seen that a significant portion of the energy lies between 3,170 Hz and 4,514 Hz.

It is not always easy to "backward engineer" a sophisticated piece of equipment as complicated as this. The chirp function was the subject of a patent application that was abandoned and is the subject of a patent application filed in 1978 and not yet issued. It is therefore not available to the public. Patent 4,209,836 states: "... the voiced excitation may be an impulse function or some other repeating function such as a chirp function. In this embodiment a chirp has been selected as this tends to reduce the "fuzziness" from the speech generated (because it apparently more closely models the actions of the vocal cords than does the impulse function) ...."

```
JLIST 160,179

160  REM  THE DATA STATEMENTS CONTAIN A LIST OF 82 VOLTAGE READINGS.
170  DATA  0,42,212,50,178,18,37,20,2,225
171  DATA  197,2,95,90,5,15,38,252,165,165
172  DATA  214,221,220,252,37,43,34,33,15,255
173  DATA  248,238,237,239,247,246,250,0,3,2
174  DATA  1,,,,,,,,,
175  DATA  ,,,,,,,,,
176  DATA  ,,,,,,,,,
177  DATA  ,,,,,,,,,
178  DATA  ,,,,,,,,,
179  DATA  ,,,,,,,,,
```

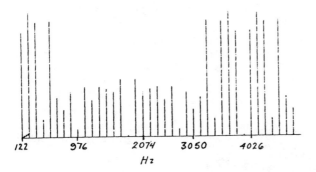

Figure 13-2. The chirp spectrum.

The writer is not inclined to take issue with the statement on the subject of the "fuzziness." One would have to have the resources to build an equivalent of the 5220 without the chirp function to test that proposition. Since the chirp has been included at some considerable cost, I would imagine that TI has tried the impulse and found the chirp to be superior.

The question of whether the chirp function "more closely models the action of the vocal cords" is another matter that remains to be demonstrated. The pneumatic action of the vocal cords is so different from the electrical action of the chirp generator and the nature of the LP filter that a number of other explanations could be equally suitable. Among other things, an impulse with significant harmonic content at the upper formant frequencies must have a very high peak-to-average ratio. An LP filter with a limited number of bits is not too well suited to handling such a signal without saturating or overflowing. The human vocal tract has no such limitation, being a passive analog device. It is therefore quite possible that the reduction in "fuzziness" could easily be due to the fact that the LP filter simply works better with the chirp than with the impulse and its attendant high peak-to-average ratio.

THE LINEAR PREDICTIVE FILTER

The very heart of the VSP is the linear predictive filter. It is called linear because there are no mathematical powers higher than 1 involved and it is called predictive because the output is the result not only of the current input but also of the previous inputs. A digital filter can exist either in hardware or in software and it may behave in a way quite different from analog filters.

For example, in the chapter dealing with security, we discussed combination locks. It is not hard to imagine a software program that examines six successive entries into the computer and tests them against a stored combination. The output of the computer would be 1 if and only if the six digits were all correct and in the proper order. Now, if the input to the computer was taken from an A/D converter on six successive samples of a repetitive wave, we see that this would be an extremely sharp filter. The output would go to 1 only when the amplitude was exactly right and only when the shape was exactly right. Furthermore, the shape can be purely arbitrary, set to any combination set in software. If the repetitive wave was thought of as sliding past a six-sample window and the combination was made pretty arbitrary, the computer would pulse a 1 only at those instants when the portion within the window was right to match the combination. If the A/D had a ten-level output, the filter would have a "bandwidth" of one in a million. Of course, there would be other "harmonic" functions that varied at a rate faster than the sampling period, which could contain the correct six points so that the filter would have harmonic responses as well.

There are a number of different types of predictive filters. The simplest is the nonrecursive, or finite impulse response (FIR), which is so called because it has no feedback. Figure 13-3 shows a simple hardware implementation of a nonrecursive filter. This circuit shows a shift register composed of four D-type flip-flops, along with a summing device shown as a circle, and three buffer amps,

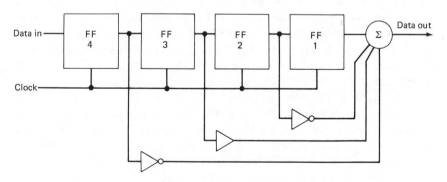

Figure 13-3. A nonrecusive filter.

two of which are inverting. Let us presume that everything except the summer is ordinary digital logic, and the summer is a summing op amp that outputs 1 V for each logic 1 it receives as input. On each rising clock edge, the data from FF4 is passed to FF3, etc., down the line.

It is fairly easy to visualize that it takes four clock pulses for a given piece of data to reach the summer. Now let us suppose that the input to the string were a steady string of all I's. The output of the summer would be a steady 2 V since it would receive a I from FF1 and FF3 and a zero from FF2 and FF4. A similar thing would happen for a continuous string of $\emptyset$'s, except the outputs would be reversed. Now, however, let us suppose that the input were a OIOIOIOIO . . . string. At one point in time, FF1 and FF3 would contain a 1 and FF2 and FF4 would contain zeros, which would be inverted to I's by the inverting buffers, thus causing the output of the summer to go to 4 V. Just one clock cycle later, the even FF's would contain a I and the odd ones a 0, thus driving the output of the summer to 0 V. For the alternating string OIOIOI . . . , the output would be a 4-V p-p square wave at just half of the clock frequency.

We note that for maximum swing the input wave must run at a frequency of half the clock. Suppose that the input frequency were slightly different. For a few cycles we might have a burst of square waves, but then we would come to a place where the clock lined up so that it might put in two zeros and then two ones in a row, and the output of the summer would fall to 2 V and stay there for a while until the slippage brought back the alternating condition. The output would be modulated by the difference in frequency between the clock and the input data. In short, this filter can be tuned by simply varying the clock frequency.

Obviously, the bandwidth is a function of the length of the shift register, with more stages making the device more sensitive to difference in frequency. Also note that the immediate input to FF4 does nothing to the summer output until the next rising clock edge, and the output at any instant is related to the history of the input over the last four cycles. For a ten-stage filter, it would be necessary that the clock and data frequency be close enough to maintain a string of ten OIOI's in order to get the full-amplitude square-wave burst out. Obviously, there are 2^N conditions for the shift register of N stages, and there will be something less than 2^N output levels from the summer.

It can be seen that this nonrecursive filter has certain properties equivalent to a tapped transmission line filter with the shift registers and clock taking the place of the propagation delay. Having no feedback, the nonrecursive filter is unconditionally stable and the output can never exceed the number of stages times the input. Unfortunately, this type of filter is less selective than the recursive type for a given number of stages.

THE RECURSIVE DIGITAL FILTER

The recursive digital filter, or infinite impulse response (IIR) filter, is one with feedback, that is, some portion of the output of either the filter or the individual filter stages is combined with the input. If this combined signal is such that it consistently increases the input (positive feedback), then the output can grow without bounds and the filter is unstable. The instability can take the form of either an increasing amplitude of oscillation at some natural frequency or of a sudden veer off toward positive or negative infinity. In an analog device this would result in either a saturation and cutoff-limited oscillation or a pinning "against the rail" in either the high or low direction.

In a digital device, the performance is somewhat different. The recursive filter we showed was a 1-bit-wide arrangement, but it need not have been thus restricted. The recursive filters used in the TI version of the VSP are 10 bits wide with 1 bit being sign. Now, most digital devices have the property of "folding" numbers. In ordinary binary notation, the number one higher than IIII on a 4-bit system is 0000, and the number one lower than 0000 is IIII, if the system neglects the carry. In twos, complement notation, we have:

Twos complementary binary	Decimal value
OIII	7
000I	1
0000	0
IIII	−1
I000	−7

Although this notation seems to be a little "backward," it is quite commonly used because there is a smooth transition between +1, zero, and −1. Furthermore, it can be easily used in binary addition and subtraction. The principal upshot of the "folding" is the fact that most simple binary systems cannot increase indefinitely in number since they reach the folding point and start over at the other end of the scale.

THE RECURSIVE LATTICE FILTER

The form of the digital lattice filter used in the TI version of the VSP is shown in Figure 13-4. This shape does not represent the real hardware but rather is a conceptual flow diagram much like a flowchart. The sigmas in the circles represent a mathematical addition and the circles with an X represent a multiplication.

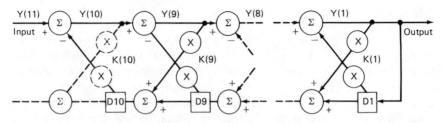

Figure 13-4. A digital latice filter.

The little box with the D represents a delay much like the flip-flop single-shift stage in the previous discussion. Each of the symbols is intended to represent a word-wide operation and the action ripples across the filter from input to output.

To begin with, the input, $Y(11)$, is applied to the summer in order to form $Y(10)$, where

$$Y(10) = Y(11) - (K(10) * D(10))$$

The term, $D(11)$, could be formed at this time, but it is not used and, therefore, omitted.

Once $Y(10)$ has been formed, $Y(9)$ can be calculated.

$$Y(9) = Y(10) - (K(9) * D(9))$$

and then $$D(10) = D(9) + (Y(9) * K(9))$$

This process ripples down through the filter, with $Y(8)$ and then $D(9)$ being calculated until we reach $Y(1)$, whereupon $D(2)$ is first calculated and $D(1)$ is set equal to $Y(1)$.

It should be remembered that the K's are 10-bit signed numbers and that the calculations for a single stage represent two additions and two multiplications. Now, TI allows 5 μsec for an addition and 45 μsec for a multiplication, as being compatible with the MOS devices on the chip. From this we see that the actual calculation for a single stage of the lattice filter would require $2 * 50 = 100$ μsec.

There is another point of great importance in the implementation of the calculation, and that is that the calculations must be carried on in series. It is necessary to calculate $Y(9)$ before $D(10)$ and $Y(8)$ can be calculated, etc. Considering that these are 10-bit signed numbers, this is a lot of calculation. A Motorola 6809, which is billed by the manufacturer as a "fast math engine," will do a 16-bit signed multiply in something over 9 μsec. However, with load and store overhead it could not handle three such operations in 45 μsec, therefore something like a five-unit multiprocessor would be required to duplicate the performance of the 5220, which manages to iterate the filter lattice at a 10-kHz update rate.

The fast update, or throughput rate, is necessitated by the fact that TI maintains that a 10-stage lattice filter updated at a 10-kHz rate (and therefore capable of reproducing to something like 5-kHz) will produce "speech which is virtually indistinguishable from actual human speech." The phrase may be a little overly enthusiastic, but the quality is good with careful encoding.

TI approached this formidable task and solved the problem with silicon. Using the inexpensive and relatively slow PMOS technology, they have structured the 5220 in what is generically a parallel pipelined processor, an architecture that is generally used only in the very largest and fastest mainframes. Without the parallel processing, it would probably have been necessary to go to ECL or GaAs or some other ultrafast technology to achieve the throughput rate. This would have, of course, put the device completely out of the market for talking toys.

Figure 13-5 shows the basis upon which the parallel pipeline works. This illustration again does not represent the physical structure but rather tends to depict the sequence of events that take place simultaneously within the machine.

Starting from the top, we see the events in the highest horizontal row, which depicts the happenings in respect to the tenth section (the input section of the filter). Since D(10) is derived by an addition, a no-op (no operation) period of 5 μsec is required before the $-K(10) * D(10)$ multiplication can commence. This

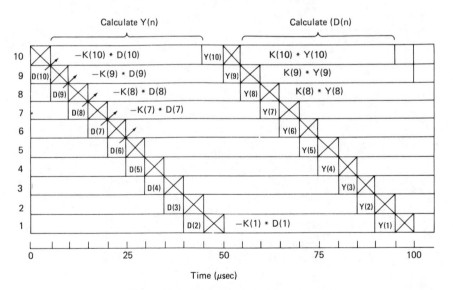

Figure 13-5. The parallel pipeline process.

factor leads to a diagonal series of no-op boxes, which are marked with an inscribed X. The term "pipelining" stems from the fact that each operation is begun at a time such that the results are available at the appropriate time for the succeeding stage; thus, the intermediate results are in the "pipeline," scheduled to arrive at the time they are required.

The elegance of this silicon solution can be compared to the Applesoft program of Figures 13-6 and 13-7 written for use on a general purpose computer. The detailed mechanism by which the parallel pipelined solution was actually achieved at the transistor level is beyond the scope of this text and can be obtained from the patent. It is probably only of academic interest unless you wish to try to duplicate the chip. It would certainly be impossibly complicated to attempt in discrete hardware.

Regarding the Applesoft program, there are several points of interest. The chirp excitation is included in the data table, lines 120 through 127. The data

```
]LIST 100,332
100  REM  A TEN SECTION LINEAR PREDICTIVE FILTER WITH CHIRP EXCITATION
105  E = .05
106  GOTO 400
120  DATA  0,42,-85,50,-51,18,37,20,2,-98
121  DATA  -70,2,95,90,5,15,38,-125,-38,-38
122  DATA  -87,-94,-93,-125,37,43,34,33,15,-127
123  DATA  -121,-111,-110,-112,-120,-119,-123,0,3,2
124  DATA  1,,,,,,,,,,
125  DATA  ,,,,,,,,,,
126  DATA  ,,,,,,,,,,
127  DATA  ,,,,,,,,,,,
130  D10 = 0:D9 = 0:D8 = 0:D7 = 0:D6 = 0:D5 = 0
131  D4 = 0:D3 = 0:D2 = 0:D1 = 0
140  READ A
150  ONERR  GOTO 400
160  Y10 = A - (K10 * D10)
180  Y9 = Y10 - (K9 * D9)
185  D10 = D9 + (Y9 * K9)
200  Y8 = Y9 - (K8 * D8)
205  D9 = D8 + (Y8 * K8)
220  Y7 = Y8 - (K7 * D7)
225  D8 = D7 + (Y7 * K7)
232  Y6 = Y7 - (K6 * D6)
233  D7 = D6 + (Y6 * K6)
240  Y5 = Y6 - (K5 * D5)
245  D6 = D5 + (Y5 * K5)
260  Y4 = Y5 - (K4 * D4)
265  D5 = D4 + (Y4 * K4)
280  Y3 = Y4 - (K3 * D3)
285  D4 = D3 + (Y3 * K3)
300  Y2 = Y3 - (K2 * D2)
305  D3 = D2 + (Y2 * K2)
320  Y1 = Y2 - (K1 * D1)
325  D2 = D1 + (Y1 * K1)
332  D1 = Y1
```

Figure 13-6.

has been converted from signed binary to decimal. Lines 130 and 131 essentially "sweep out" the delay flip-flops. Lines 160 through 332 represent the multiplications and additions represented for the lattice in equations 11-1 through 11-3.

In the TI implementation, the values of K are interpreted as 10-bit signed numbers less than ± 1 and, as a matter of fact, they must be generally considerably less than ± 1 if the system is to be kept from violent oscillation. Note that

```
]LIST 334,800

334  IF Y1 > 255 THEN  GOTO 700
335  IF Y1 < - 255 THEN  GOTO 700
340 C = C + 1
342  IF C > 79 THEN  GOTO 520
343  IF Y1 < N1 THEN N1 = Y1
344  IF Y1 > Y0 THEN Y0 = Y1
350  IF C < 79 THEN  GOTO 140
360  IF C = 79 THEN  GOTO 460
400  RESTORE
402 E = E * .81
403 K10 = 10 * E:K9 = 9 * E:K8 = 8 * E:K7 = 7 * E
404 K6 = 6 * E:K5 = 5 * E:K4 = 4 * E:K3 = 3 * E
405 K2 = 2 * E:K1 = E
410  GOTO 140
460 N2 = 190 / (Y0 - N1)
470  HGR2
480  HCOLOR= 3
490  POKE  - 12524,0
500  POKE  - 12529,255
510  POKE  - 12525,64
520 Y2% = 190 + (N1 * N2) - (.9 * (Y1 * N2))
521  IF Y2% > Y3% THEN Y3% = Y2%
522  IF Y2% < Y4% THEN Y4% = Y2%
523  IF Y2% > 190 THEN Y2% = 190
524  IF Y2% < 0 THEN Y2% = 0
525  IF C = 79 THEN N3 = 0:N4 = Y2%
530  HPLOT N3,N4 TO X%,N4 TO X%,Y2%
540 N3 = X%
550 N4 = Y2%
560 X% = X% + 1
570  IF X% > 270 THEN  GOTO 590
580  GOTO 140
590 Y2% = 190 + (N1 * N2)
600 X% = X% - 1
610  HPLOT 0,Y2% TO X%,Y2%
612  PR# 1
614  PRINT "CYCLES=",(C - 79)
615  PRINT "Y3%=",Y3%,"Y4%=",Y4%
616  LIST 100,127
617  LIST 400,410
618  PR# 0
620  END
700  PR# 1: PRINT "OSCILLATING"
710  PRINT C,A,Y1
720  PR# 0
730  END
```

Figure 13-7.

Y1 is equal to Y2 minus the product of K1 * D1. Now, if Y2 remains positive and K1 is negative, the output of the single lattice can grow at a pretty rapid rate if K1 departs much from zero.

Since the writer was using the program to investigate the effects of different coefficient distributions (Ks) it was found necessary to place an oscillation test in lines 334 and 335 to prevent the program from spending a great deal of time calculating trash. More properly, the program should test each of the operations between lines 160 and 325, with some GOSUB overflow routine to actually simulate the operation of the 5200. This operation would "fold" the data appropriately. Unfortunately, this would add 19 GOSUB's to what is already a relatively time-consuming program, and GOSUBs do not run particularly fast on an Apple in any event.

Program line 340 is used to keep track of the number of passes through the filter, and lines 343 and 344 are intended to keep track of the maximum and minimum values of the output for scaling purposes when the run is completed. The latter operation is performed in line 460 at the start of the plotting routine.

Experimentally, it was found that any distribution in which the sum of the Ks was large enough to produce any significant filtering action in the first 3 to 5 cycles of the chirp frequency would always oscillate violently if allowed to stay in place for a longer period. As a matter of fact, nearly any magnitude of K will result in violent oscillation if allowed to persist for more than a few hundred or thousand cycles through the complete filter. As noted in the Moser chapter, the pitch repetitions tend to run between 3 and 11 cycles. Therefore, it seems to be generally necessary to employ coefficient magnitudes that would surely result in oscillation if allowed to persist. Line 402 contains a term by which the Ks can be caused to decay with time, thereby obtaining a quick response and controlling oscillation.

Figure 13-8 shows an interesting result in which the Ks were distributed in a linear manner, that is, tapering either from input to output or vice versa. It may be seen that the output wave scarcely differs from one to the other and that the 0.81 decay coefficient is slightly too large in this case. The shape of the chirp has been altered and the exponentially decaying section has been added as a tail.

Figure 13-9 shows, respectively, a nearly half-sine distribution (low at the edges and high in the center) and a nearly full-cycle sine distribution. In this case, the chirp has been considerably tailored and a "ringing" term has been added in the dead portion of the chirp. All of the above curves represent the third through the fifth cycles of the wave. It is relatively easy to see that the spectrum of the original chirp has been considerably altered and that shaping to obtain the formant frequencies is possible with simple control of the Ks for the filter.

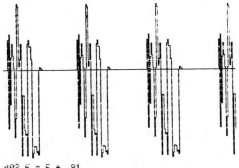

All Ks = 0
The chirp

```
402 E = E * .81
403 K10 = E:K9 = 2 * E:K8 = 3 * E:K7 = 4 * E
404 K6 = 5 * E:K5 = 6 * E:K4 = 7 * E:K3 = 8 * E
405 K2 = 9 * E:K1 = 10 * E
410  GOTO 140
```

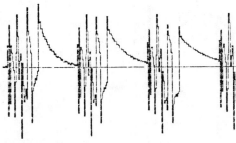

Linear tapered Ks

```
402 E = E * .81
403 K10 = 10 * E:K9 = 9 * E:K8 = 8 * E:K7 = 7 * E
404 K6 = 6 * E:K5 = 5 * E:K4 = 4 * E:K3 = 3 * E
405 K2 = 2 * E:K1 = E
410  GOTO 140
```

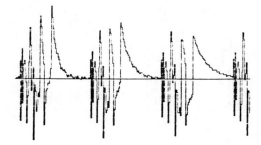

Figure 13-8. LPF outputs.

```
100   REM   A TEN SECTION LINEAR PREDICTIVE FILTER WITH CHIRP EXCITATION
105 E = .5
106 B = .2856
120   DATA  0,42,-85,50,-51,18,37,20,2,-98
121   DATA  -70,2,95,90,5,15,38,-125,-38,-38
122   DATA  -87,-94,-93,-123,37,43,34,33,15,-127
123   DATA  -121,-111,-110,-112,-120,-119,-123,0,3,2
124   DATA  1,,,,,,,,,,,
125   DATA  ,,,,,,,,,
126   DATA  ,,,,,,,,,
127   DATA  ,,,,,,,,,,

400   RESTORE
402 K10 = E *  SIN (B):K9 = E *  SIN (2 * B):K8 = E *  SIN (3 * B)
403 K7 = E *  SIN (4 * B):K6 = E *  SIN (5 * B):K5 = E *  SIN (6 * B):K4 =
      E *  SIN (7 * B):K3 = E *  SIN (8 * B)
404 K2 = E *  SIN (9 * B):K1 = E *  SIN (10 * B)
410   GOTO 140
```

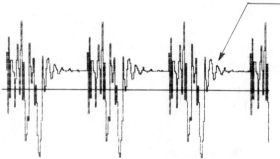

≈1924 Hz Ring
for 125 Hz Pitch

105   E = -.3
106   B = .6238

```
402 K10 = E *  SIN (B):K9 = E *  SIN (2 * B):K8 = E *  SIN (3 * B)
403 K7 = E *  SIN (4 * B):K6 = E *  SIN (5 * B):K5 = E *  SIN (6 * B):K4 =
      E *  SIN (7 * B):K3 = E *  SIN (8 * B)
404 K2 = E *  SIN (9 * B):K1 = E *  SIN (10 * B)
410   GOTO 140
```

≈1467 Hz RING

Figure 13-9.

As noted earlier, the formants move much more slowly than the individual pitch cycles. Therefore, the 5220 linearly interpolates each K from the last to the next value in eight cycles of the pitch. This provides a very substantial level of data reduction at the same time, resulting in a smoother blending of the formants.

SPEECH ENCODING

The actual encoding of the speech for use with the 5220 is by no means a trivial task. At the time of this writing, it is, to the best of the writer's knowledge, beyond the capabilities of a small microcomputer. Texas Instruments is offering a system with approximately 1 Mbyte of read/write memory and additional disk storage to permit the logical blending of phonemes and allonemes into connected speech for something on the order of $40,000. Using this system, the operator is prompted through a dictionary with text-to-speech editing rules. The system will run on a DS990 computer from TI, and the cost includes approximately $5,000 for software charges. They maintain that an 8K-byte rule will generate (in this system) LPC-10 code with something like 90% accuracy. To obtain a somewhat higher accuracy, on the order of 96% to 97%, the complexity of the rule rises sharply, to approximately 50K-bytes.

If it is desired to go directly from speech to digitization, TI offers an audio system for collecting and recording speech data at a cost of about $15,000, of which $5,000 is again a software charge.

This system requires something like the capabilities of a "professional level" minicomputer, such as the TI DS990 model 20, and close to 10M bytes of disk space. Even so, the digitization lags behind the speech input by a ratio on the order of 12 to 1, resulting in an overall throughput of about 100 analyzed words per hour, including the recording session time.

The present standard against which phoneme conversion can be tested is the "Brown Corpus." This is a text-to-phoneme dictionary of the 20,000 most commonly used English words, listed in order of frequency of occurrence. TI has developed this in a text-to-alloneme form. However, the entire list takes a prodigious amount of memory and is extremely expensive. Furthermore, the large amount of content searching causes it to run very slowly, even on a large, high-speed computer.

For a further discussion of this system, the reader is directed to: Tom Brightman, Mgr. Speech Technology Engineering, TI Corp., "Speech-synthesizer Software Generated from Text or Speech." *Electronic Design Magazine.* Aug. 20, 1981, pp. 107–112.

HOW WELL DOES THE LPC WORK?

After all of the discussion, it seems fair to ask just how well the LPC system actually works. Since this is a book and not a record it can only be described. In the experience of the writer, the quality is very good, except if one listens quite critically. On the Tel-Trak machine, the numbers *three* and *six* leave something to be desired, and the number *two* has an odd sound to it. However, all are perfectly clear and understandable. The connected speech phrases come through much more realistically than the disconnected words and numerals. As it happens, the machine answers the phone with a very realistic salutation. Therefore, most listeners are highly impressed at the outset and are not inclined to be critical of the subsequent pieced-together speech that is message-dependent.

Perhaps the best thing which can be used to illustrate the quality is to show the spectrograms of the LPC systhesizer furnished by Dr. Doddington. Figure 13-10 is our familiar "782" reproduced by LPC. Compared to the original spectrum of Figure 10-1, we see that the phonemes are much less detailed. Whereas the original was striped like the sides of a bass, the LPC reproduction simply has "islands" of energy centered upon the formants. However, we see that the waveforms below quite faithfully mimic the original and the phoneme travel does indeed follow the original. Similar comments apply to Figure 13-12, containing "Zero 98," which is to be compared to Figure 10-3. All in all, the reproduction of the formants and waveshapes is remarkable when one considers the amount of data that has been rejected in the encoding.

THE FUTURE

It is the writer's expectation that future developments in the form of FFT chips, etc., will eventually bring the encoding of speech by the LPF technique more nearly within the grasp of the small laboratory. This solution in the silicon is probably no more difficult than the development of the 5200 LPF processor. Unfortunately, the economic reasons seem less compelling since it probably would not be incorporated into a low-cost toy. Thus, we must wait a bit longer for the gentler market forces to bring the development to fruition.

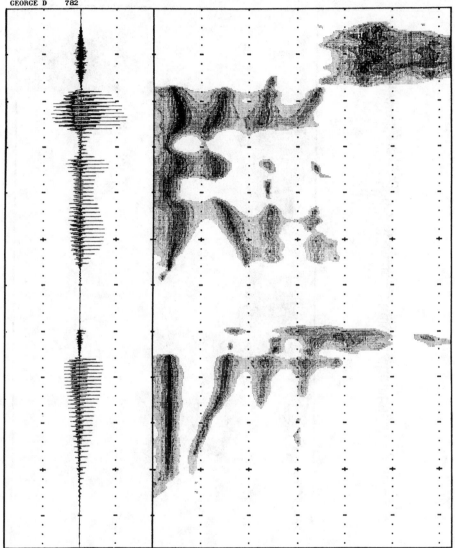

DBB1:[SPCH3.3DIGITS]CRD782.;1   14-th order LP model   6-AUG-81 09:13:40
30.00 msec window, preemphasis = 0.9375, starting time = 0.00 sec, 1.17 secs plotted at 20.00 cm/sec
    bottom =   0 Hz, top = 6250 Hz, dark = 0.00, cont = 0.00, ago = 0.50, sample period =   80 microsec
GEORGE D   782

Figure 13-10.

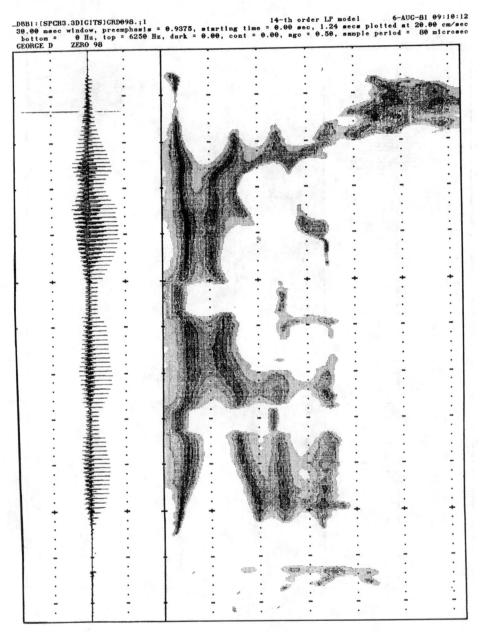

_DBB1:[SPCH3.3DIGITS]GRD098.;1   14-th order LP model   6-AUG-81 09:10:12
30.00 msec window, preemphasis = 0.9375, starting time = 0.00 sec, 1.24 secs plotted at 20.00 cm/sec
  bottom =   0 Hz, top = 6250 Hz, dark = 0.00, cont = 0.00, ago = 0.50, sample period =   80 microsec
GEORGE D   ZERO 98

Figure 13-10. (Continued).

14
Speech Recognition

The successes achieved in speech synthesis have led to a large amount of research into the topic of speech recognition. There are even speech recognition devices being marketed currently to run on small computers like Apple II+ and TRS-80. IBM is working on a speech-recognition typewriter, and Bell Labs is working on a speech-recognizing telephone service.

The possible payoffs are tremendous for a successful speech-recognition system. In the preparation of the manuscript for this book, it would certainly have been a tremendous boon to have a machine take dictation and produce properly spelled error-free copy without a touch to the keyboard.

In the telephone field, imagine the advantage of having a speech-recognizing PBX. One could eliminate the use of extension numbers. One would simply call and say "Fred Fotzengargle" and the machine would instantly recognize his name and connect you to the correct extension. An employee reporting ill or late would simply read his name and pay number to the machine and his foreman would receive a list of absences.

In the field of communications, the police dispatcher would notify cars of a robbery in progress by speaking into the microphone. The machine would encode and then encrypt his announcement, and the radio at the police car would decrypt and either speak or print the message. The transmission would require only a fraction of the time and bandwidth used for voice transmission, thereby effectively enlarging the radio system and reducing the queing of messages. Because of the encryption, the "wheelman" with his scanner would not be informed of the alarm.

At inventory time, the clerk would simply speak the items into a microphone and the computer would produce a printed list. The requirement for a computer operator at the bank would be eliminated since the tellers would simply speak the entries into a microphone.

Those are the dreams; how about the realities?

In order to answer that question, let us take a look into the technical requirements of speech recognition. Along the way we shall encounter some of the technological realities of speech recognition.

To begin with, most speech-recognition schemes are separated into two categories, vocoder-based machines and Inverse Digital Speech Synthesis (IDSS) types. In the vocoder type, the input speech is split up by a vocoder bank of filters and the energy in each is recorded as a function of time. In the IDSS type, the speech is digitized directly. Both types then begin a set of pattern, or "template," matching operations.

The vocoder operation has the advantage of parallel processing the input data, which simultaneously emerges as an amplitude descriptor from each of the filters. In this sense the operation parallels that of the human hearing faculty, which sends parallel processed data from the ear to the brain.

The IDSS machines, on the other hand, tend to serialize the data. They may then attempt the template matching on either the pressure wave itself or on the Fourier-derived spectrum. In the latter case, the operation after spectrum derivation parallels that of the vocoder.

TEMPLATE DERIVATION

All speech-recognition schemes begin with an operation in which one or more individuals speak words or phrases into the machine, usually several times. The data thus acquired is then tagged with an entry the machine can understand (from the keyboard) to identify the meaning. The digitized speech data is then examined for characteristic signatures, or "templates," to associate with the meaning.

If the template is formed from a number of repetitions by the same speaker, the system is termed *speaker dependent,* and will generally respond only to that speaker. If the template is generated by processing speech input from many different speakers, the system is termed *speaker independent.* The process of reading the speech into the machine is termed *training.* This is usually done a number of times to permit averaging or correlation of the input.

The applications suitable for the two types of machines are quite different. A wheelchair designed for self-propelled voice-controlled operation by a paraplegic (a device under active investigation) would benefit little from speaker independence, but would have severe reliability requirements. On the other hand, a system for voice-recognition to give stock quotations over the telephone would have to be extremely speaker independent. However, the consequences of an occasional error in recognition would not be severe. A TV game might be acceptable if it only worked "most of the time." The possibility that the wheelchair might go forward when told to stop or go back could be very dangerous in certain circumstances.

ACCURACY

The terms *accuracy, reliability,* and *error rate* generally refer to much the same thing. However, there is little agreement on just how a speech recognition system is to be tested. For example, certain of the commercially available units are quoted as operating with 95% accuracy. This is not as good as it might at first seem. If it refers to word accuracy, it would mean that the average page of this book would have five completely wrong words on it. On the other hand, if the accuracy term refers to phoneme accuracy, the errors would rise to approximately twenty-five per page and the work would be almost completely unreadable.

In addition to this, there is no standardization regarding the conditions under which the test was conducted. On a speaker-independent condition, was the speaker possessed of a Texas drawl or a Georgia drawl? Was there any background noise such as office machinery or conversations, or was the room as quiet as a recording studio? Hewlett-Packard has suggested a testing technique in which a synthesized voice is used with measurable noise added in evaluating error rates.

In actuality, the accuracy of speech identification has a long way to go before it can be considered useful for a great many applications. A radio teletype circuit (which is more error prone than a land-line circuit) is generally considered to be only marginally operational at an error rate of 10^{-3}. At that rate, there would, on average, be two wrong letters on this page. This is not quite the same thing as an incorrectly identified word.

VOCABULARY

There are considerable differences in the size of the vocabulary required for different applications. In general, the user-dependent systems are capable of recognizing more different utterances than the user-independent types for the simple reason that it generally takes more memory and more processing to identify a given utterance in a user-independent system. On the other hand, there are certain applications in which a very limited vocabulary might be acceptable. For example, certain data entry applications might succeed where only numbers from zero to nine were recognized, along with a simple yes or no. The machine could then prompt the user by reading speech synthesized phrases:

> *Please enter your account number.*
> 2-1-4-6-8-1.
> *Please enter the item number.*
> 4 8 9.
> *Do you want the purchase shipped?*
> No.

The key question in a system such as this is the matter of user acceptance and time. The announcements would have to be read slowly for clarity to newcomers and will tend to be painfully slow to the initiate. Secondly, there is a psychological factor involved in the user being a passive responder to the machine. Furthermore, there are liable to be a certain number of people who could not use the system, no matter how hard they tried, because of a slight speech impediment or a regional accent. This could be very frustrating after having a machine play "20 questions" with you.

CONNECTED SPEECH

Perhaps the most difficult part of the speech-recognition problem stems from connected speech. Certain words and phrases are run together in normal conversational speech and are thus referred to as "connected speech." In the spectrogram of Figure 10-1, we see that the only break in the wavetrain exists as the 140 msec pause that is an integral part of the /t/. There is really scarcely a break between the unvoiced /s/ and the voiced /eh/. By and large, the wavetrain and spectrum simply slide smoothly from phoneme to phoneme. An even more pronounced example is to be found in Figure 10-3, where the phrase "Zero98" blends smoothly from wavetrain to wavetrain, with only the final pause in the /t/.

Perhaps just as significant is the fact that in Figure 10-3 the "eight" and the "two" share a single /t/, whereas they require two /t/'s to be spelled properly. An experienced radio operator reading the alphanumeric 7A2 would actually read "seven able two" to prevent it from being copied "782." This is common in other areas of speech where a large portion of a central word may be omitted. For example, the phrase, "John'n Henry went out," really will not reveal "and" between the names. As a matter of fact, the pressure oscillogram will show only a diminution of energy in the location marked by the apostrophe and not an actual pause. The English-speaking human brain apparently has a built-in algorithm for inserting an "and" following a word ending in /n/ when the trailing /n/ is slightly lengthened.

TEMPLATE MATCHING

Eventually, all current speech-recognition schemes get down to matching a pattern of some sort picked out of the speech with some standard library of patterns contained in memory. This pattern could be from either the spectral distribution with time or from the shape of the pressure wave.

An example of the spectral characteristics can be seen on both Figure 10-1 and 10-3. In the /e/ taken from "eight," we see the characteristic that the middle formant climbs from about 1,300 Hz to about 2,000 Hz in about 150 msec, while the upper and lower formants are essentially stationary. This is a fairly reliable "signature" for the phoneme. It can be seen even more clearly in the LPC models of Figures 13-10 and 13-10 (Cont'd).

Even such a clear-cut signature is not without its identification problems. In a woman's voice, the pitch would be considerably higher. However, the formant would not be proportionally higher, although it does raise somewhat. This means that our signature description cannot be as specialized as to specify the formant frequencies and the frequency slope of the central formant if we are to recognize both men and women using the phoneme. In other words, we would have to allow for some shifting of the formant location as a function of pitch. Note also that even a single speaker will change pitch on a given phoneme when moved by a desire to stress a word or phoneme.

A fairly strong case of the phoneme and pitch shift is presented by the terminating /ol/ of the "two." This is more a problem of connected speech than a characteristic of the phoneme. In discrete (nonconnected) speech, or if used in the middle of a connected sequence, the /ol/ will not show this extreme pitch droop. In the case of this central phoneme, we see from Figure 13- that it starts at about 2,400 Hz in /eh/ and droops to about 2,100 Hz to meet the /v/, when it climbs to 2,300 Hz to meet /n/, and nearly disappears for about 60 msec to the start of /e/.

Because of this complexity of behavior, only the largest and most complex speech-recognition systems are even attempting to handle anything in the way of connected speech. By forcing the speaker into a pattern of discrete speech, the problem is immensely simplified. First of all, the machine knows the start of the word because of the pause and, secondly, the formant movement, because of blending requirements to adjacent phonemes, is reduced to those blendings required within the word. Presumably, a word will respond to a single template.

The mechanics of the situation also prove to be a bit of the problem. If there is anything that one learns when working with a computer, it is that computers are terribly literal-minded. The statement:

$$100 \text{ FOR } Q = 1 \text{ through } 10$$

will bring back a:

$$\text{SYNTAX ERROR}$$

every time because the machine was looking for:

$$100 \text{ FOR } Q = 1 \text{ TO } 10$$

Human utterances are simply not as repeatable as they have to be in order to have the computer consider a word "equal" to a template. For a computer, *equal* means "identical," and a human being never says a word or phrase the same way twice. The pitch is slightly different, the amplitude and formant shaping changes, and the time duration varies. As a matter of fact, it is virtually impossible to insert or splice a correction into connected speech and have the result sound natural because of this. The spliced-in part is always obvious.

To overcome this problem, most speech-recognition schemes employ a form of scoring. Suppose we had the zero-to-nine-yes/no machine discussed previously and were attempting to identify the utterance "six." To begin with, we could assign a score of 10 to candidates "six" and "seven" because they both begin with /s/. The remaining numbers and yes/no might get a zero in this department except for "two," which also starts with a thermal agitation sound with a spectrum similar to /s/. The distinction between the /s/ and the /t/ can be made on the basis of the sharp start of the /t/ compared to the ogive amplitude contour of /s/. A second distinguishing feature is the short duration of /t/ (60 msec) compared to /s/ (120 msec). In order to make the time comparison, we would have to first make some estimate of when the /t/ phoneme ended. "Three" also would probably get a 10, as might "four."

Generally, the end of a phoneme is not accompanied by a reduction to zero energy, as is the /t/. The phonemes blend smoothly into one another within the individual word in discrete speech and from word to word in connected speech. Therefore, some other criterion must be applied, such as the shape of the spectrum, which does show a discontinuity from phoneme to phoneme.

In our special limited vocabulary, we could classify "six" because it ends with an unvoiced sound. This would give a score of 10 to "six" and to "yes." It could also give a score of 10 to "eight" unless we recognized and rejected the stopped fricative.

Because of the overall duration, which is short, we could give a 10 to "one," "two," "five," "six," "nine," "yes," and "no."

At this juncture the scoring is:

1	10
2	20
3	10
4	10
5	10
6	30
7	10
8	10
9	10
Zero	0
yes	10
no	0

It can be seen that the discriminant is not overly strong, with "six" coming out only slightly better than "two."

It is also fairly apparent that we cannot treat "six" as a special case. In order to create a discriminant to pick out some of the other numbers, it is obvious that we must have a mechanism for matching and selecting the voiced sounds. This would be done on the basis of either the pressure wave contour or the spectrum.

The pressure wave contour has the advantage that it is directly available from the initial digitization. Unfortunately, we saw from Figure 12-3 that the detailed contour of the wave is a function of the phasing of the harmonics. Two waves with very different appearance can contain exactly the same harmonics and will sound the same. It is also noteworthy that electronic processing, such as a transit over a telephone circuit, will not necessarily preserve the phase relationships. This means that the pressure wave itself is a poor discriminant since it would reject a sound that was indistinguishable to the human listener from the template.

On the other hand, two sounds with identical spectra will sound alike and the spectrum is not phase sensitive. Furthermore, a change in spectrum does accompany a change in sound. It is in this area that a vocoder-type machine with a series of hardware filters has an advantage over the IDSS types. The IDSS machine must perform a Fourier analysis to obtain the spectrum, whereas the spectrum emerges directly from the vocoder. At any given state of the art, the analog processing of the vocoder will yield the required spectrum much faster. For this reason, a number of the larger and more powerful speech-recognition machines are vocoder types replete with the bank of hardware filters. This is neither cheap nor compact, but it is fast and effective. A bank of sixteen filters is frequently used for the spectrum measurement.

In one mechanism for comparison, the time history for each filter output is compared on a point-for-point basis with the averaged template by subtraction, and the absolute magnitudes of the differences are added. Obviously, two identical patterns would yield a zero result. However, human speech is not really that repeatable. For one thing, the absolute magnitude of the individual utterance will usually not be identical to the original utterance stored in the template. Secondly, the speed of the word will not be identical to the template. In order to perform the matching with reasonable accuracy, it is generally necessary to scale the utterance in both time span and peak amplitude. It is in this area that discrete speech becomes much easier to work with since a definite start and end is detectable.

All by itself, this scaling is a bit tricky since we are working with a discrete digital machine. Suppose, for example, that there are 42 points in the time history of the spectral line of the template and 47 points in the time history of the utterance. In order to obtain a match, we somehow have to get rid of 5 of the points of the utterance, which means providing a reading "in the cracks," or between digitized points. To do this, it is often necessary to curve fit and interpolate. The easiest interpolation is a straight-line interpolation with the data points for the utterance presumed to be connected by straight lines and the new data derived from the height of the line above the new data point.

A slightly more elaborate scheme involves fitting an arc of a circle to three adjacent points with the desired new point between a pair. An even more elaborate scheme involves fitting two circles. Suppose that we label the points A, B, C, and D and we need a data point halfway between B and C. We could construct a circle using points A, B, and C and another circle with B, C, and D. We would then use the circle with the largest radius of curvature for the interpolation. These techniques are generally more accurate than the straight-line interpolation but they are also more time-consuming.

These comparisons are generally made at 10 to 20 msec intervals, using averaged values over the intersample period. Some machine time can be saved by refusing to scale if the disparity between the template and the utterance is too great as, for example, when an inherently short word like *no* is compared with an inherently long word.

An optimum strategy might be to first compare the spectral lines for the middle formant of the utterance with all of the templates and reject those with a relatively high difference score. In the remainder of the testing, the remaining spectral time histories would be compared only with those templates that had not "flunked out." This technique provides greater savings in time as the vocabulary gets larger.

ACTUAL SCORES

At the time of this writing, one of the best comparative tests of speech-recognition devices and machines was published by George R. Doddington and Thomas E. Schalk: *Speech Recognition – Turning Theory to Practice* (IEEE Spectrum, Sept. 1981, pp. 26–32). A series of seven machines ranging from $65,000 units from Verbex and Nippon Electric down to a $500 VET/1 plug-in for the Apple II+ were tested. Of these machines, only the Verbex was rated as speaker independent and only the Verbex and the Nippon Electric were rated as capable of connected speech operation.

It is probably not surprising that the error rate is approximately inversely proportional to price. In approximately 5,120 utterances, the Verbex scored the best, with only 10 substitutions, 2 by men and 8 by women. The Scott Instruments VET/1 did worst, with 646 (12.2%), 11.2% substitutions for men and 14% for women. Consumers Union would probably rate the Interstate Electronics VRM as a "best buy" at $2,400. It made 147 substitutions (2.9%), with 2% for men and 3.7% for women.

In the TI evaluation, a 20-word spoken vocabulary was used, including 10 spoken digits, zero through nine, and 10 command words: start, stop, yes, no, go, help, erase, rubout, repeat, and enter. The speakers were eight men and eight women, about half of whom had previous experience with word recognizers. Only discrete speech was used and only speaker-dependent operation was attempted despite the fact that the top two machines were claimed to have the capability of recognizing connected speech.

From a user standpoint, the nature of the substitutions was very interesting in some cases. In the three lowest scoring devices, the substitution of "stop" for "start" and "start" for "stop" was quite frequent. In particular, the VET/1 substituted on 63 different occasions for "stop." Of these, in 45 instances the substituted word was "start." The next most frequent error was "no," for which the machine substituted "go" 30 times. "Start" was missed 55 times, of which "stop" was substituted 46 times. "Go" was missed 48 times, with "no" substituted 12 of those times. "Help" was missed 40 times, with "start" substituted 9 times.

From a control standpoint, the nature of these errors is most telling. If the computer were used to control a vehicle or any form of moving machine, the substitution of "start" for "stop" or "help" would constitute a severe safety hazard.

Also noted in the report is that the Verbex machine made an insertion on 9 occasions when nothing was uttered. This is in addition to 4 occasions in which "repeat" was substituted for "eight" and 2 occasions in which "no" was substituted for "go."

CONCLUSION

At the present state of the art, the speech-recognition machine is far behind the speech synthesis machine in terms of suitability for wide application. The TI tests were conducted under studio conditions and yet errors, even with a severely restricted vocabulary, were significant. In a more noisy office or factory environment, the operation would be marginal for even the best of the machines. A great deal of development work remains to be done before an inexpensive machine is suitable for economically sensitive applications (the CAD plotter might destroy the drawing). In applications where a safety hazard could be created by a substituted word, usage seems even further off.

The prospect of a large vocabulary (20,000 words), connected speech, speaker-independent machine awaits some major advances in hardware development to permit FFT manipulation in real time and reasonable response lags. A number of hardware silicon houses are working on solutions to these problems, and only time will tell how soon they can be solved.

Index

Active filter, 46
A/D conversion, 166
aether, 86
ALC amplifier, 62
aliasing, 164
aloneme, 142
alveoli, 121
Ampere, Andre Marie, 2
amplitude control, 30
anvil, 91
apodizing, 150
Apple II+, 146
audible ring, 37

Basic english, 141
Baud, 63
Bell, Alexander Graham, 1, 2, 7-9
Bell, Melville, 8
Berliner, Emile, 7
Besky, G., 94
bit error rate, 63
Boyle's Law, 90
Brantlingham, G., 199
Brown, Sir Thomas, 1
bulk modulus, 89
businessmen, 5
busy signal, 37

Chamberlin, H., 155
Charles Law, 90
chirp, 207
connected speech, 133, 228
consonants, 139
cochlea, 92
Cooley, J., 154

D/A conversion, 166
decibel, 41
delta modulation, 178, 193
detection of tones, 44

dial tone, 29
differentiation, 183
digitization, 186
double lock, 79-80
DTMF, 35-36, 40, 44, 45, 53
DTMF detector, 55-63
DTMF tone generator, 64-68
Du Fay, C., 1

Ear, the, 91
Edison, T., 2, 7, 17
Ethernet-Xerox, 21

Filters, 129
Fletcher, Dr. H., 130
formant, 129, 133
Fourier Transform, 125, 146
Franklin, B., 1
frequency shift keying, 63
fricatives, 139

Gauss, K., 71
Gauss Error Function, 86-87, 152
Gilbert, W., 1
glides, 140
glottis, 121
Gould, J., 6
Gray, E., 6
Ground resistance measurement, 71

Hammer, 91
Hamming Window, 150
harmonic generation, 124
harmony, 103
Helmholtz, H., 93, 99
Henry, J., 2, 12
Hubbard, G., 5
human voice, 121
hybrid isolator, 68-70

Incoming ring detector, 39
inventors, 6

Johnstone and Boyle, 95

Ladder network, 168
larynx, 121
lattice filter, 213
levels of security, 77-79
lightning protection, 74
linear predictive filter, 211
longitudinal voltage, 74
LPC, 199

Miller, D., 129
misdial tone, 38
Morse, S., 2
Moser, F., 181
Mossbauer Technique, 95

Natural scale, 108
non-recursive filter, 211
notch filter, 48

Octave, 97
Oersted, H., 2
Ogden, C., 141
Ohm, G., 2
Orton, W., 5
oscillogram, 133

Phase-locked-loop tone detector, 49
phoneme, 137-142
pipeline processor, 215
pitch period repetition, 187
Pixii, H., 2
polarity reversal, 28
Polo, M., 1
Pope, F., 18
pressure wave, 86
production of sound, 112
Pythagoras, 98

Ranke, O., 94
read only memory, 65
receiver-off-hook, 29
recursive filter, 213
reference noise, 43
repeat bit, 206

ringer equivalence number, 41
rotary dialing, 31

Schmitt trigger, 51, 52
security techniques, 77
Shannon, C., 163
sound, 85, 89
sound and hearing, 85
Speak-and-Spell, 141
spectrogram, 133
spectrum analyzer, 144-146
Spoedlin, H., 96
star network, 22
station-protector limiting voltages, 75
stirrup, 91
stop consonants, 139
surge and test voltages, 71
syllable, 186

Telephone, 14
telephony, 1
TEL-TRAK, 202
tempered scale, 108
template matching, 228
Thales of Miletos, 1
thermal agitation oscillator, 118
thoracic cavity, 122
tip and ring, 28
tone decoder, 153
tone detectors, 39
tone useage, 45
touch tone dialing, 32
transverse metallic voltage, 74
triads, 104
TTL leveler, 30
tuned interruptor, 13

Unvoiced sound, 119, 131

Velocity of sound, 89
visible speech, 8
vocabulary, 141
VOCODER, 142
voiced, 139
voicegrams, 133
Volta, A., 2
Voltage controled oscillator, 49
VOTRAX, 140
vowels, 139
VSP, 200

Waggener, G., 155
Wiggins, R., 199
window, 146, 148-150
wire tap, 80-81
word frame, 205

X-period zeroing, 193

Youngs hodulus, 90

Zero-phase encoding, 181, 190
Zwislocki, J., 93-95